TOUR DE FRANCE
CHAMPIONS
AN A-Z

TOUR DE FRANCE
CHAMPIONS
AN A-Z

GILES BELBIN

The
History
Press

Quotes from *The Monuments* kindly reproduced with permission ©
Peter Cossins, 2014, *The Monuments*, Bloomsbury Publishing Plc.

Quotes from *Pedalare! Pedalare!* kindly reproduced with permission ©
John Foot, 2011, *Pedalare! Pedalare!*, Bloomsbury Publishing Plc.

Quotes from *Maglia Rosa* kindly reproduced with permission © Herbie
Sykes, 2013, *Maglia Rosa*, Bloomsbury Publishing Plc.

First published 2020

The History Press
97 St George's Place, Cheltenham,
Gloucestershire, GL50 3QB
www.thehistorypress.co.uk

© Giles Belbin 2020

British Library Cataloguing in Publication Data.
A catalogue record for this book is available from the British Library.

ISBN 978 0 7509 9200 8

Typesetting and origination by The History Press
Printed and bound in Great Britain by TJ International Ltd.

FOREWORD

I remember my first glimpse of the Tour de France as if it were just yesterday; in fact it was over fifty-four years ago in Luxembourg, as I pedalled through my first European trip from my home on the Wirral.

There was a feeding station where riders snatched their flimsy 'musettes' and took basic food and drink. The finish was still a few hours away in Metz, but the centre of the city of Luxembourg was packed with people.

And there, in the centre of the peloton was *le maillot jaune* – the leader of the Tour. His name was Bernard Van De Kerckhove, a Belgian who would never lead the race again but had left his mark on one of sport's most iconic events.

My chance to be part of the Tour came in 1973 as a driver for ITV's commentator, David Saunders. I jumped at it.

Since that July, a red-hot summer, I have followed every single day of the race for forty-six years and I am not done yet! There is no cure for Tour fever.

'What do you see in following the same event, year in and year out,' my fellow journalists have often said. My answer is always the same: 'You never see the same race twice.'

Since 1903, when a chain-smoking chimney sweep won the first edition by almost three hours, the public quickly realised that this was no ordinary race. The fact he was disqualified the next year for cheating only served to highlight how significant winning the Tour was – and nothing's changed today.

This is a remarkable book by Giles Belbin and, although millions of words have been written about La Grande Boucle, I do not think any have been written in such a way as here.

Each winner getting his moment, while even those who caused such controversy having been caught doping, getting their moment, too.

In 1973, everything was new to me. Since my first chance sighting of the Tour in Luxembourg in 1964, I had not seen it since.

That year, the sun never stopped shining and the French-loving Spaniard, Luis Ocaña was, in the absence of the brilliant Belgian Eddy Merckx, the dominator.

Luis had hoped for a revenge meeting with Merckx, whom he was on course to beat in 1971 when he crashed out of the race. Merckx had decided not to ride, so Ocaña took it out on everyone else, winning six stages and the race by almost sixteen minutes.

I have been lucky to commentate on all of the English-speaking winners beginning in 1986 with the American Greg LeMond and ending (so far) with a succession of British winners from Sir Bradley Wiggins in 2012, to Geraint Thomas in 2018.

Along the way, the irrepressible Stephen Roche gave Ireland a first win in 1987 and my immortal words of: 'It's Roche, it's Stephen Roche,' as he climbed La Plagne, fighting to limit his losses to race leader Pedro Delgado where he saved the day, resulted in hundreds of T-shirts being sold in Ireland.

In that same race of 1987, there was also a sad farewell to one of the race's finest riders. From 1957 to 1964, Jacques Anquetil dominated the Tour, winning it five times, so becoming the first member of the famous Five Club.

Rumour had spread around the Tour caravan that Maître Jacques was dying from cancer. So typical of the man, he refused surgery until he had finished his work as a radio reporter on that Tour.

But every second had counted and the handsome French aristocrat died four months later aged 53. Jacques has a magnificent, almost life-sized, granite headstone in the cemetery of his home city of Rouen.

Anquetil was the first rider to win all three Grand Tours – France, Italy and Spain – he also became the first modern-day rider to lead the race every evening from start to finish in 1961.

I say 'evening' because in the morning's opening stage, the French sprinter André Darrigade had won, and was given a yellow jersey. But in the afternoon's time trial, he lost out to *Monsieur Chrono* – Anquetil's other nickname, and so saw the jersey pass on to a man who would not concede it for the next three weeks and would win by 12 minutes and 41 seconds in Paris.

As this great race continues to evolve perhaps the 107th edition will see membership of the Five Club, which stands at four, with Eddy Merckx, Miguel Induráin, and Bernard Hinault, welcome its first British member in 2020. Chris Froome, stopped by a crash when preparing for the 2019 race, will write the next chapter as he goes for five in 2020.

Enjoy this unique book.

Phil Liggett MBE
The Voice of Cycling,
Hertfordshire

INTRODUCTION

From the inaugural Tour de France held in 1903, through to the 2019 edition, some sixty-two men have entered the record books as registering at least one Tour de France victory. Three of those sixty-two never had the experience of standing triumphantly in Paris as the winner of cycling's greatest race, their victory only coming after an investigation into an allegation of cheating, or into a positive anti-doping control result, had concluded and stripped those who had taken the acclaim in Paris of the title they had initially been awarded.

From Aimar to Zoetemelk, this book seeks to provide an insight into the lives and careers of the sixty-two riders in the history books as winners of the Tour de France (as well as providing an entry on those who were subsequently disqualified). Some of the names – those such as Eddy Merckx, Fausto Coppi or Bradley Wiggins – will be familiar to even the most casual cycling fan. Others such as René Pottier or Léon Scieur, perhaps less so. All have fascinating stories, sometimes glorious, sometimes distressing: from the winner who was celebrated for carrying wartime resistance messages hidden in his bike on training rides, to the rider who was shot dead by his lover some twelve years after his victorious ride into Paris. Some tasted Tour victory at the first time of asking, while for others it took many years of building towards the top step of the podium. Some never found another major win; others dominated the sport for years. Whatever their story they all have one thing in common: they have all claimed the one cycling race that transcends the sport.

For ease of reading I have shortened references to cycling's three most important stage races – the Tour de France, Giro d'Italia and Vuelta a España – to the Tour, Giro and Vuelta respectively. Collectively they are referenced as the Grand Tours. All references to other bike races are given their most familiar name when referenced in English language cycling texts, for example I use the Tour of Flanders rather than De Ronde van Vlaanderen but retain use of the GP des Nations. The most important one-day races – Milan–Sanremo, the Tour of Flanders, Paris–Roubaix, Liège–Bastogne–Liège and the Tour of Lombardy – are collectively referenced as the Monuments. Unless otherwise stated, all references to world titles, rainbow jerseys or 'the Worlds' refer to elite road-race world championships only and do not include world titles in other disciplines. All the translations from foreign language texts are my own.

Finally, while putting the final touches to this book, normal life was turned upside down by the Covid-19 global pandemic. The cycling world was completely shut down, with many major races postponed and no replacement dates confirmed. At the time of writing it remains unclear whether the 2020 Tour will go ahead as planned, with no one from the organisers of the race – Amaury Sport Organization – offering formal comment. Throughout its 117-year history, only the two world wars have prevented the Tour from being held – but right now it seems inevitable the 2020 edition will be affected. Perhaps there will be a scaled-down version: no spectators, a smaller peloton and televised coverage only. Perhaps it will be postponed to early autumn. Perhaps it will be cancelled completely. But whatever happens, the Tour will still be the Tour, and it will surely return as strong as ever. It has to. For the Tour de France *is* cycling.

Giles Belbin
March 2020

Aimar, Lucien

FRA

BORN: 28 APRIL 1941, HYÈRES, FRANCE

Described by some as a one-hit wonder and as 'one of the more forgettable Tour winners',[1] Lucien Aimar first rode the Tour in 1965, his debut professional season. His entrance into the pro ranks had started well with a podium finish at Paris-Camembert and fourth at the Dauphiné Libéré, the second most important stage race in France. They were very decent returns for a rider fresh out of the amateur ranks.

That fourth place at the Dauphiné Libéré had been achieved in the service of the Ford-Gitane leader, Jacques Anquetil. Anquetil had won three stages and the overall, and Aimar was impressive enough in his supporting role to earn a spot on the team for the Tour, which started a little over three weeks later. Anquetil was the reigning Tour champion but had set other targets for 1965 (see Anquetil entry for more) and so wasn't on the start line for the opening stage in Cologne. Instead, Aimar had number one pinned to his jersey. Some pressure for a Tour debutant.

Unfortunately for Aimar his Tour ended early, on the slopes of the Aubisque in the Pyrenees, on a day of unbearable heat that claimed a number of other riders. As Aimar climbed the Aubisque he had become disorientated and unable to keep his balance. He left his bike lying on the road and continued a few paces on foot before falling 'stiff on his back, like a knocked-out boxer'.[2] The Tour's chief medical officer, Doctor Dumas, who was growing concerned at the growing number of strange illnesses suffered by riders during races, suspecting doping products as the cause, was furious, reportedly exclaiming 'Ah! Les Vaches!' (a French expression of shock, literally translated 'the Cows') before ordering an oxygen mask be placed over Aimar's nose and mouth and blaming sunstroke.

Aimar had turned professional after a notable 1964 amateur season during which he had been selected to represent France at both the world championships and the Tokyo Olympic Games. Second place at the Tour de l'Avenir, widely regarded as the amateur version of the Tour, had helped earn him those selections. Aimar had finished just 42 seconds behind the Italian Felice Gimondi at the race despite having been hit with a one-minute penalty following an exchange of jersey pulling with the Belgian rider Jos Spruyt during the eighth stage. Many felt the penalty unduly harsh, especially as reports suggested Spruyt had started the argument. 'The next day the two men shook hands and there was nothing left of the trouble,' reported René De Latour. 'Nothing except the loss of the most important race (world championship apart) for an amateur.'[3] Aimar was lying third behind race leader Ginés García and second-placed Gimondi before the final stage but attacked impressively on a hill at Chateaufort, 25km or so from the finish. Aimar had been so sure of his form that he had actually told De Latour of his plan before the start. Garcia was distanced but Gimondi held fast, sticking to Aimar's wheel 'as if it were a Derny'.[4]

Forty thousand spectators watched the end of the stage in Paris, won by Gerben Karstens. Gimondi may have left with the overall win but Aimar had gained plenty of admirers, among them Raphaël Géminiani, Anquetil's sports director at Ford, who made sure a contract was drawn up to add him to the team.

Twelve months after abandoning his debut Tour Aimar was back. This time Anquetil was alongside him at the start in Nancy, aiming for his sixth title. But it was Aimar that made the earliest strike, joining a breakaway on stage 10, from Bayonne to Pau, and going over the Aubisque, scene of his meltdown the previous year. Aimar arrived in Pau a couple of minutes behind stage winner Tommaso de Pra but more than seven minutes ahead of Anquetil and Raymond Poulidor, Anquetil's great rival. Aimar was now Ford's best-placed rider.

As the race progressed Anquetil, struck by bronchitis and the realisation he could not win the race, put himself in the service of Aimar. During the stage to Turin, which went over the Montgenèvre and Sestriere climbs, Poulidor attacked, taking five riders with him, and quickly gaining 150m. Aimar was in the peloton with the yellow-jersey-wearing Jan Janssen sat right behind. 'I did not know what to do,'[5] Aimar said afterwards. Then, Anquetil came alongside, pledged his support and towed his young teammate up to Poulidor before then immediately encouraging him to attack on the straight and rising road. Aimar followed Anquetil's word, surprising both Poulidor and Janssen with his move. That night in Turin he wore the yellow jersey for the first time.

Aimar held yellow all the way to Paris. His winning margin 1min 7sec over Janssen. It was not a popular win – Poulidor was France's favourite and many wanted to see him take the Tour title. But Aimar had scaled the summit of his sport in just his second season as a professional. He would never again hit such heights.

In 1967 Aimar was awarded the title of national champion despite finishing second when Désiré Letort, the man who had crossed the line first, was disqualified after failing a doping test.[6] Aimar refused to wear the national jersey, saying he'd been fairly beaten, receiving fines as a result of his stance. Twelve months later he claimed the title national championship properly, beating Roger Pingeon after the two launched a long-range breakaway on the Aubenas circuit in the Ardeche.

By 1973 Aimar was riding for the short-lived De Kova-Lejeune team. Géminiani, looking for a backer for his team, had been introduced to a wealthy widow in her seventies called Miriam De Kova. De Kova was a singer and dancer who wanted badly to perform in France. She had money to burn but needed publicity. Géminiani had a cycling team but needed money. De Kova reportedly required little convincing that her best way of getting publicity was to have her name plastered all over the cycling jerseys of Géminiani's team, which of course included Aimar in its ranks.

Their jerseys were bright pink; their results were terrible. The team only picked up one win of note with Aimar winning stage 5 of the Four Days of Dunkirk and claiming what would prove to be the final win of his professional career. The team rode the Tour with Aimar claiming 17th overall. That was as good as it got and De Kova's short reign as a cycling sponsor ended after just one season.

Aimar retired at the end of the 1973 season and in 1974 established the Tour Méditerranéen, a race which ran until 2014.

> ## MAJOR WINS
> Tour de France: 1966
> National Champion: 1967, 1968

Anquetil, Jacques
FRA

BORN: 8 JANUARY 1934, MONT-SAINT-AIGNAN, FRANCE

'To be good on the bike you have to be good at the table and to enjoy life. I'm going to eat oysters and veal stew with a bottle of Gros Plant.'[7] That is Jacques Anquetil, as described by the French author Paul Fournel, at 8 a.m. on the morning of the final stage of the Tour du Var. It distils the essence of one of France's greatest champions into just two sentences. Here was a man that loved the finer things in life but was also a fierce competitor. Fournel writes that Anquetil consumed this fare in front of the disgusted Antonin Magne, manager of his great rival Raymond Poulidor, and then went on to win the stage in Saint-Tropez, proclaiming: 'And at the finish I'm the one snatching the bouquet.'[8] Anquetil's talent was such that this should surprise no one.

In 1964 Maître Jacques (he was also known as Monsieur Chrono) became the first rider to win five Tour titles. He had announced his arrival into the sport eleven years earlier at the GP des Nations. The GP des Nations took the form of a long individual time trial and Anquetil was supremely gifted at riding alone against the clock. He dominated the event from the mid 1950s until the mid 1960s, claiming a record nine victories.

His first win there came in 1953 after he had attracted the interest of Francis Pélissier, head of the team La Perle. Pélissier had been scouring race reports looking for France's next big champion and in Anquetil – talented, enigmatic and good-looking – he thought he might have found his man. When Anquetil destroyed the field during Paris–Normandie in the summer of 1953 Pélissier was convinced and promptly signed the 19-year-old to a 30,000 francs per month contract. Just over one month later Anquetil, riding as an *indépendant* (a semi-professional category) but wearing the jersey of La Perle, stunned the cycling world by winning the 140km GP des Nations by nearly seven minutes at his first attempt. French cycling writer Pierre Chany wrote: 'We truly did not know Jacques Anquetil before we had seen him on the slopes of Saint-Remy-les-Chevreuse or of Châteaufort. In this sector he massacred all of his rivals.'[9] Chany described Pélissier as watching on, cigarette dangling from the corner of his mouth, as admirers crowded round his new rider, and murmuring: 'You have not seen anything yet. It is just beginning.'[10] A truer statement has perhaps never been uttered.

Born into a family of strawberry farmers, Anquetil's first club was the Association Cycliste de Sotteville. He won the amateur French national title in 1952 before taking the call to join La Perle, though notably he would never claim France's professional national championships. Nor would he ever wear the rainbow jersey of world champion despite his pedigree, but we'll get to that.

Four years after his GP des Nations debut, Anquetil rode the Tour for the first time. Just three days in he won his first stage, a 134km race into his home town of Rouen. There is a photograph of him taken before that day's racing. Anquetil is sat on a grass bank, hair swept back, hands interlocked over his knees which are pulled towards his chest. He looks completely relaxed, more like a man on a picnic than a man ready to ride a stage of the world's most important race. Indeed, it is only his cycling jersey that betrays the fact he is about get on his bike. Two days after that photograph was taken, he was in the yellow jersey for the first time. He later lost it briefly but reclaimed it in the Alps, with two weeks still to race. Despite later coming under pressure in the Pyrenees, Anquetil held the jersey until the end. His first Tour and his winning margin in Paris was nearly fifteen minutes.

Louison Bobet, the three-time champion who had taken six years to win his first Tour, had been absent, targeting instead the Giro d'Italia. With the Tour run in national teams at the time, the press immediately wrote of the dilemma now facing the French. 'One took six years to win it, the other less than a month. Bobet v Anquetil in next year's Tour?' ran the headline in *Coureur*. 'With 1957

Tour de France bikes still lying around track centre [at the Parc des Princes velodrome] there was already a lively discussion among race followers. Will Anquetil and Bobet both be among the starters in the 1958 Tour?'[11] As it turned out the answer was yes, both were there, yet neither would feature in the final reckonings – Anquetil abandoned and Bobet came seventh.

Anquetil was held to be a cold and calculating racer, a rider who knew exactly what he needed to do and often did no more. In the mountains he was described as a man who could not drop anyone but who could not be dropped himself. Given his supremacy against the clock that was often all he needed – to match his rivals in the mountains and then beat them in the time trials. This is not to suggest Anquetil was poor when the road rose skyward. He raced in the era of great climbers, Charly Gaul and Federico Bahamontes among them, and often matched and sometimes beat those with greater climbing reputations. In 1961 he took the yellow jersey at the end of the first day and held it to the finish, three weeks later. The public and press didn't enjoy such ruthless domination. The director of the Tour, Jacques Goddet, wrote a scathing article in which he accused other riders of being 'helpless, resigned and satisfied with their mediocrity'.[12]

The following year he won again but was booed in Paris. 'Each time he wins the ill-feeling grows,' reported Miroir des Sports. 'He says it can't be helped but it is obvious he's disturbed. He can't be blamed for the incompetence of the rest.'[13] In 1963, faced with fewer time-trial kilometres, he rode aggressively in the mountains. He took yellow after winning stage 17, a day of four major climbs in the Alps. Before the stage Anquetil's sports director, Raphaël Géminiani, hatched a plan for an illegal bike-change at the bottom of the day's hardest climb, enabling his rider to benefit from better gearing for the climb. 'Changing bikes is forbidden,' Anquetil is said to have told Géminiani. 'That's my business,'[14] his DS allegedly replied.

And so it was that at the bottom of the Forclaz, Anquetil faked a mechanical problem. The race officials confirmed the cable running to the derailleur had snapped, unaware of the wire cutters in the hands of Anquetil's mechanic, and authorised the change. Anquetil was able to stay with the great climber Bahamontes to win the stage in Chamonix. He took the yellow jersey by twenty-eight seconds over the Spaniard, courtesy of a thirty-second stage-win bonus. The gap would grow to over three minutes come Paris.

If the feeling in late summer 1957 was that Anquetil's great rival would be Bobet, that would prove not to be the case. Instead Anquetil would come to be defined by his mid-to-late career rivalry with Raymond Poulidor. Poulidor was a warm individual and quickly grew into a firm favourite with the French public despite being regularly beaten by Anquetil. Quite simply Anquetil could not understand why he, a proven winner, would garner less affection than Poulidor, a very good rider but one who would never win the Tour.

Their Tour battles came to a head in 1964, on the Puy de Dôme, in what remains one of the great Tour moments. With the Tour having reverted to trade teams and with just three days to go, fifty-six seconds separated the two Frenchmen before the 237km stage from Brive to the summit of Puy-de-Dôme. Anquetil was of course in yellow, Poulidor second. On the final climb Anquetil and Poulidor engaged in a very personal battle. For more than 3km they rode the steep slopes of the Puy-de-Dôme side by side, Anquetil on the inside, Poulidor on the outside. Shoulder to shoulder and head to head. Then they came together. Heads bowed, arms clashing, bikes leaning, eyes fixed downward. Flashbulbs flared. One of the Tour's most famous photographs had been captured.

With less than 1km to go Anquetil fell away. Poulidor rode to the line, the prospect of snatching yellow from Anquetil lit large in front of him. But he still couldn't do it. Anquetil came in forty-two seconds down but he'd done enough to save the jersey. Paul Howard's biography of Anquetil, *Sex, Lies and Handlebar Tape*, describes Anquetil collapsing onto Géminiani's car:

'How much?' he asked
'Fourteen seconds.'
'That's thirteen more than I need.'[15]

Maître Jacques – always calculating. He would beat Poulidor in Paris by fifty-five seconds.

Such was the intensity of their rivalry that Anquetil sometimes sacrificed his own chances just to ensure Poulidor couldn't win. The world championships, where they had to ride for the same national team, was a prime example. Neither could bear to help the other win and the French team was divided, racing not just against other countries but also against each other. Paralysed by their rivalry, Anquetil and Poulidor finished second and third respectively in the 1966 Worlds, unwilling to work together when away alone in the closing moments and allowing Germany's Rudi Altig to come back and take the win. Neither would ever wear the rainbow jersey. In the words of Pierre Chany, for three successive years (1964–66) such was their obsession with each other they 'offered gifts'[16] to others. At the 1966 Paris–Nice race the rivalry split the peloton, with Anquetil enlisting the support of the Salvarani and Molteni teams and Peugeot riding for Poulidor.

Anquetil at least won some much-needed public affection with his exploits in 1965. With five Tour titles to his name, Anquetil had opted to skip the race and instead focus on a unique challenge – to win both the Dauphiné Libéré stage race and the mammoth one-day Classic Bordeaux–Paris in the same season. Simple enough you may think, until you realise Bordeaux–Paris started just seven hours after the Dauphiné finished.

It had been Géminiani's plan. Anquetil at first thought the idea ludicrous but Géminiani was clever, telling his rider that it was 'a feat that only you are able to achieve',[17] and explaining it would capture the imagination of the public.

And how right he was. First Anquetil beat Poulidor at the Dauphiné before rushing to a hotel for a massage and a meal of steak tartare, camembert and strawberry tart, washed down with beer. Then to a waiting aeroplane at Nîmes, reportedly provided by none other than Charles de Gaulle, and a brief flight to Bordeaux. Seven hours after collecting the winner's bouquet in Avignon, Anquetil felt ready for bed. He just had the small matter of 557km to ride before he could finally turn in.

In the silent pre-dawn hours on the road to Paris, Anquetil struggled to retain enthusiasm for Géminiani's idea. He climbed off and said he was quitting but France was following this story intently. Géminiani convinced his rider to continue, mainly by accusing him of betrayal and telling him it was over between them. He was making him, the great Gém, look like an idiot, he told Anquetil before kicking him out of the car. Anquetil got back on his bike, carried on, and ultimately rode into Paris alone at the head of the race. Thousands chanted his name in the Parc des Princes, the place where they had booed him just three years before. It was an extraordinary achievement and the press lavished praise on him, with *Cycling* urging readers to salute 'the greatest cyclist that the world has ever seen'.[18] Anquetil was overcome by the reaction, later admitting to shedding tears in the sanctuary of the team car, away from prying eyes. 'He cried precisely because this time he'd taken risks, something he normally never did in a stage race,'[19] wrote Chany.

Away from cycling Anquetil's life was complicated. His first wife, Janine had been married to his doctor and a personal friend before Anquetil took her away. He then had a child, Sophie, with Janine's daughter, Annie – his stepdaughter. To the outside world Sophie was portrayed as Janine's daughter. 'I was a little girl with two mothers,' Sophie later wrote in her book *Pour L'amour de Jacques*. 'One of my mothers was the daughter of the other one.'[20] It should be made clear that there was no incest here, but there was a very complicated living arrangement with Anquetil, according to Sophie's book, bed-hopping between Janine and Annie. If that wasn't enough, he later had a son, Christopher, with the ex-wife of his stepson.

As well as his five Tour wins Anquetil also won two Giro titles and the Vuelta, the first rider in history to win all three Grand Tours. In 1956 he claimed the prestigious hour record in Milan at his third attempt, to a soundtrack of Italians shouting '*Forza Jacques!*' Days earlier they had been chanting for the previous record holder, Fausto Coppi, while watching Anquetil's failed second effort. True to form, Anquetil prepared for his third try by dancing in a nightclub on the shores of Lake Como before returning to the Vigorelli velodrome and smashing Coppi's mark by 312m according to the UCI's own records[21] (which differ slightly to other published sources).

Anquetil died in November 1987 of stomach cancer. He was 53.

MAJOR WINS
Tour de France: 1957, 1961, 1962, 1963, 1964
Giro d'Italia: 1960, 1964
Vuelta a España: 1963
Liège–Bastogne–Liège: 1966
Bordeaux–Paris: 1965

Bahamontes, Federico

ESP

BORN: 9 JULY 1928,
SANTO DOMINGO-CAUDILLA, SPAIN

'Don't lose time on the flat stages, and you must win the Tour.'[1] Those were the words spoken by the Italian cycling maestro, Fausto Coppi, to Spain's Federico Bahamontes in the weeks running up to the 1959 Tour. Coppi had two Tour and five Giro titles to his name by then so he knew a thing or two about what it took to win a three-week-long bike race. And Bahamontes, who had signed to the Tricofilina-Coppi trade team for the season, listened.

Bahamontes was a fine climber, perhaps the finest ever to have turned a pedal. There is a terrific cartoon, drawn by René Pellarin and published during the 1963 Tour, that highlights the Spaniard's prowess in the mountains – depicting Bahamontes parading over the Alps, chased by Jacques Anquetil who is twirling a rope over his head in an attempt to lasso the Spanish rider and bring him to heel.

Despite his mountain-climbing talents, before the 1959 Tour wins of the highest order remained scarce on Bahamontes' *palmarès*. He always lost too much time against the clock, or on the flat, or when descending. In five years of professional racing the rider known as the 'Eagle of Toledo' had collected stage wins at the Tour and Vuelta and a brace of mountain titles at each, as well as a national championship and a Giro stage, but little else of consequence. His best result at the Tour had been fourth in 1956 when he finished more than ten minutes behind Roger Walkowiak.

The 1959 Tour was run in national teams. It started in Mulhouse and ran anti-clockwise around the north of France, heading down to the Pyrenees, before calling in on the Massif Central. Four stages in or around the Alps followed en route to the finish in Paris.

Bahamontes waited until the Pyrenees to start his bid but was unable to make serious inroads. By the time the race exited the mountain range he remained more than thirteen minutes behind race leader Michel Vermeulin. Fast-forward four stages and he was lying third, just ten seconds off the new leader, Eddy Pauwels, thanks to a storming ride during the Puy de Dôme mountain time trial, which he won by 1min 26sec over Charly Gaul.

The race would be decided in the Alps. And as those great mountain passes loomed large events were falling the Spaniard's way. The French team was in disarray with Jacques Anquetil and Roger Rivière at each other's throats, refusing to work together for fear of helping the other increase the value of lucrative post-Tour criterium contracts at the expense of their own. The French team manager, Marcel Bidot, had anticipated the problem. Indeed, before the race Anquetil had told Bidot he and Rivière could 'not be real team-mates'.[2] Bidot had tried to address the issue, inviting a group of senior riders, including Anquetil and Rivière, to a meeting in Poigny for discussions. But it was all to no avail and as the race developed so did the acrimony. There was also the problem of the newly crowned French national champion, Henry Anglade, who was riding for the regional Centre-Midi team. Anglade was well placed going into the Alps and while Anquetil and Rivière didn't want the other one to win, neither did they want Anglade standing in yellow in Paris.

All of which goes to explain why when Anquetil and Rivière found themselves in a break of six alongside Anglade, with torrential rain falling and a five-minute lead over the now yellow-jersey-wearing Bahamontes, neither contributed to the effort to stay away. 'The other one did not want to lead,'[3] Rivière said by way of an explanation at the finish. The result was that Bahamontes clawed his way back and easily retained the race lead, holding it until Paris to become the first Spaniard to win the Tour.

If Spain rejoiced heartily – Bahamontes reflected that given the size and noise of his reception in Toledo it was as if 'he had returned from winning a war',[4] – the reaction elsewhere was muted and the crowds at the Parc des Princes booed the French team. 'Bahamontes, did he win a tinpot Tour,'[5] asked the front page of the *Miroir-Sprint*. [A] great winner of a modest Tour,'[6] wrote Jock Wadley in the pages of *Coureur*. All of which seems a little cruel on the man from Toledo who had just secured the greatest win of his career.

Bahamontes was born in 1928 into a poor family and a country just eight years away from civil war. In a 2017 interview with the Spanish daily *ABC*, he recalled working on his father's road gang, aged 12, crushing stones. His family lived for a week under a tarpaulin in Madrid and ate only what they could find. 'The meat we ate was the cats that I hunted at night with a slingshot or with sticks,' he said. 'We ate cats, we were very hungry.'[7] He honed his cycling legs 'engaged in the black market',[8] riding 60km every morning to collect bread, flour and chickpeas that his family then sold on at a profit. 'I went hungry, very hungry,' he said. 'That's why I became a cyclist.'[9]

Bahamontes was selected for his first Tour in 1954 and immediately won the first of an eventual six Tour mountain titles. At the top of the Col de Romeyere he famously had to wait for his mechanic to arrive to repair a broken spoke, taking an ice cream from a nearby seller while he waited much to the amusement of the watching crowds. As a result he quickly gained a reputation for eccentricity.

A temperamental figure – there are tales of bikes and shoes being thrown from mountains and photographs of him sitting on the roadside in complete despair – Bahamontes had a fierce rivalry with fellow Spaniard Jesús Loroño. The feud dated from the 1957 Vuelta where they were both riding for the Spanish national team. The pair nearly came to blows after a stage during which Bahamontes was prevented from chasing his compatriot, literally being held back by Loroño's allies on the squad while team manager Luis Puig blocked the road with the team car.

That rivalry would develop into Spain's version of Bartali and Coppi. Coppi himself said that Bahamontes was 'a job to handle. He's as stubborn as a mule,' while his sports director at the 1959 Tour, Dalmacio Langarica, said: 'All you have to do with Federico is calm him down nine days out of ten. If you didn't, he would kill himself fighting just when he felt like it, no matter how unimportant the rider [attacking] was.'[10]

Six years after his Tour win, Bahamontes rode the race for the last time. He abandoned in the Pyrenees in typically eccentric fashion, riding away from the peloton before the climb of the Portet-d'Aspet and then hiding in bushes to let the peloton pass before climbing off his bike out of sight from his fellow riders. 'Bahamontes abandoned in view of the peaks where once he reigned,'[11] ran *ABC*'s headline. He would retire at the end of the season.

In 2013 the French sports daily *L'Équipe* assembled a nine-strong panel of experts that included riders, team managers, race organisers and journalists, to decide the best climber in the Tour's history. Seven of them voted for the same man, the man who holds the race record for leading over the most mountain passes (forty-five according to the Tour's Guide Historique[12]): Federico Bahamontes.[13]

> ## MAJOR WINS
> **Tour de France: 1959**
> **National Champion: 1958**

Bartali, Gino

ITA

BORN: 18 JULY 1914, PONTE A EMA, ITALY

Nicknamed *Gino the Pious*, Gino Bartali was born to a hard-working and deeply religious family. He attended Mass during races and had his first yellow jersey blessed by a priest. God may have been on his side but his rivals gave him another nickname: The Iron Man.

A rider who famously said the weather could never be too hot nor too cold for him, Bartali burst onto the scene in 1935, taking the first of four national championships, winning his first stage at the Giro and claiming the mountain title. The following year he won the Giro for the first time. Riding for Legnano he won stage 9 taking the race lead by over six minutes. While Bianchi's Giuseppe Olmo would whittle away at that lead over the next week and a half, winning a total of ten stages, Bartali would hold on to take his first

Giro title. Over the course of his career he would win another two Giri (1937, 1946) and claim a total of seven mountain titles at his homeland tour.

After his 1937 Giro win he went to the Tour for the first time, taking a stage win and wearing yellow before abandoning following a crash. He would return in 1938, winning by 18min 27sec. His director was none other than the Italian legend Costante Girardengo – 'I brought my muscles and my capacity for suffering and you, your wisdom and experience,'[14] Bartali told Girardengo at the finish.

After the war Bartali returned to the Tour in 1948, starting as he had finished a decade earlier, by taking the race lead on day one after winning a twelve-man sprint into Trouville. It was a great start but from there things didn't quite go to plan.

A young Frenchman called Louison Bobet was riding his second Tour. Bobet had abandoned the previous year but now on stage six he took the biggest win of his career so far, breaking away with three other riders before outsprinting them on the finish line in Biarritz. Bartali had already lost his grip on yellow, slipping out of the top ten after only the second day. Now Bobet had the jersey and he wasn't about to give it up without a fight.

Bartali won two consecutive stages in the Pyrenees but Bobet managed to maintain a huge lead. As the race headed east towards the Alps the Frenchman had over eighteen minutes on Bartali who was down in eighth spot overall. Bartali grabbed some time back but then, on stage 12 Bobet lit the afterburners and left the Italian standing, taking 7min 39sec out of him on the stage from Sanremo to Cannes. France had a new darling and Italy's great hope was over twenty-one minutes down. Bartali was carrying the hopes of his nation on his broad shoulders. But twenty-one minutes! His Tour was surely done, wasn't it?

Stage 13 was a brute. From Cannes to Briançon the peloton would take in three major climbs – the Allos, Vars and the Izoard – over 274km of racing across three mighty mountains.

But before that the peloton had a rest day to enjoy. Legend has it that as Bartali relaxed in his Cannes hotel, readying himself for the efforts to come, he took a phone call from the Italian Prime Minister, Alcide De Gasperi.

In Italy a dire situation was unfolding. De Gasperi's Christian Democrats had been voted into office three months earlier and it had seemed Italy had taken its first steps towards political stability after the Second World War. But, as the Tour's riders rested on the Mediterranean coast, the chairman of the Italian Communist Party, Palmiro Togliatti was shot three times. Immediately Italy descended into anarchy. Strikes were called, demonstrations held. Unrest pervaded the country. Civil war was in the air. All the good work of the previous two years was in danger of being thrown away.

De Gasperi needed a diversion to save his country. He called Bartali and told him of the crisis in his homeland. De Gasperi said that the country needed Bartali to win, telling him that it could make a difference. Bartali said that he'd do his best.

And that was what he did. On stage 13 Bartali launched an almighty attack on the Allos. Bobet went with him initially but the Italian accelerated away from the Frenchman, chasing stage leader Jean Robic. By the time Bartali topped the Izoard, drenched by freezing rain that was now falling, the Italian was at the head of the race with a lead of over six minutes. He rolled into Briançon in 10hr 9min 28sec, to win the stage. Bobet crossed the line over eighteen minutes down. That night Bartali lay second, just fifty-one seconds behind Bobet, who was still in yellow. Just.

The next day. Stage 14. Another massive day in the Alps. Over 263km, from Briançon to Aix-les-Bains, Bobet and Bartali locked horns. Over the Lautaret, the Galibier and the Croix de Fer they matched each other, attack for attack, pedal stroke for pedal stroke. It snowed, the terrible roads turned to mud, and still they fought. Then, finally, cruelly, Bobet cracked. On the Porte his will failed him and Bartali rode away. Over the Porte, Cucheron and Granier, Bartali was ruthless. In another extraordinary display of power, the Italian won the stage by nearly six minutes. Bobet finished over seven minutes back. As night fell in Aix-les-Bains the yellow jersey was hanging in the wardrobe of the Italian master. He had a lead of 8min 3sec. Bartali had fought back to gain nearly thirty minutes in two simply astonishing days in the Alps.

Bartali paid tribute to the young Bobet's fighting spirit. 'He will be a great, great champion,' he said. 'He will win the Tour [one day] I'm sure of that.'[15] The next day the *Dauphiné Libéré* newspaper described 'a life and death struggle between two great champions'.[16] It also carried a story from across the border. 'Peace in Italy,' it said. Bartali's exploits had proven the ultimate diversion.

After his Alpine heroics it was plain sailing for Bartali. He took one more stage win to take his tally for the race to seven. He had won every major mountain stage the race had thrown at him, claiming the mountains title in the process. By the time they rolled back into Paris, Bartali's winning margin was 26min 16sec from second-placed Alberic Schotte.

Bobet? He finished fourth, over half an hour back. But, just as Bartali predicted, his day would come.

Bartali's career was defined by his rivalry with Fausto Coppi. Coppi, who initially joined Bartali's Legnano team to ride in his support before leaving for Bianchi, won more than Bartali but scandalised the country with his extra-marital affairs. Bartali, the elder by five years, was the God-fearing veteran who also won more than his fair share of major races. Their rivalry divided the country, reaching its nadir in 1948 when both men opted to climb off their bikes rather than help the other at the world championships. (See Coppi entry for more.)

The Iron Man was more than just a stage racer and added seven Monuments to his palmarès, claiming Milan–Sanremo four times and winning three Tour of Lombardy titles. His final Sanremo win came in 1950 when he took advantage as Coppi punctured on the Capo Berta climb, accelerating and taking three riders with him. Coppi fought back to force a bunch sprint. No matter. Despite his efforts on the Capo Berta, Bartali still prevailed to win the sprint by a couple of bike lengths. He was 35 years old and at the time was the race's oldest winner; he has since been overtaken by three others.

The gap of ten years between his first Tour win and his second in 1948, explained in part by the war, remains a record. During the conflict Bartali worked as a military bike messenger but was secretly helping Jewish families, harbouring them in his house and running fake papers and money that he hid in his bike during so-called 'training rides'.

His actions only came to light after his death from a heart attack in 2000, Bartali never really speaking of them. 'Good is something you do, not something you talk about,' he said. 'Some medals are pinned to your soul, not to your jacket.'[17]

MAJOR WINS
Tour de France: 1938, 1948
Giro d'Italia: 1936, 1937, 1946
Tour of Lombardy: 1936, 1939, 1940
Milan–Sanremo: 1939, 1940, 1947, 1950
National Champion: 1935, 1937, 1940, 1952

Bernal, Egan

COL

BORN: 13 JANUARY 1997, BOGOTÁ, COLOMBIA

'Welcome to the Egan Bernal era.'[18] That was the opening line of the *Sunday Times*' Tour report that was published on the morning of the 2019 race's final stage. Those words were written by the paper's chief sports writer, David Walsh, a man who has been writing about cycling for more than thirty years and not someone prone to hyperbole. 'Yesterday was the first victory,' Walsh continued. 'It will not be Egan Bernal's last.'[19]

As Walsh's words hit the newsstands Bernal was at the Alberta Hotel in Val Thorens with the rest of his INEOS team. Having safely negotiated the final mountain stage in the yellow jersey all that remained for the young Colombian was the ceremonial ride into Paris. His real work was done. All he needed to do now was to catch the plane transfer north with the rest of the Tour's peloton before then making sure he managed to stay upright on his bike while holding a champagne glass and posing for photographs. He also had the small matter of working out what on earth he was going to say when the microphone was passed to him on the Champs-Élysées, knowing that the eyes and ears of the world would be on him.

Life was about to change dramatically for the quiet man from the city of Zipaquirá, some 40km or so north of Bogotá. At just 22 years and 196 days old, Bernal was about to become the youngest winner of the Tour for over 100 years. He was also about to become the first from Latin America. That's not to say that his win was a surprise – he was many people's favourite before the race started. *L'Équipe* had rated him 8/10 on the eve of the race, the highest of any contender for the overall win. 'A sense of the spectacular and of attack is his trademark since his debut in mountain biking,' was the paper's view. 'He is not afraid to take risks, to be adventurous.'[20]

His status as one of the favourites for the race despite his tender years had been earned because of a meteoric rise through cycling's ranks. He had already won Paris–Nice in 2019 and had been lined up to lead INEOS at the Giro, but a crash while training in Andorra resulted in a broken collarbone just one week before the race started. 'We'd been in Colombia and then in Andorra preparing for the Giro,' INEOS team coach Xabi Artetxe told *Cyclingnews* a fortnight after the accident. 'After I got to where he was after the crash, he told me, "I know I've broken my collarbone." But as soon as he was out of the operating room on the Sunday, he wasn't thinking about the Giro any more, he was thinking about the next race he could do.'[21]

That race would turn out to be the Tour de Suisse where he won a stage and the overall to cement his place as a stage racer of the highest quality.

The accident meant a reshuffling of his programme and a spot on INEOS' Tour squad as one of their protected riders. He lost time early during the race, most notably on the 27km Pau time trial, leaving him 2min 52sec off the lead. He was still over two minutes down on race leader Julian Alaphilippe as the race entered its Alpine climax. As France dared hope that Alaphilippe could end their thirty-four-year wait for a Tour winner, Bernal started to climb the standings. In Valloire he jumped to second overall, 1min 30sec behind the Frenchman and then the next day he launched his attack on the race, breaking away from the group of favourites on the slopes of the Iseran, the highest mountain on the race route.

It would turn into one of the most memorable stages in recent Tour history. Bernal crested the Iseran at the head of the race, some fifty-eight seconds ahead of his teammate and defending champion Geraint Thomas and more than two minutes ahead of Alaphilippe. The stage was due to finish at Tignes after a descent of the Iseran and a final climb to the ski-station. But a sudden and dramatic hailstorm hit the mountain, causing a number of landslides and giving the organisers no choice but to stop the stage on the descent. The decision was made to take times from the top of the Iseran. And that meant yellow for Bernal. He said after the stage:

> To be honest, I didn't know what was happening. I'd been told on the radio that the race was finished and I said 'no I want to keep going' ... Only after I stopped and my director told me that I was in yellow, I felt relieved ... I want to ride full gas tomorrow and then arrive in Paris and once I cross the line, I'll start believing this is true.[22]

Bernal needn't have doubted his position as race leader. With the last day in the Alps also cut short because of landslides there was no opportunity for anyone to seriously challenge his lead. He finished with a winning margin of 1min 11sec over Thomas. In Paris he hugged his family and stood on the podium, still in a sense of disbelief. 'I think it's going to take me a few days to realise what I have done,' Bernal said. 'This is the first Tour de France for Colombia. It's not just mine, but for everyone. Our country deserves it.'[23]

Ten days later he returned to Colombia as a hero. Fans started arriving at 5 a.m. in Zipaquirá's main square to get a glimpse of the history-maker. As he donated his yellow jersey to Colombia's cycling federation, Bernal told the thousands that had come to see him: 'It was my dream to win the Tour de France, and now I've done it. I'm not sure I'll be able to win it again.'[24] He might just be the only person in cycling who thinks that.

Bernal started cycling aged eight, joining his father, German, on weekend rides. 'One day there was a race for the kids in our town, but my dad didn't want me to compete,' Bernal told *CyclingTips* in 2016. 'Another friend signed me up and gave me a helmet.'[25] Naturally, Bernal won.

With Zipaquirá lying at 2,650m above sea level, most of Bernal's early cycling was done on mountain bikes, claiming silver and bronze junior cross-country medals at the world championships in 2014 and 2015 respectively. He had ridden comparatively little on the road when his climbing potential was touted to Gianni Savio, manager of the pro-continental team Androni Giocattoli. After seeing Bernal's test results Savio snapped him up with a four-year contract. Two years later, and after wins at the Tour des Pays de Savoie and Tour de l'Avenir and an impressive 13th at the Tour of Lombardy, Team Sky (now Team INEOS) swooped.

In his debut WorldTour season Bernal won the Colombia Oro y Paz and the Tour of California as well as recording a podium spot at the Tour de Romandie and riding impressively at the Tour in the service of Thomas. One year later and the roles had been switched. 'I don't want to put pressure on the lad but he's 22, he's got ten years in front of him,' Thomas said after the Colombian's Tour win. 'He could become one of the greatest ever.'[26]

Time will be the judge of that of course. For his part Bernal refused to look too far ahead after his win. Bernal said during his homecoming:

> I don't want to be focused only on Tour de France. I want to focus on each of the races and continue doing what I've been doing so far. I want to live this moment, enjoy it with my people and then think about the future ... I don't want to win a Tour of France and that's it for Egan.[27]

It surely won't be. Welcome to the Egan Bernal era indeed.

MAJOR WINS
Tour de France: 2019

Bobet, Louison

FRA

BORN: 12 MARCH 1925, SAINT-MÉEN-LE-GRAND, FRANCE

When Louison Bobet crossed the finish line of the 1955 Tour wearing yellow, there was a special guest among the welcoming committee that had formed to greet the riders.

In 1920 Belgium's Philippe Thys had become the first man to win three Tours (see Thys entry for more) and he had been on holiday with friends in France when word reached him that the paper *L'Équipe* had invited him to the Tour's finish. The reason? Bobet was about to both match and better the Belgian's record. As Thys changed his plans and travelled north from the Auvergne, Bobet was riding towards Paris, about to become only the second man to win three editions of cycling's greatest race. But the man from Brittany had gone one better than Thys. He had won them in succession.

Bobet's winning margin was 4min 53sec over Jean Brankart and more than eleven minutes over his hated rival Charly Gaul who finished third. A tremendous ride over Mont Ventoux in terrible heat set the foundations of a win which was sealed by a strong performance in the Pyrenees. Over two days Bobet battled Gaul over the Aspin, Peyresourde, Tourmalet and Aubisque, taking the race lead for the first time despite suffering sores that meant he found it difficult to sit on his saddle. Thirty-five thousand fans cheered France's favourite son at the Parc des Princes while Philippe Thys presented a commemorative bouquet before the pair took a ceremonial lap of honour. 'I salute him because he is a great champion,' Thys said before adding: 'I think that if the war had never taken place, I too could have won three consecutive Tours,'[28] thus proving in a single sentence that a cyclist's competitive fire still burns strongly even decades after retirement.

For a while it had seemed that Bobet would never win the Tour. He had first ridden the race in 1947, the year he turned professional, abandoning in the Alps halfway through. One year later he captured French hearts, winning stages and wearing the yellow jersey for the first time while engaging in a fierce battle with Gino Bartali (see Bartali entry for more). He would end that Tour fourth, more than thirty minutes down, but France had fallen for him.

'Tonight, all the girls in France will cry,'[29] wrote Roger Louis Lachat the day after Bobet finally lost the jersey to Bartali.

If the scene seemed set for an imminent Bobet win it wouldn't be until 1953 that the Breton finally took the honours. Before then he had either been forced to abandon or to settle for minor placings, although he stood on the bottom step of the podium in 1950. 'In the Tour de France it [had] seemed that Bobet just did not seem to have the resistance necessary for total victory,'[30] wrote Jock Wadley in 1956, reflecting on those early disappointments.

In 1952 Bobet didn't even start the race, suffering from saddle sores and announcing his decision in a letter in *L'Équipe* five days before the opening stage. Twelve months later and with the race again fast approaching it wasn't certain Bobet would start. He had abandoned the Giro just weeks before, once more with saddle sores. But this time he recovered sufficiently to take his place in a strong French team. Faced with issues of team leadership and team infighting over the first two weeks of the race, team manager Marcel Bidot decided to call a meeting before the race reached its climax in the Alps.

'I will ask one question, only one, to each of you,' Bidot said. 'I'm waiting for a clear answer. Which of you is sure they can take the yellow jersey to Paris?'

Raphaël Géminiani replied that ten days earlier he would have said yes, but now he had a chest infection. Nello Lauredi said he could make the top-five. Then came Bobet's answer.

'If we ride together, I think I can win. If I do, I will give up my winnings.'[31]

And so Bobet became the leader of the French team, with the promise that any winnings would be divided between the team. Six days later he scaled the mighty Izoard alone and sped into the town of Briançon more than five minutes before anyone else to take over the race lead. His final margin in Paris was 14min 18sec. Over his career Bobet would become synonymous with the Izoard and Briançon, three times leading over the Alpine giant and winning in Briançon. Today a memorial to Bobet is mounted in the Casse Déserte, a desolate cathedral of rock a couple of kilometres below the summit on the southern flank of the Izoard, alongside one commemorating Fausto Coppi's exploits on the same mountain.

So what changes had Bobet made in his approach in order to finally become a Tour champion? Wadley wrote:

> More and harder training, a rigid diet and a life of utter simplicity were prime factors in this transformation ... Plus the trust and confidence of his soigneur Raymond Le Bert. From being a rider who always cracked

somewhere on the month-long journey of the Tour de France, the new Bobet became a rider who seemed incapable of cracking even if the race were to go on for another month.[32]

Bobet's second Tour win the following year was even more emphatic. 'I no longer recognised him,' his brother and fellow professional rider, Jean, later wrote. 'He had been liberated; Louison the worrier had become a warrior.'[33]

Bobet had first met Le Bert after the 1948 Tour while in the middle of the post-Tour criterium circuit. Le Bert ran an athlete's surgery in Saint-Brieuc and examined Bobet, who was covered in boils and physically wrecked after his exertions in the Tour, at his parents' house. There were many criteriums still to race but Le Bert was shocked by what he saw and told Bobet's father he was taking his son home with him. 'There is no address. There is no point in looking for us. I have no telephone,' he said. 'The organisers will have to do without him. In any case he is not a racing cyclist anymore, he is a wreck and it is high time he was salvaged.'[34] Thus started a relationship that would take Bobet through his peak years.

Those years were from 1951 to 1956. Bobet was a talented one-day rider as well as a stage racer, claiming a number of important Classic wins including Paris–Roubaix, the Tour of Lombardy, Milan–Sanremo and the Tour of Flanders. That Flanders win came in 1955 when he beat the likes of Rik Van Steenbergen and Bernard Gauthier in the final sprint, a result so unexpected that Pierre Chany wrote that the spectators 'dropped their cartons of frites'[35] in surprise. Bobet was wearing the rainbow jersey at the time, having won the world championship in Solingen some seven months earlier on a devilish course that was described as a 'journalist's dream and the rider's nightmare'.[36] Only twenty-two riders made it to the finish, led in by Bobet under a cold rain that sapped the spirit of many. On the final lap Bobet was away with Switzerland's Fritz Schär when disaster struck the Frenchman after he punctured. But fortune favours the brave and Bobet was lucky to be close to the feed zone and able to collect a replacement bike. He launched a terrific pursuit and caught Schär with 7km to go before striking out alone on the final climb. He won by twelve seconds to become the first French world champion for eighteen years. At the presentation ceremony he grabbed a microphone and shouted: 'Maman, je suis champion du monde!'[37] Later he told journalists 'You can never imagine how much I suffered after my puncture ... No, for nothing in the world would I like to relive those moments ... That was hard. Good God. You have to have suffered on a bike to understand.'[38]

Bobet's Tour de France story ended in 1959 when he climbed off his bike at the summit of the Iseran on Bastille Day, beaten by the mountains he had once conquered. A photograph captured the moment he walked away, coat thrown over his shoulders, the Tour's medical supervisor, Dr Dumas, at this side – 'surely the saddest picture in his personal album',[39] wrote Wadley.

Two years later Bobet retired from cycling to open a thalassotherapy centre in Brittany after a car accident alongside his brother. He died in March 1983 at the age of 58.

MAJOR WINS
Tour de France: 1953, 1954, 1955
Paris–Roubaix: 1956
Tour of Flanders: 1955
Tour of Lombardy: 1951
Milan–Sanremo: 1951
World Champion: 1954
National Champion: 1950, 1951
Bordeaux–Paris: 1959

Bottecchia, Ottavio

ITA

BORN: 1 AUGUST 1894, SAN MARTINO, ITALY

On 3 June 1927 Ottavio Bottecchia, by then a two-time Tour champion, was out training on his bicycle in the Friuli area of north-east Italy. From humble beginnings Bottecchia had grown into a major sports star in Italy and after the disappointment of not finishing the previous year's race, he was focused on trying to add a third Tour title to his palmarès. Bottecchia woke early that day and got ready to go out on his bike even though he didn't really want to go training. He wasn't feeling well and he had failed to convince any fellow cyclists to accompany him. They all had other things they needed to do but Bottecchia knew he needed to train. He was a professional cyclist and this was what he did. And so he went alone, telling his wife he'd be back mid afternoon.

Around 30km north-west of Udine is the village of Peonis. The road into the village from the south runs alongside the Tagliamento, a river that rises in the Alps and flows into the Adriatic Sea. It was here that later that day two locals found Bottecchia lying on the roadside with head injuries, some distance from his seemingly undamaged bike. He was taken to a nearby inn and a priest summoned to administer the last rites before being placed in a cart and taken to hospital, some 12km away along bumpy roads and under a fierce sun. Twelve days later he was pronounced dead.

Today that road into Peonis is called the Via O. Bottecchia and a memorial stands where the champion cyclist was found. Exactly what happened that day has long since been the source of much debate. Theories abounded, from the mundane to the fantastical: he fell from his bike; he was hit by a car; he was caught stealing grapes by a farmer who threw a rock at him which hit him on the head (even though grapes aren't ripe in June the farmer apparently confessed on his deathbed); he was killed by a hitman contracted by fascists who wanted to stop him popularising his socialist leanings in Italy (an Italian in New York supposedly admitted to doing the 'hit' in another deathbed confession); he bent down to adjust a toe strap, suffered a dizzy spell, fell and hit his head; he was killed because he had insulted a friend of Mussolini's by rejecting a compensation offer after the friend had run over and killed Bottecchia's brother in an accident.

No theory truly stacks up. The formal verdict was death by 'malaise, sunstroke and a fall'.[40] But whatever the truth of his death, in life he made a huge impact on cycling and the Tour, becoming the first Italian to win cycling's greatest race. 'His name will remain inseparable from the Tour de France,'[41] wrote André Reuze in a tribute piece.

Accounts vary regarding Bottecchia's pre-cycling life: some have him working with horses, some as a vegetable grower, some as a mason making bricks and building walls. All portray a hard life spent in a family with seven siblings and no money. His cycling abilities were spotted during the First World War when he rode to the top of mountain passes carrying heavy loads. A friend, Alfonso Piccin, convinced him to try bike racing – Piccin would also ride professionally – and by 1923 Bottecchia was riding as an *indépendant*, finishing in the top ten of Milan-Sanremo and then fifth at the Giro.

That ride earned him an invite to the Tour on Henri Pélissier's Automoto team. Pélissier would win that Tour and Bottecchia would finish second having worn yellow and won a stage, a remarkable debut. Twelve months later it would get even better.

The first stage of the 1924 Tour ran 381km from Paris to Le Havre. A little over fifteen hours after they had set out Bottecchia led the sprint into the port, 'a brilliant, Italian triumph',[42] according to *L'Auto*. After Pélissier abandoned in controversial circumstances (see Pélissier entry for more) Bottecchia became Automoto's main man. In truth he was by far Automoto's strongest rider anyway, a fact recognised by Pélissier who said, 'in this form, Bottecchia is head and shoulders above the rest of us',[43] before he abandoned.

Bottecchia wore yellow from the end of the first day to the last, the first rider in history to do so. He was imperious in the Pyrenees, transforming a three-minute lead into 30min 21sec, attacking on the Aubisque and not resting until he powered into Luchon four mountains later. His winning margin in Paris was 35min 36sec and he reportedly wore his yellow jersey on the train back to Italy so proud he was of his win. He would repeat the feat the following year, winning by an even greater margin.

Regarded as taciturn and quiet by the French – he possessed just a smattering of the language – he rode simply to earn money. 'Once I have my house I will not ride anymore,'[44] he said after his first Tour win. He was well respected if not quite loved. 'In truth he was not well known,' wrote Reuze. 'I saw him sneaking behind the official cars, the finish line crossed, to escape congratulations. Modesty? Without a doubt. Timidity? Perhaps. The victor's bouquet was, for him, nothing but clutter.'[45]

MAJOR WINS
Tour de France: 1924, 1925

Buysse, Lucien

BEL

BORN: 11 SEPTEMBER 1892, WONTERGEM, BELGIUM

The legend of Lucien Buysse was forged on 6 July 1926, the tenth stage of what remains the longest Tour in the record books, some 5,745km over seventeen racing days. The nine preceding stages had been something of an anticlimax. A nervous and uncertain peloton, concerned at the long distances, had ridden conservatively, meaning the majority of stages had ended in bunch sprints. The one notable exception had been the solo escape of Jules Buysse, younger brother of Lucien, on the opening stage where he raced into Mulhouse to claim the race's first yellow jersey by more than thirteen minutes.

However, it was Belgium's Gustaaf Van Slembrouck who was in yellow at the start of stage 10. Lucien Buysse was eighth overall, more than twenty minutes back. How things were about to change. The day's racing started in Bayonne, on France's southern Atlantic coast, and ran for 326km to Luchon, in the heart of the Pyrenees. On the way the peloton faced the climbs of the Aubisque, Tourmalet, Aspin and Peyresourde, the four Pyrenean peaks that combine for the so-called 'circle of death'. As that moniker suggests it was a stage to be feared, considered by far the toughest of the race. While it was already known that the race was entering its 'decisive phase',[46] what hadn't been anticipated was the weather that hit the Pyrenees that day. That made it a stage the likes of which the Tour has rarely seen.

The horrendous conditions that day made an already supremely difficult day all but impossible. The unleashed elements brought a gale that cut to the bone and torrential rain that drenched the skin. Ice formed on the mountains and the dirt roads became nothing but trails of mud. Henri Desgrange, a man not known for sympathising with the travails of those who rode his race, described the conditions as glacial. 'Our men suffered terribly,' he wrote in the pages of L'Auto before detailing their ordeal as a 'true martyrdom'.[47] In his book Le Tour de France et les Pyrénées, Dominique Kérébel simply labels the stage as 'Dantesque'.[48]

The rain had started to fall at Eaux-Bonnes, on the lower slopes of the Aubisque. Buysse was at the head of proceedings and led the race over the climb. While he then trailed by more than one minute over the Tourmalet, by the time he had reached the foot of the third climb, the Aspin, he was alone and in the lead by more than five minutes. As thunder roared and lightning danced over the Pyrenees, Buysse rose over the Aspin and Peyresourde in glorious isolation. He rolled into Luchon 25min 48sec ahead of the next rider. He had been in the saddle for more than seventeen hours but was now in yellow with a margin of more than thirty-six minutes.

Behind had been nothing but carnage. Only fifty-four riders made it to Luchon. Many had abandoned or taken shelter in bars, unable to carry on. At midnight search parties were sent out to round up the missing men. Normal race controls were abandoned, the time cut-off forgotten. In the pages of Le Petit Parisien, the journalist L.C. Royer questioned whether the 'massacre' counted as sport:

> I leave here the numbers. The first, Lucien Buysse, whose performance, according to the specialists, is a miracle, only arrived two hours late. At the time when, following the letter of the regulations, the control was to be closed, only 31 riders had arrived ... Thirty-five riders, out of the 76 starters in Bayonne, still remained on the road. Finally, we decided to accept all the arrivals, I mean all the survivors, whatever the time in which, dead or alive, they would come to the control ... At 2 o'clock in the morning there were still statues of mud seeking race control in the streets of Luchon. How did they come? On foot, on horseback, by car or by train? Nobody knows.
>
> If this is sport, I will never really understand anything ... Bottecchia refrigerated to the point of not being able to speak; Cuvelier, whose frozen hands could not change a tyre; Detreille, too weak to unscrew his pump ... Pfister, a big kid of twenty-three, half-unconscious at the bottom of Tourmalet ...You will tell me that all this makes even more remarkable the effort made by Buysse and all those who have arrived behind him. I agree with that. But all the same, I think about the others too.[49]

What made Buysse's effort even more astonishing, and perhaps goes some way in explaining how he found the strength to carry on in such conditions, was that he had already suffered far worse. Shortly before the race his daughter had died of meningitis but his family had urged him to continue. Bad weather wasn't about to stop him trying to win in the name of his daughter. Buysse won the next stage into Perpignan and rode into Paris with a winning margin of 1hr 22min 25sec. He later said that he had thought of his daughter 'during all the hardest hours of the race'.[50]

Buysse's 1926 Tour win was the only major victory of a career that spanned fifteen war-interrupted, years. Other notable results of his are top-three placings in Paris–Roubaix, Bordeaux–Paris and Liège-Bastogne-Liège. Buysse retired from cycling in 1930 and later opened the Café Aubisque, named after the first mountain he scaled on the day he forged his legend and where today a bust of him stands to commemorate his 1926 Tour win.

Buysse died in January 1980, aged 87.

MAJOR WINS
Tour de France: 1926

Contador, Alberto

ESP

BORN: 6 DECEMBER 1982, MADRID, SPAIN

'Un año más,' they chanted. When Alberto Contador stood on a balcony in September 2017, overlooking the Plaza de La Constitución in his home town of Pinto, two days after he completed his final race as a professional cyclist, the message from the thousands that stood below him was clear. They wanted more. Contador had heard it before. Throughout the 2017 Vuelta the echo of 'one more year', had followed him. From the roadsides, from the mountaintops, through the windows of the hotel. 'Even my colleagues on the bus began to sing it,' he told the Spanish sports newspaper *AS*. Contador was moved but he was also determined to stand firm, resolute against the imploring for one more dance. 'I think there's no better time to leave,' he said.[1]

And how could there have been a better time? Three days earlier on the Angliru, the final climb of the Vuelta, Contador had distilled into 15km of racing everything that he had brought to professional cycling over the preceding fifteen years or so. With the tantalising prize of a second stage win on the Vuelta's most feared mountain dangling right in front of him, Contador went for it. He could have sat in and waited. He could have let other teams do the work while he waited to try to outfox his rivals for the stage, maybe hit them further up the climb with a single deadly hit of trademark acceleration. But no. That wasn't how Contador rolled. He had one day in the mountains left and he wasn't going to let it pass him by. Forty-five minutes of effort stood between him and the summit and he wasn't about to retire thinking, 'What if?' Take the chance. Roll the dice. Glory or nothing. Do it.

And so it was that Contador closed his career with one of his greatest stage wins and created another piece of history in the process – the first man to win twice atop the Angliru. No better time to leave.

Contador had entered the professional peloton in 2003, aged 20 and having signed for Manolo Saiz's ONCE after three months as a *stagiaire*. In September that same year he won his first race, a 19km time trial at the Tour of Poland. All seemed set fair but at the 2004 Tour of Asturias he collapsed and left the race. Ten days later he collapsed again. The congenital condition, cerebral cavernoma, was the diagnosis and brain surgery was required. Eight months later he was back riding with a metal plate in his head. In January 2005 he announced his return by winning stage 5 of the Tour Down Under, ripping the race to shreds on the final climb of Willunga Hill alongside his Liberty-Seguros teammate Luis Leon Sanchez. In the run-in to the finish Sanchez, who was leading the race overall, started celebrating and pointing to his teammate, leaving Contador to take the stage. Contador took his teammate's hand before blowing kisses to the sky as he crossed the line. In 2017 Contador reflected on that moment:

> I have always said that the most important victory for me, even if it was not the biggest sporting event, was the victory in the queen stage of the Tour Down Under that I won just after recovering from the cerebral stroke that I suffered in 2004. Some months before, I did not know if I would be a cyclist or even if I was going to be able to have a normal life. That's why that victory will always mean a lot to me.[2]

It was in 2007 that Contador entered the sport's upper echelons. He won the prestigious Paris–Nice race and went to the Tour hoping for a top-five overall finish and the white jersey of best young rider. It turned out to be much better.

Contador was lying third going into the stage to the Pyrenean ski-station Plateau de Beille, more than two minutes behind the yellow jersey of Michael Rasmussen. In a frenzy of climbing action, the Tour's finest mountain men attacked and counter-attacked for kilometre after kilometre. Contador and Rasmussen dropped everyone else in their pursuit of the lone breakaway rider Antonio Colom who they caught with just over 3km to go. Contador and Rasmussen matched each other pedal stroke for pedal stroke until the Spaniard jumped ahead of the Dane in the closing metres, crossing the line with what would become his trademark pistol gesture to claim his first Tour stage win. Two days later the two men went head-to-head again on the slopes of the Aubisque. This time the Dane rebuffed attack after attack of Contador's, before pulling away in the final kilometre. Rasmussen came with some baggage though. Before the stage it had been revealed that he had missed three drug tests and had lied to the authorities about his whereabouts. Rasmussen was booed by fans on the mountainside and that same evening, under intense scrutiny, he was thrown off the Tour by his Rabobank team. Contador took yellow and held it to Paris. In only his second Tour, Contador had reached cycling's pinnacle.

From that first Tour win Contador grew into the king of the Grand Tours. By the end of the 2015 season he had two Tour, two Giro and three Vuelta titles to his name – a stellar return bettered by no one during that time. But it was not always smooth going. Contador also had questions asked of him.

First, Contador's name had come up during the Operación Puerto investigation into doping practices by Eufemiano Fuentes that broke just prior to the 2006 Tour. Many of Contador's then Astana-Würth squad were implicated and the team was denied a start to the Tour. Contador's name was also mentioned in the documents investigated but it was later ruled that his name appeared only in reference to team training and Fuentes himself denied any connection. For his part Contador said he was guilty only of being on the wrong team at the wrong time and was subsequently cleared of any wrongdoing.

Then came 'chaingate' at the 2010 Tour when Contador attacked on the Port de Balès while the yellow-jersey-wearing Andy Schleck stopped to deal with a slipped chain. Contador, who was the defending champion, gained thirty-nine seconds and took the jersey from Schleck before holding it to the top step in Paris with a winning margin of, yes, thirty-nine seconds. It was Contador's third Tour win in four years but many thought it a slap in the face of cycling's unwritten rules of not benefitting from the mechanical misfortunes of the race leader. Commentators and fans were divided and Contador was rattled enough to issue a YouTube video statement explaining his perspective, saying that maybe he had made a mistake.

That race would again come into the spotlight a couple of months later when the biggest controversy of Contador's career broke. In late September 2010 the UCI announced that the Spaniard had tested positive for a small amount of the prohibited drug clenbuterol during the race. Contador claimed he had ingested the drug unwittingly by eating contaminated meat and there followed a lengthy investigation with multiple cases heard. In early 2011 Contador was provisionally cleared by the Spanish federation and resumed riding, adding the 2011 Giro to his palmarès, but the UCI and WADA appealed. The ultimate verdict was delivered by the Court of Arbitration for Sport (CAS) in February 2012 which concluded:

> the Athlete's positive test for clenbuterol is more likely to have been caused by the ingestion of a contaminated food supplement than by a blood transfusion or the ingestion of contaminated meat ... no evidence has been adduced proving that the Athlete acted with no fault or negligence or no significant fault or negligence.[3]

CAS upheld a two-year ban, retrospectively applied. That meant the wiping of all Contador's results from the time of the 2010 positive test, with Andy Schleck awarded the 2010 Tour and Michele Scarponi the 2011 Giro.

Contador would never win the Tour again. His final major victory came at the 2015 Giro. Now riding for the Tinkoff-Saxo team he inherited the race lead on stage 5, then lost it after being held up in a crash on stage 13, before regaining the jersey the following day and holding it until Milan. *En route* he survived an assault on his lead on the Mortirolo when Katusha and Astana attacked after Contador had punctured on the penultimate descent. The reaction was typical Contador: nearly one minute down on his rivals at the start of the final climb he immediately left the wheel of teammate Roman Kreuziger, who had towed him along the valley, and danced his way up the Mortirolo.

He didn't win the stage but make no mistake, Contador on the Mortirolo in 2015 was a ride for the ages. Here was a race leader pitted against a legendary mountain in a bid to save his race. And Contador had read the script. Ahead of him Astana's Mikel Landa was towing his team leader Fabio Aru up the road with Steven Kruijswijk for company, while Contador doggedly picked his way through the remnants of the leading group that had splintered on the Mortirolo's precipitous road. With 7km of the climb still to go he'd made it back. Landa went on to win the stage while Contador rolled into Aprica alongside Kruijswijk. Not only had Contador saved his Giro but he had increased his gap at the top of the standings from 2min 35sec over Aru, to 4min 2sec over Landa. 'These are the kind of stages that people remember,' Contador said afterwards.[4]

Five days later Contador stood on the podium in Milan wearing pink, joining Bernard Hinault as the only men to have won all three Grand Tours more than once. 'I think I have achieved everything I could dream of as a rider,' Contador said after his 2017 retirement. 'I have not won a world championship or a great cobbled classic, but those are not goals for a climber like me. A specialist of stage races.'[5]

MAJOR WINS
Tour de France: 2007, 2009
Giro d'Italia: 2008, 2015
Vuelta a España: 2008, 2012, 2014

Coppi, Fausto
ITA

BORN: 15 SEPTEMBER 1919, CASTELLANIA, ITALY

In the early evening of 28 June 1952, the French cycling writer René De Latour knocked on the door of Fausto Coppi's hotel room in Roubaix. De Latour had just watched France's Pierre Molinéris win a Tour stage and his teammate, Nello Lauredi, slip on the yellow jersey. It was early in the race and Coppi was sitting outside the top ten, nor had he featured in the action to Roubaix. You might therefore have expected De Latour to be more focused on the two French riders on this particular evening but Coppi was cycling's greatest draw and De Latour had been contracted by two French journals to file stories on the Italian. That meant seeking regular chats with the *Campionissimo* and so it was to Coppi's room that he headed.

De Latour knew Coppi well, later writing that 'in 25 years of cycling journalism I have never met a rider so informative or willing to help',[6] but this night he found the Italian in a fury. He was pacing the room and shouting at his soigneur, aggressively throwing his towel against the wall. De Latour said he'd come back later but Coppi told him to stay, adding that they should go out and eat together. And so De Latour found himself in a car, with Coppi dressed only in a tracksuit and bedroom slippers, driving out of Roubaix in search of a quiet restaurant. 'What's wrong with you tonight?' De Latour asked. 'I may as well tell you,' Coppi said. 'I just can't stand the sight of that hypocrite Bartali anymore. He ruins my appetite.'[7] Over the course of the next three hours Coppi cut loose. 'That interview with Coppi was the greatest scoop of my journalism career,' De Latour wrote five years later.[8]

Coppi had started the 1952 Tour unhappy that his great rival Gino Bartali was on the Italian team with him. He had questioned team manager Alfredo Binda about the decision, saying that all he needed to win the race was a handful of loyal teammates and that Bartali could hardly be counted as such. Coppi and Bartali's rivalry was fierce and divided Italy. Five years earlier the two riders had been sanctioned by the Italian cycling federation for what they judged to be a lack of competitive spirit at the world championships, with neither man willing to chase down a move made by Belgium's Alberic Schotte for fear of towing the other to victory. The French daily *Le Monde* reported that the two Italians were 'only concerned to watch each other',[9] while *La Stampa* accused the pair of 'playing an ugly game', describing Bartali as 'a lead ball and chain'.[10] Things had barely improved between the two in the years since.

'I should never have agreed to start in this Tour with him as a teammate, if I can call him that,' Coppi told De Latour. 'He is not there to help me but to watch me ... It's just like having a traitor in our group. It makes me sick.' Coppi went on to say that he felt he was riding strongly and would perform well in the mountains. 'But riding strongly is not enough,' he said. 'There is another great quality necessary to back up "form" and that is to have a good morale – to be happy and content during a race instead of being in a bad temper as you found me this evening ... the presence of Bartali is a terrible handicap to me.'[11]

A terrible handicap? If so, goodness only knows what Coppi would have achieved at the Tour in 1952 had Bartali not been present. Two days after that meal with De Latour, the Italian won the first time trial of the race. Three days later he rode away from France's Jean Robic on the slopes of l'Alpe d'Huez, becoming the first rider to win on what is now the Tour's most famous mountain and taking yellow. Two days after that he put on a masterclass on the stage to Sestriere, leading over the climbs of the Croix de Fer, the Galibier and Montgenèvre on the way to a 7min 9sec stage win. That night his overall lead stood at nearly twenty minutes. In Italy's *Corriere della Sera*, Orio Vergani likened Coppi's performance more to an orgy than a mere triumph, claiming he was turning the Tour into a demonstration of his 'phenomenal talent'.[12] 'From the very long ascent to the Croix de Fer, that separates the Dauphiné from Savoy, the yellow jersey had started to apply brushstrokes to his masterpiece,'[13] was Vittoria Varale's take in *La Stampa*. By the time Coppi entered Paris his winning margin was 28min 17sec. One month earlier Coppi had won the Giro d'Italia for the fourth time. His win in France had secured his second Giro/Tour double, a feat he had first achieved three years earlier. Until Coppi had arrived the Giro/Tour double was considered an impossibility: the races were too long, too arduous and too close together for anyone to win both in the same year. But Coppi did the impossible. Twice.

Angelo Fausto was the fourth of five children born to Domenico and Angiolina Coppi in Castellania, north-west Italy, and discovered his talent for cycling in his work as a butcher's delivery boy. He was introduced to a masseur and former cycling team manager, Biagio Cavanna. The blind Cavanna took the young Coppi under his wing, taught him how to train as a professional and would be a mainstay in Coppi's life from that moment on.

After turning professional in 1939 with the Legnano team, which was led by Bartali, Coppi secured his first Giro title the following year. Aged just 20, Coppi had been selected to ride in support of Bartali but outshone his leader. Their rivalry was years away and Bartali actually helped Coppi to secure the win. The star of a new generation had been born. 'His sensational revelation is the mark with which this Giro will go down in history,'[14] wrote Giuseppe Ambrosini in *La Stampa*. Twelve months on, aware that he could not exist for much longer on the same team as Bartali, Coppi moved to Bianchi, the team with which he is most famously linked to this day.

Coppi was photogenic and graceful on a bike, with an ability to 'turn on the windmill with devastating effect more than any other rider in the game.'[15] Fellow rider André Leducq spoke of Coppi caressing rather than gripping the handlebars – 'all the moving parts turn in oil. His long face appears like a blade of a knife as he climbs without apparent effort, like a great artist painting a water colour.'[16]

Without the kick of the natural sprinter, Coppi often won his races alone, choosing the right moment to attack and then staying away to the finish. This meant that his victories often came with a certain flair, exploits that served only to cement his reputation. Stage 17 at the 1949 Giro is just one example. Coppi put in a huge attack over five Alpine passes in terrible weather, gliding up the mountain slopes, building more and more time as he went. The majestic Coppi arrived in Pinerolo after more than nine hours of riding having completely destroyed the field, taken control of the race and confirmed his status as the best rider in the world. The radio commentator Mario Ferretti described to his listeners a lone rider leading the race, wearing a white and blue jersey: 'His name is Fausto Coppi.'[17]

Such rides earned him the title Il Campionissimo (champion of champions). Under Cavanna's guidance he revolutionised training techniques, replicating racing conditions by getting riders to attack him in the final 100km of long training rides, or putting in huge efforts for short periods of time before returning to tempo. Jacques Goddet, journalist and long-time director of the Tour, said that 'Merckx was the strongest cyclist of all time, and Coppi the greatest ...'[18]

Away from the bike Coppi's private life was complicated. He was close to his brother Serse, who was also a professional cyclist, and was devastated when he died after an accident at the 1951 Giro del Piemonte, shortly before the Tour. Just under a month later Coppi won the Tour stage over the Izoard and into Briançon but his grief, coupled with illness, meant he could only finish tenth overall. Then there was his affair with the so-called 'White Lady', Giulia Locatelli, which led to the very public failure of both his marriage and hers at a time when adultery in Italy was a criminal offence. Such was the extent of the scandal that the Vatican intervened in a vain attempt to encourage Coppi to repair his marriage. Coppi, who already had a daughter with his wife, eventually fathered a son, Faustino, with Locatelli.

In 1953, as rumours about Coppi and Locatelli's relationship were growing, Coppi landed the one jersey that had been missing from his wardrobe – the rainbow jersey of road world champion. Again, he put on a stunning solo performance, this time on the roads of Switzerland, escaping on the climb of the Crespera to record a huge win. A cartoon drawn after the race depicts Coppi in full flight but without a bike, pedalling only air, such was the freedom of his movement. His margin of victory was such that he had reportedly completed much of the post-race protocol before the next rider arrived, though whether 6min 22sec is really enough time for all the actions that follow a bike race to be completed before the runner-up comes home is surely a matter a of debate.

> He was hugged, kissed, carried, cheered, taken to the UCI's president, invested with his championship vest, presented with flowers, stood to attention whilst his country's national anthem was sung, and the Italian flag went to the masthead ... and then it was that the second man in the world's professional road championship, 1953, crossed the finishing line![19]

Or so reported *Cycling,* perhaps with more than a hint of poetic licence.

Locatelli had been in Switzerland and was actually photographed with Coppi as he celebrated on the podium. Also there was Coppi's wife, Bruna. In a bid to avoid further controversy, that night Coppi went home with Bruna and Cavanna rather than attend the celebratory dinner. Five days later Coppi recorded the fastest 5km individual pursuit recorded at the famous Vigorelli velodrome in Milan. Thousands stood outside, chanting for their hero, hoping for a glimpse of the great man.

Coppi's life ended prematurely. He was a keen hunter and fisherman and in 1959 had been invited to Africa, to ride some races and take in some hunting. While there he fell ill. Two weeks after his return, on 2 January 1960, Coppi died of malaria in hospital. He was 40 years old. Ten thousand mourners attended his funeral.

MAJOR WINS
Tour de France: 1949, 1952
Giro d'Italia: 1940, 1947, 1949, 1952, 1953
Paris-Roubaix: 1950
Tour of Lombardy: 1946, 1947, 1948, 1949, 1954
Milano–Sanremo: 1946, 1948, 1949
World Champion: 1953
National Champion: 1942, 1947, 1949, 1955

Cornet, Henri

FRA

BORN: 4 AUGUST 1884, DESVRES, FRANCE

Eighty-eight riders assembled at the Réveil-Matin café in Montgeron, a suburb south-east of central Paris, on 2 July 1904 for the Tour's second edition. Among them was Henri Cornet, a 19 year old sponsored by the little-known Paris company, Cycles JC. Actually, Cornet wasn't his real name, that was Henri Jardry, but by 1904 he had adopted the Cornet name. He would also be known as '**Le Rigolo,**' – the joker – due to his sunny demeanour.

If Cornet wasn't a particularly noteworthy rider before the Tour started, he certainly was afterwards. Four months afterwards to be precise, as it wasn't until December 1904 that the results of the second Tour were confirmed by the UVF – the French cycling federation – and which declared Cornet the winner. To say such an announcement was unexpected is something of an understatement, mainly because Cornet had actually finished fifth in Paris.

If the first Tour in 1903 had captured France's imagination like no one in the offices of *L'Auto* had dared hope, the 1904 Tour was nothing short of a disaster. With huge rewards on offer cheating was rife. Riders drafted behind cars, took the train, accepted lifts or traded places at stage finishes.

And it wasn't just the riders that took things beyond acceptable limits. On the race's second stage, from Lyon to Marseilles, the route went over the Col de la République. Maurice Garin, the winner of the first edition, was leading the race much to dislike of a number of locals. Antoine Fauré, a 21 year old from Gerzat, had strong ties to the area unlike Garin who had been born in Italy but later taken French nationality. Fauré was a favourite of the people that lived around the République and they decided to try to help him win. Their method? Simple: batter the other riders into submission.

So it was that on the République locals armed with sticks and rocks formed a barrier. They let Fauré pass and then set about the other riders, raining stones down on them and beating them about the head. Pierre Chany described the events: 'A swarm of fanatics, sticks raised, insults on their lips, fall on the other riders. Maurice and César Garin are beaten, the eldest [Maurice] gets a stone in the face ... *"Vive Fauré!* Down with Garin! Kill them!" they scream.'[20]

The Garin brothers weren't the only ones attacked: Italian rider Giovanni Gerbi had his fingers broken and had to abandon. The beatings only ended when officials arrived, firing pistols into the air in a desperate attempt to rescue their racers.

After three weeks of mayhem it seemed that Maurice Garin had defended his title despite the best efforts of certain spectators when he finished more than three hours ahead of second-placed Lucien Pothier. But Henri Desgrange was embarrassed by what had happened and the UVF wasn't happy either. Two days after the race finished Desgrange penned a front-page article that announced that the second Tour would also be its last – 'killed by its own success, by the blind passions that it unleashed and the insults and dirty suspicions of the ignorant or the wicked'.[21] For their part the UVF stated Garin's win was only provisional until it was able to unravel what had gone on.

It took the UVF over four months to do that unravelling. On 30 November 1904 they announced that Garin, along with twenty-eight others, including the rest of the top four, were disqualified. Two days later the revised results of the race were officially issued, with Cornet declared the winner. Cornet had been just shy of his 20th birthday when the Tour ended and remains the youngest winner of the race to this day. The race organisation, the disqualified riders, and their sponsors, were furious, and *L'Auto* made no effort to conceal that fury, speaking to the various slighted parties and quoting them at length:

> 'By what right,' says M. Hammond [director of Maurice Garin's sponsor, *La Française*] 'does the UVF stand up in a court of law without appeal? ... I did not spend several thousand francs to hire several riders for the Tour de France, to now come and hear them say: "You are disqualified," and no more. Why? I ask why they are disqualified?'

Garin himself called it a 'flagrant injustice'. Cornet, meanwhile was said to be: 'stunned when he learned of the sentence pronounced by the UVF, but the amazement quickly gave way to joy, not before, however, making sure that the news was accurate.'[22]

Cornet rode the Tour another seven times before retiring from cycling, an eighth-place finish in 1908 his only other top-ten result. He was sometimes portrayed unfairly as a weak rider, beset by health problems, a beneficiary of officialdom. Away from the Tour his best result came in 1906 with a win at Paris-Roubaix, beating Marcel Cadolle in a two-man sprint.

Cornet retired from cycling before the outbreak of war. In April 1915 he wrote a letter from the trenches to Henri Desgrange which was published on the front page of *L'Auto* and in which his light-hearted nature came across despite the terrible conditions he must have faced. He gave updates on his own health and that of other Tour winners now engaged in fighting a war – the likes of Octave Lapize and Odile Defraye – before offering a little insight into life on the front:

> Look, yesterday, I had established my headquarters in a building where only the roof was missing, when a shell came and burst 10 metres from me ... I first finished lighting my pipe, then, scornfully and marking my contempt, I spat over my shoulder in the direction of the shell ... Am I not a first-class soldier?[23]

Cornet owned a bike shop after retirement. He died in 1941.

MAJOR WINS
Tour de France: 1904
Paris-Roubaix: 1906

De Waele, Maurice

BEL

BORN: 27 DECEMBER 1896, LOVENDEGEM, BELGIUM

Going into stage 15 of the 1929 Tour, Belgium's Maurice De Waele was in yellow. His margin over the second-placed Joseph Demuysere was more than fourteen minutes. There remained a long way to go to Paris but De Waele, a member of the Alcyon team, was in prime position, surely destined to win and become the sixth Belgian to win the race.

Then, just before that fifteenth stage, 329km from Grenoble to Évian over the passes of the Lauteret, Galibier and Aravis, disaster struck. *Le Miroir des Sports* takes up the story:

An hour before the stage, Maurice De Waele found himself suddenly inconvenienced and, taken with violent vomiting, had to go to the bathroom. Fortunately, Meunier, the devoted second of Ludo [Feuillet, director of the Alcyon team], was present and had accompanied De Waele, for the leader of the Tour de France suddenly fell unconscious. If no one had noticed his absence, De Waele could very well have remained shut up in the bathroom, though he would have been vainly sought everywhere else.[1]

De Waele was in trouble. He had eaten something bad and had been ill all night – according to Jacques Sys's book *Top 1000 van de Belgische Wielrenners* he had been 'more on the toilet than he was in his bed'.[2] In agony with violent stomach cramps, he was 'dragged at two o'clock in the morning, wailing, to the start'.[3] Three hundred grams of sugar, mixed with water was all he could stomach, and then he was sent on his way.

De Waele's Alcyon team was strong, with a number of talented riders on the roster. But the autocratic Henri Desgrange had reverted to type and outlawed teamwork in his race. It was every rider for himself and so, in theory at least, De Waele could not seek assistance from his teammates when he most needed it. He was on his own.

Except of course that wasn't quite how things played out. Instead his team, and riders from other outfits who had been convinced to help by the influential Feuillet, protected De Waele, blocking the road, keeping the pace low and pushing the all-but-incapacitated leader of the race when the commissaires looked elsewhere. 'We cut off our arms to help him save the jersey,'[4] future Alcyon rider Marcel Bidot said, who was at the time on the La Française team. Incredibly, De Waele rolled into Évian in eleventh position and still in the overall lead.

Desgrange couldn't believe that a man who was so ill only moments before the stage had survived and retained the race lead. He was convinced his regulations had been broken. 'My race has been won by a corpse,' he complained. 'Why were his opponents so ineffective? What to think of their tactics and the real value of the winner.'[5] But Alcyon was too powerful an outfit for Desgrange to do much about it. He couldn't disqualify De Waele – Alcyon often took out large, quarter-page adverts in his paper, celebrating their regular successes.

Instead Desgrange had to content himself with pouring further scorn on De Waele's rivals. After De Waele won the 270km Charleville to

Malo-les-Bains stage – held six days after his survival in the Alps and in which the peloton was started in two separate bunches as a result of another Desgrange regulation which held that if the pace of a stage dropped below 30km/h the bunch would be split up like naughty schoolkids the next day – the editor of *L'Auto* and father of the Tour accused the Belgian's rivals of offering De Waele 'A lovely gift'. He wrote:

> This morning, our riders had a very touching thought, which is more due to their sensitivity than their understanding of the race. They decided to give De Waele a gift, probably to celebrate his bravery and courage, to give him – I say – ten minutes in the overall standings. So his victory ... is now consolidated and it would need a kind of disaster for him to be removed now.[6]

There was no further disaster for De Waele and he won in Paris with a margin of nearly forty-five minutes. Desgrange, as was clear, was unimpressed. The Belgian had inherited the yellow jersey in the first place only when Victor Fontan abandoned in the Pyrenees after his forks broke. And so De Waele was never considered a grand champion by Desgrange even though he had twice finished the Tour in the top three previously, won the Tour of the Basque Country, and podiumed at both the Tour of Flanders and Bordeaux–Paris. The disparaging comments were a little harsh and more a reflection on the Tour's continuous battles with cycling's manufacturers than De Waele himself.

A talented cyclo-cross rider – he won the national title in 1922 before turning to the road and track as a professional – De Waele had a reputation for consistency and was nicknamed 'the metronome'. The Tour remained his only major victory. He retired from professional cycling at the end of the 1931 season after finishing sixth in the mammoth Paris–Brest–Paris, going on to build a successful cycle business. He died in 1952 aged 56.

MAJOR WINS
Tour de France: 1929

Defraeye, Odiel

BEL

BORN: 14 JULY 1888, RUMBEKE, BELGIUM

Described by the writer Jacques Sys as 'the forgotten Godfather',[7] in 1912 Odiel Defraeye, sometimes spelled Odile Defraye, became the first Belgian to win the Tour. For the last time the race's general classification was calculated using a points-based system, with the rider with the fewest points declared the winner (see Trousselier entry for more on the points system). Defraeye's final tally of forty-nine was comfortably the lowest – second-placed Eugène Christophe amassed some 108 points – but it would be wrong to suggest that this was a completely dominant performance and an easy win for Defraeye. In truth, had the classification been decided on elapsed time, as has been the case for the vast majority of the Tour's 117-year-and-counting history, Christophe would have been leading the race going into the final day by some eleven minutes.

As it turned out Christophe reportedly sat up in the final stage, having suffered a puncture and knowing that overall victory was impossible. He trailed into Paris eighteen minutes behind Defraeye who finished fifth on the stage, in the same time as the stage winner. Defraeye's elapsed time was 190hr 34min, some seven minutes faster than Christophe's. It meant that the same result would have been achieved had the Tour been decided on time, but Christophe would have surely ridden the final stage very differently had he been in with a chance of winning.

Defraeye had only ridden the Tour once before – in 1909 – during his first year as a professional having turned his back on his job as a brush-maker. He'd abandoned on the second stage. Three years later he had not been included in the initial Alcyon team selected for the race and it took the angry intervention of the company's Belgian representatives to push for his involvement. Initially tasked with riding for Alcyon's leader Gustave Garrigou, Defraeye won the Tour's second stage and then beat his nominated leader on the third stage as well, coming second behind Christophe. By the time the race reached its midway point the Belgian was firmly established as Alcyon's leading rider, and sat at the top of the classification with a fourteen-point margin over Garrigou having placed better than the Frenchman in all but one stage.

In the end Defraeye claimed three stages on the way to his overall win, including a solo win into Luchon, over the Port, Portet d'Aspet and Ares climbs, a stage during which his main rival in the standings, Octave Lapize, abandoned, taking his entire La Française team with him. *L'Auto* reported:

> A dramatic twist marks the ninth stage of the Tour de France ... While he could still expect first place in the overall standings, Lapize gave up. His marvellous rival, Odile Defraye, remains alone in the lead now, and he is likely to maintain his command to Paris. In the formidable duel long-engaged between the champion of France and the champion of Belgium, one of them had to let go; it is Lapize who has yielded; and if there is some patriotic regret as far as we are concerned we will not conceal the admiration we feel for Defraye, a superb athlete, triumphing in the Perpignan-Luchon [stage] in special circumstances.[8]

While not without controversy – one of the reasons offered for the abandonment of Lapize and La Française was that they had grown frustrated at Belgian collusion and the assistance they claimed Defraeye was receiving from other teams, Defraeye was acclaimed by *L'Auto* as 'an excellent and wonderful champion,'[9] and returned to Belgium a hero. 'All hardships and tiredness are gladly forgotten with a smile and I really feel the happiest man in the world!' Defraeye said after his win.[10] His prize money amounted to 32,000 gold francs, forty times the average annual wage of his former occupation.[11] With the money he bought a large parcel of land in his hometown of Rumbeke and built a villa. He also constructed a dirt track which was later converted to concrete. The velodrome would be used as a training venue by such future Belgian luminaries as Briek Schotte, Rik Van Steenbergen, Marcel Kint and Albert and Patrick Sercu.

Such was the impact of his win in Belgium that Defraeye has been credited as inadvertently assisting in the founding of the Tour of Flanders, a race that remains one of cycling's most important one-day Classics. In 1912 plans were afoot in Flanders to form a new sports newspaper – *Sportwereld* – to rival the already established *Sportvriend*. Defraeye's win, and the reaction to it from the public, accelerated those plans and ensured they came to fruition. On 13 September, a little over six weeks after Defraeye's Tour win, *Sportwereld* launched onto the newsstands and five months later the paper announced the launch of a new race – the Tour of Flanders.

Defraeye never rode the Tour of Flanders, his French Alcyon team were far more interested in Paris–Roubaix, his best result there being fifth in 1912. Alongside his Tour title, the 1911 national championship and the 1913 edition of Milan–Sanremo stand out as his only other major wins. In Milan–Sanremo, Defraeye was part of an eight-man break that went over the summit of the Turchino pass together, alongside his fellow Belgian and Alcyon teammate, Louis Mottiat. The two Alcyon riders then rode everybody off their wheels until, with 30km to go, they were alone. At Sanremo their lead had grown to four minutes at which point Defraeye won the sprint to the line. Three months later he was again on the start line of the Tour looking to defend his title but after leading the race for three stages he left on stage 6, finding himself two hours behind the leaders on the Tourmalet and complaining of a leg-muscle injury. He would later describe suffering from leg pains that 'felt like his nerve endings were being cut'.[12]

After the First World War, Defraeye returned to racing but never again finished the Tour. He retired in 1924 and opened a bar and hotel, enjoying a drink with his regulars. Later in life he suffered a number of strokes and died in a nursing home aged 77. In 2012 the centenary of his Tour win was commemorated with the unveiling of a statue in his home town. 'A hundred years after his victory, Odiel is once again given the status of cycling icon,' said Dirk Lievens, one of the people behind the idea. 'We give his image to the city, its residents and all cycling enthusiasts.'[13]

MAJOR WINS

Tour de France: 1912
Milan–Sanremo: 1913
National Champion: 1911

Delgado, Pedro

ESP

BORN: 15 APRIL 1960, SEGOVIA, SPAIN

Sometimes it rains, sometimes it is cold or you feel ill, you have a really depressing day, fed up with the hardship and you feel like saying 'enough is enough'. But when you get to the hotel, you shower, you put clean clothes on and get your daily massage ... not only the outside of you changes but also the inside. Then it doesn't seem like you've had such a bad day ... and then you go on the next day and the next.'

Those are the words of Pedro Delgado, talking about the challenges of riding a bike, of keeping going when every fibre of your body is telling you to stop this madness and climb off. He is recalling a memory of racing at the Baby Giro in 1980 during his amateur days, riding like 'the devil' in strong crosswinds. 'Next to me was my teammate from the Spanish National Team, Angel Camarillo,' he remembered. 'We looked at each other and during a small lull in the race we both realised we were in exactly the same state of mind. "I can't carry on; cycling is not made for me. When I get home, I'll study like mad and leave cycling to the others."'[14]

But Delgado went back to his room, he had his shower and his massage. He put on clean clothes. He went on to the next day, and to the next, and he left that Baby Giro with a stage win and the mountain's classification to his name. Two years later he turned professional.

Delgado had already had offers to turn professional three years previously, after he put in a good performance at the 1979 Tour de l'Avenir, winning the race's Queen Stage. But military service beckoned and he was still studying, unsure of whether riding a bike could really offer a career. By 1982, with enough good amateur results behind him, those doubts had dissipated enough for him to sign a professional contract with the Reynolds team, though he hedged his bets by continuing his studies for another year before finally committing everything to cycling.

A gifted climber but average time trial rider – when reflecting on his career in 2016 Delgado said he joined the Dutch team PDM in 1986 to try to improve his time trialling and to find out why the Dutch were so good at it only to discover that 'Dutch riders' legs are burning just as much in a team time trial'[15] – Delgado rode his first Grand Tour in 1982 as a domestique for Angel Arroyo at the Vuelta. He finished twenty-ninth, returning the following year and riding strongly until suffering from a cold and finally ending up fifteenth. Steady, if unspectacular, progression. And then came the Tour.

After a poor showing in the flatlands of northern France, Delgado sprang into life in the mountains. He finished second on the four-climb stage to Bagnères-de-Luchon, coming home just six seconds behind stage winner Robert Millar. That result propelled the Spaniard into the top ten overall and he rose steadily through the standings thanks to a series of terrific rides until he was in second place, just 1min 8sec behind the yellow jersey of Laurent Fignon (see Fignon entry for more on his first day in yellow). With two days left in the Alps the Spaniard seemed poised for a final assault on the race lead.

Delgado had been a sickly child, 'not much to look at physically'.[16] He recalls his mother giving him orange juice as he lay in bed, remembering that 'she would say loving words to me to help me get better soon'.[17] And while he grew into a formidable athlete a sense of vulnerability remained around Delgado, a faint sniff of there being something bad waiting just around the corner to derail him. That 1983 Tour was one such time. A bad case of food poisoning after the stage to l'Alpe d'Huez meant that he endured a terrible ride on the next stage, crawling into Morzine some twenty-five minutes down. Any chance of a debut Tour win had been left shredded by the mountain roads on which he was normally so at home. He ended his first Tour fifteenth, a decent display for a 23-year-old debutant, but perhaps not as good as it could have been.

Delgado has described his association with the Tour as 'a real love and hate relationship'.[18] After that first Tour he knew it was a race suited to him but in the years that followed he was dogged by ill-fortune. In 1984 he crashed on the Joux Plane, breaking his collarbone, fighting on to finish the stage but abandoning that evening. The following year he finished sixth, having suffered ill-health despite having confirmed his position as one of the best three-week racers in the world by winning the Vuelta two months earlier – a race that itself was not without incident with Delgado winning by escaping on the penultimate stage and gaining six minutes over then-leader Robert Millar. The rest of the Spanish-majority peloton did nothing to help pull Delgado back, preferring that a home rider win rather than the foreign Millar. On the podium Delgado thanked the 'directeurs sportifs of the other Spanish teams. Without their support, this win would have been impossible,' while Millar said he was 'disgusted with it all ... You can't compete against the whole peloton.'[19]

In 1986 he abandoned the Tour after the death of his mother and then fought a famous duel with Stephen Roche during the 1987 race (see Roche entry for more).

Delgado returned to the Tour for the sixth time in 1988. He assumed the yellow jersey by finishing third on the stage to l'Alpe d'Huez, won the following day's mountain time trial to strengthen his position in yellow and steadily built a commanding lead over the rest of the race. A tremendous ride in the final time trial gave him an overall margin of victory of 7min 13sec. But again, his victory was not without controversy. Reports that Delgado had returned a positive doping test were leaked late in the race. All hell broke out, the French and Spanish governments even got involved with Delgado on the verge of quitting the race as the fallout continued.

It emerged that the substance found was probenecid, a masking agent. At the time probenecid was not on the UCI's controlled list (though it was banned by the IOC) meaning the finding could not be classified as a positive result. Delgado was free to continue riding though for some the clouds of suspicion remained. Delgado said in 2016:

> I had no idea what probenecid was or how it got into my body ... Regardless, it wasn't a banned substance, so the official that announced that I was positive made a huge mistake. And today it is still frustrating, because I have to explain something that I should not have to explain.[20]

Delgado rode into Paris as just the third Spanish rider to win the race. *El Pais* gushed:

> Bahamontes, Ocaña and Delgado. Three completely different riders who go on to set up the Spanish Holy Trinity of the Tour de France. We would distinguish the first one by his genius, the second by his passion, and the third by his intelligence. The three have reached the top, but Perico [Delgado] has an advantage over the other two: at 28 he can still dream of winning again.[21]

But Delgado would never win the race again. He entered the 1989 Tour in tremendous form having won his second Vuelta title just six weeks earlier but effectively lost the race before it had even started, farcically missing his prologue start time. As defending champion, Delgado was the last to start but was nowhere to be seen as his start time approached. With baffled officials looking on the clock started with the Spaniard still not in sight. Eventually a harassed-looking Delgado fought his way through the television cameras and quickly rolled down the ramp, more than two and a half minutes late. If that wasn't bad enough, Delgado couldn't sleep that night and suffered terribly during the next day's team time trial, losing more time. Remarkably he battled back and finished the race third overall.

Delgado retired from racing after the 1994 season. His final race was the famous Montjuic hill climb, celebrated as his 'grand party'. He finished fifth but was still taken to the podium for an interview and presented flowers. Watched by his family, he threw a bouquet to his wife and his glasses and gloves to the crowd. *'Moltes gracies i adeu,'*[22] he said, before stepping down from the podium one last time. He went on to work in the media.

> ## MAJOR WINS
> Tour de France: 1988
> Vuelta a España: 1985, 1989

Disqualified (Various)

Four riders have had Tour wins struck from the record books after standing in Paris and being hailed as the race's winner. Maurice Garin was the first in 1904 (see Cornet entry for more) while the most recent was Alberto Contador in 2010 (see Contador and Schleck entries for more).

In 2006 the American rider Floyd Landis staged an incredible ride in the Alps to reclaim the yellow jersey after cracking on the stage to La Toussuire, where he lost ten minutes and the jersey on the final haul up to the ski-station. The next day, fuelled by anger and wounded pride (and, as we would soon discover, some illegal substances) Landis went on a 130km romp through the Alps, churning a huge gear while continually dowsing himself in water. Over the Saises, Aravis, Colombiere, Châtillon-sur-Cluses he roared and on the early slopes of the Joux Plane, Landis rode away from Patrick Sinkewitz, the only man who had been able to stick the heat the American had been dishing out. Landis won by well over five minutes and set himself on the way to regaining the yellow jersey he would later wear in Paris.

The escapade was hailed as one of the great stages in the race's history. But the story didn't end there. Landis tested positive for elevated levels of testosterone and was stripped of his title, which passed to Spain's Óscar Pereiro. His appeals were rejected and in 2010 he admitted to using performance-enhancing drugs throughout the majority of his career, telling *ESPN* 'I made some misjudgements and want to clear my conscience. I don't want to be part of the problem anymore.'[23]

The most notable rider to have been stripped of his titles is, of course, Lance Armstrong. Armstrong stood in Paris wearing yellow a remarkable seven times after surviving cancer. From 1999 until 2005 Armstrong and his US Postal and Discovery teams ruled the Tour with an iron fist. It was the only race he was interested in winning, with each year dedicated to that singular pursuit. His seven titles meant that he surpassed all other Tour legends – Anquetil, Merckx, Hinault and Induráin – all five-time winners, all beaten. He became a household name and appeared on late-night chat shows. He hung out with presidents and Hollywood stars, wrote best-selling books. He transcended the sport. But there were some who simply didn't believe what was billed as the greatest comeback in sporting history.

Armstrong was dominating in an era when the use of performance-enhancing drugs in the peloton was known to be widespread. Some found it inconceivable that a clean rider could be so commanding at such a dirty time. Armstrong fought any allegation like he rode, that is to say fiercely. He lodged legal actions. He dismissed those with doubts as haters. Riders who were perceived as being in the enemy camp were ostracised, sometimes even humiliated during races.

After his final Tour win, Armstrong stood in Paris and told the watching millions: 'You need to believe in these riders. I'm sorry you can't dream big and I'm sorry you don't believe in miracles.'[24]

In the summer of 2012, the US Anti Doping Agency (USADA) brought a series of charges against Armstrong, his former team manager Johan Bruyneel, doctors Pedro Celaya, Luis Garcia del Moral and Michele Ferrari, and team trainer Jose 'Pepe' Marti. Armstrong was accused of: the use and/or attempted use of prohibited substances; possession of prohibited substances; trafficking of EPO, testosterone, and/or corticosteroids;

administration and/or attempted administration to others of EPO, testosterone, and/or cortisone; assisting, encouraging, aiding, abetting, covering up and other complicity involving one or more anti-doping rule violations and/or attempted anti-doping rule violations.[25]

Armstrong tried to challenge USADA's jurisdiction but when that failed he stated he would not contest the allegations, saying enough was enough, but adding that 'I know who won those seven Tours, my teammates know who won those seven Tours, and everyone I competed against knows who won those seven Tours.'[26] A lifetime ban was imposed and in one sweep of the brush Armstrong's titles were gone. 'We wish that there is no winner for this period,' Tour director Christian Prudhomme said. 'For us, very clearly, the titles should remain blank. Effectively, we wish for these years to remain without winners.'[27]

On the night of 17 January 2013 an Oprah Winfrey interview with Armstrong was broadcast in which he admitted doping during all seven of his Tour victories. 'This story was so perfect for so long,' he said. 'You overcome the disease, you win the Tour de France seven times. You have a happy marriage, you have children. I mean, it's just this mythic perfect story, and it wasn't true.'[28]

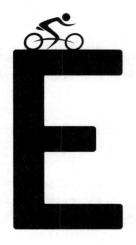

Evans, Cadel

AUS

BORN: 14 FEBRUARY 1977, KATHERINE, AUSTRALIA

When Floyd Landis had stood in yellow in Paris in 2006, amid all the fallout that came afterwards (see Disqualified and Pereiro entries for more) the Australian cycling quarterly *Ride Cycling Review*, had put the American slap bang on their front cover. Dimly lit, slouched casually on a chair, eyes hidden by shadows, Landis was pictured wearing the yellow jersey, with the headline 'Floyd honestly?' Five years later the same magazine was celebrating the first Tour win by an Australian. On the front cover was Cadel Evans, stood on the Paris podium, chest puffed out, pride etched on his face. The headline was 'Cadel honestly'. No question mark needed this time.

A talented mountain-bike rider with a number of World Cup wins to his name, Evans had moved to fulltime road racing in 2001, joining the Saeco team and taking his first win in June's Tour of Austria. He rode his first Tour in 2005, finishing eighth (later promoted to seventh), highlighting his Grand Tour credentials. Two years later he finished second behind Alberto Contador with a losing margin of just twenty-three seconds. Twelve months on he was second again, this time to Carlos Sastre by just fifty-eight seconds. If it seemed that the ultimate breakthrough would surely come then poor finishes in 2009 and 2010, when he finished thirtieth and twenty-sixth respectively, cast doubt on whether he would ever take the next step up the podium.

Evans was in danger of getting a reputation as a nearly-man, a rider who was always a real threat but one that never quite delivered. While he'd had a disappointing 2009 by his standards, struggling with his Silence-Lotto team and having to fight hard just to ride the races he wanted, Evans went some way to erasing that tag by taking the first major victory of his career as the season neared its end. In Switzerland, Evans became the first Australian road-race world champion, breaking away from a small escape group in the final kilometres. 'It really just turned my year around,' Evans said when reflecting on his win. 'I'd had a year of people just doubting my ability as a bike rider and here I was riding towards the finish line and a rainbow jersey.'[1]

The following year was spent riding in those rainbow bands for a new team – BMC Racing. Evans rode well at the Giro, wearing pink before being hit by a fever and ultimately finishing fifth. At the Tour he was well placed but crashed on stage 8, breaking his elbow. He remounted and carried on, actually taking the yellow jersey at the end of the stage. He continued in the race but the pain was too much for him to remain a contender. In 2016 he said:

I was really in a position to really do something. I'd won Flèche Wallonne earlier in the year ... I was having a good year but I had a bit of bad luck at crucial moments. I didn't even know I'd broken my arm when I crashed ... I wasn't going to pull out of the Tour – I had the yellow jersey.[2]

An unpredictable character, sometimes with little time for, or understanding of, cycle sport's media – 'everyone's perception of you changes so much [when you win] whereas if you get second no-one's [interested] despite you still having a good race,'[3] he once said – Evans returned to the Tour in 2011 on the back of good form. He had won Tirreno-Adriatico early in the year; he had won the Tour de Romandie; he'd placed second at the Dauphiné Libéré; all was set for one more serious assault on the Tour and with the BMC wholly structured around supporting him, the Australian was considered among the top contenders.

> The maillot jaune ... This is what transfixes a rare breed of bike rider. It's a symbol of success at the highest level of a sport with a long history and an event that is part of French culture. And it's now significant in distant lands. The face of the man who wore the yellow jersey on the final podium of the 2011 Tour de France is now known. Cadel Evans is now a household name in Australia.[4]

So wrote Rob Arnold in the post-Tour pages of *Ride Cycling Review*. And indeed he was. Evans had been a study in consistency over the three weeks, never out of the top five on the general classification. On stage 19, a 109km blast over the Télégraphe and Galibier to the summit of l'Alpe d'Huez, Evans had mechanical trouble but got back to the lead group in time for the final climb, taking second on the stage and getting himself within fifty-seven seconds of race leader Andy Schleck with just a time trial and the parade in to Paris to come. Schleck was not in the same calibre as Evans against the clock and so the next day the Australian easily assumed the race lead, turning that fifty-seven-second deficit into a 1min 34 sec lead over the course of the 42.5km time trial. History had been written, the first Australian to win the race: it was Cadel. Honestly.

The 2011 Tour was Evans' final major win. He retired in 2015 and today works for BMC bikes.

MAJOR WINS
Tour de France: 2011
World Champion: 2009

Faber, François

LUX

BORN: 26 JANUARY 1887,
AULNAY-SUR-ITON, FRANCE

In August 1908, two days after he won his second Tour in a row and becoming the first rider to record back-to-back wins in the process, the French rider Lucien Petit-Breton reflected on his record-making ride on the front page of *L'Auto*. He had beaten François Faber by thirty-two points, but among the stories of his own daring escapades, completed despite 'extreme fatigue', he took the opportunity to offer his opinion on the man who had just placed second: 'Faber is excellent in the sprint,' he reflected. 'I am convinced that this man will be unbeatable next year ... I do not think I have ever met a competitor as powerful as him.'[1]

To say that Petit-Breton's words would prove prescient is to underplay the dominance with which Faber won the following year's race. After finishing second on the opening stage Faber won the next five stages in a row, something no one had ever done before (the previous record for successive stage wins had been four – achieved by René Pottier in 1906). By the mid-point of the race he had amassed fewer than half the points of the second-placed rider, his Alcyon teammate Gustave Garrigou. What made this feat even more impressive was that the 1909 Tour was hit with frankly atrocious conditions. The wind blew an icy gale and rain fell continuously, causing huge floods and turning already poor roads into rivers of mud.

'In an abominable weather, on roads dangerously slippery and muddy, under continual showers, the 142 riders who arrived in Roubaix on Monday resumed yesterday with the intention of covering in similar conditions the 398km separating Roubaix de Metz', is just one example of *L'Auto's* reporting from the race.[2] That had been the paper's reflections on stage 2, the stage on which Faber had opened his stage-winning account and taken his place at the head of the standings, arriving in Metz more than thirty minutes ahead of the second-placed rider, Octave Lapize, after riding alone for more than 175km. On the following stage, held two days later, he did it all again. This time snow fell but he again rode alone to the finish, over the Ballon d'Alsace, for another thirty-minute-plus stage win. On the next stage his margin of victory was ten minutes, despite falling twice. 'His sloping shoulders seemed to move cubes of earth, his legs seemed to want to dig the ground with the pedals,' reported Henri Desgrange, 'None of them got the better of his thighs.'[3]

Faber won in Paris by twenty points, leading home an all-powerful Alcyon team which took all top-five placings. His half-brother, Ernest Paul, riding as an *independent*, came sixth. It was an astonishing display from a rider who had truly earned his nickname, the Giant of Colombes.

Described variously as 'a force of nature',[4] and 'looking more like a wrestler or weight lifter than a cyclist',[5] both of which give some idea of the man's physical presence, Faber entered history as the first foreign rider to win the Tour – sort of. He was actually born in France, to a French mother with family history in Luxembourg, and a Luxembourger father. The law in France stated that a child born in the country to a foreign father took French nationality on adulthood unless they specifically declined to do so. So it was that for the early part of his life Faber was considered French. Indeed, it wasn't until January 1909 that he repudiated his French nationality and assumed that of Luxembourg. 'Today the doubts still persist as to the motive that then drove the champion, on the verge of a glorious season, to opt for the nationality of his father,' writes Pascal Leroy in his biography of the rider. 'Some interpreted it as a desire to escape military service, then of a duration of two years in France.'[6]

Regardless of the motives, Faber won the Tour as a Luxembourger, meaning he is in the books as the first foreign rider to win the race. Never mind the fact that he had lived in France all his life, making the village of Colombes his home. 'How to celebrate tonight in Colombes?'[7] had been his first thought in Paris.

Faber had first ridden the Tour in 1906 as a complete novice. He didn't win any stages and finished outside the cut-off time on the sixth stage. But he had caught the eye and was offered a place on Alphonse Baugé's Labor team. Two years later he finished third at Paris-Roubaix (only a collision with a child stopped him from winning) and second at the Tour, before claiming his first major race – the Tour of Lombardy – riding across to the leading Giovanni Gerbi and then attacking in the final 50km to record a near fifteen-minute win. He would also win the 1911 edition of Bordeaux-Paris, riding away with more than 200km still to go and winning by 22min 10sec. In 1913 he claimed Paris-Roubaix, emerging victorious from a seven-rider sprint in the Roubaix velodrome.

Faber died during the First World War while with the French Foreign Legion, shot while carrying a fallen colleague on his back. He was 28 years old.

MAJOR WINS
Tour de France: 1909
Paris-Roubaix: 1913
Tour of Lombardy: 1908
Bordeaux-Paris: 1911

Fignon, Laurent

FRA

BORN: 12 AUGUST 1960, PARIS, FRANCE

On the first page of Laurent Fignon's autobiography, *We Were Young and Carefree*, is a pull quote that perfectly sums up some people's perception of the career of the Frenchman. 'Ah, I remember you:' runs the quote, 'You're the guy who lost the Tour de France by eight seconds!' 'No monsieur,' comes the reply. 'I'm the guy who won it twice.'[8] Laurent Fignon: perhaps the only rider more famous for losing the Tour than for winning it.

Born in Montmartre, Paris, Fignon was an energetic child whose first sporting love was football. Some of his footballing friends also rode bikes and Fignon eventually decided he wanted to give cycling a go. In his family's cellar was an old bicycle that had belonged to his father. 'It was an antique but I didn't care about the sneers,' Fignon wrote in 2010. 'Nothing fazed me.'[9]

Fignon discovered he could ride faster and for longer than his friends. He got himself a racing licence at 16 years old only to be immediately told that he had started too late to ever amount to anything unless he really focused. That was all Fignon needed to hear. He won his very first race, a 50km road race in Vigneux-sur-Seine, by getting in a late breakaway and then attacking, surprised at the ease with which he rode away from the others. Soon he was dominating the local scene, working his way up the amateur ranks.

In May 1981 Fignon's telephone rang. On the other end of the line was Cyrille Guimard, head of the Renault team. Guimard had been impressed by the 20-year-old's amateur performances and had decided he wanted him in his team for the 1982 season. 'I'll take you next year,' Guimard told Fignon. 'You'll sign for me.'[10] Fignon could scarcely believe his ears. Tears welled up in his eyes. Renault was the home of Bernard Hinault and was one of the dominant forces in the peloton. They had collected four Grand Tour titles and three Monuments in the preceding four seasons, all courtesy of Hinault. 'I was going to Guimard's. I had ended up with Hinault,' Fignon would reflect. 'It was the cycling equivalent of taking a degree at Oxford or Cambridge.'[11]

The student was a fast learner. He won the Criterium International and placed fifteenth in the Giro within six months of turning professional. The following year, just over two years after taking that call from Guimard,

Fignon was on the start line of his first Tour as the nominated leader of his team – Hinault having been ruled out by injury. One can only imagine the pressure the young Frenchman must have felt as he lined up for the start of the biggest bike race in the world as the leader of Renault, France's most famous team.

With expectations for Renault suitably low, Fignon made an unspectacular start. He didn't place in the top ten on the prologue, he suffered over the cobblestones of northern France and came down with conjunctivitis. He later said that had it been any other race he would have quit. But he carried on, gradually improving, and on stage 10, the Tour's first big day in the mountains, he joined the day's main breakaway and rode into Bagnères-de-Luchon in seventh place. It was enough to propel him up the overall standings into second, 4min 22sec behind Pascal Simon, who had taken over the race lead from Ireland's Sean Kelly.

Fignon's first yellow jersey in that 1983 Tour should have passed into legend, coming as it did at the top of the fabled l'Alpe d'Huez. But it arrived only after Simon finally abandoned the race having ridden with a broken shoulder for an incredible six days. Simon had crashed the day after taking the yellow jersey in Bagnères-de-Luchon, but the power of yellow had given him almost superhuman strength to carry on. Everybody has their limits though and on stage 17, from La Tour-du-Pin to l'Alpe d'Huez, Simon was forced to climb off his bike and the jersey passed to Fignon. The result was that some felt Fignon's yellow jersey came a little tainted, a feeling exacerbated by the fact that he had yet to win a stage. In Dijon, on the penultimate stage of the race, he rectified that, winning the time trial by fifty seconds. He had his stage win with the yellow jersey on his back and entered Paris as the winner of the Tour for the first time. 'Rather than being a winner by sheer happenstance, Fignon made it clear that he was the best of all the contenders who were there and none of the famous non-starters could claim he might have been better,' wrote Pierre Chany.[12]

Hinault left Renault for La Vie Claire the following year and the former teammates went head-to-head in the 1984 Tour. In the build-up Fignon had placed second at the Giro, only losing the race lead to Francesco Moser in controversial circumstances on the final day, with Fignon claiming he was hampered by helicopter downdraft during the final time trial. Nevertheless, he entered the Tour as the national champion and one of the main favourites.

Renault took control of the race and early in the first week had Fignon's teammate, Vincent Barteau, firmly in yellow. There he stayed until Fignon was ready to take over custody of the jersey. Again, the jersey came on l'Alpe d'Huez but this time in very different circumstances. Hinault was two and a half minutes behind Fignon going into the stage and relentlessly attacked on the mountains that came before the Alpe, trying desperately to claw back time. But Fignon repelled each assault with ease and even took the lead in the final valley roads before the final climb. With the leading bunch back together as the race hit the final climb, Hinault attacked again. 'I started laughing,' Fignon later wrote. 'I honestly did ... for real, physically, there on the bike. Bernard was just too proud and wanted to do everything gallantly.'[13] Fignon finally rode Hinault off his wheel to impose a crushing victory after one of the great battles ever played out in the Alps. Hinault simply shrugged, said his efforts hadn't worked out but that he'd keep on trying. But it was over. Hinault finished second in Paris, 10min 32sec behind his young rival.

While he hadn't taken yellow until the final week, Fignon had been imperious throughout the entire race – winning three individual time trials, the team time trial and a brace of mountain stages. 'The wearer of the yellow jersey conquered his opponents, his team controlled the race with mastery, and no one disputed his extraordinary superiority,' wrote Chany.[14] A period of Fignon supremacy seemed assured.

But the dominance that was expected after his 1984 Tour win never materialised. Fignon suffered a series of injuries that badly affected his career although he still managed to claim back-to-back Milan–Sanremo titles (1988, 1989) and the Giro in 1989. That Giro win came just weeks before the start of the infamous eight-second Tour (see LeMond entry for more).

With his blond ponytail, rimless glasses and headband, Fignon cut an unorthodox figure in the peloton. He was disparagingly dubbed 'Le Prof', partly because of his academic looks, partly because of his university background. He was a charismatic and controversial figure right from the start, described variously as headstrong and outspoken. After his career he admitted to experimenting with cocaine once while racing in Colombia. 'Thinking back today, I realise it was idiotic,' he wrote in his autobiography. 'Not just because of the chance of testing positive, but because of that night on the town where I could have come to the worst.'[15]

Fignon contributed to changing a cycling team's financial model. When Renault pulled the plug at the end of the 1985 season he established a company alongside Guimard in order to run their own team, approaching commercial backers for sponsorship. Most cycling teams operate on this basis today.

Fignon died from stomach cancer, aged 50, in 2010; the same year his autobiography was first published in English. 'Sometimes when I was physically at my best,' he wrote, reflecting on his early experiences of riding as a teenager, 'I could sense moments of utter ecstasy, those rare fleeting times when you are in total harmony with yourself and the elements around you: nature, the noise of the wind, the smells. Let's not get carried away. But I have to confess: I was happy.'[16]

> ## MAJOR WINS
> Tour de France: 1983, 1984
> Giro d'Italia: 1989
> Milan–Sanremo: 1988, 1989
> National Champion: 1984

Frantz, Nicolas
LUX

BORN: 4 NOVEMBER 1899, MAMER, LUXEMBOURG

'Nicolas Frantz seized the glorious yellow jersey, object of all desires, from the first stage, and I don't think there was anyone who doubted he would never lose it,' reported Raymond Huttier in *Le Miroir des Sports* after the finale of the 1928 Tour. 'In total, this Tour de France was won, we can say, without struggle.'[17]

Frantz and his Alcyon team had ruled the 1928 Tour with an iron-like grip, claiming the top-three placings in the standings. Frantz, already wearing yellow as the winner of the previous race, started as he meant to go on, winning the opening stage from Paris to Caen and holding the jersey until he rode back into Paris the winner by 50min 7sec a little under a month later.

This was a time when Henri Desgrange was experimenting with the format of his race, concerned that the mountains were having a disproportionate effect on the results. In 1927 he decided that flat stages would be run as a series of team time trials, of a kind at least, with teams sent on their way separately but with individual rather than team times awarded. The result was a race that was difficult to follow, deprived spectators of head-to-head racing and meant that those without a team, known as *tourists-routiers*, stood little chance of winning anything.

Having previously twice placed second in Paris, the new format would turn out to suit Frantz perfectly, even if he still took over the race lead courtesy of a strong ride in the Pyrenees – winning the now traditional four-climb monstrous stage from Bayonne to Luchon – the very result Desgrange was hoping to avoid. He held it all the way to Paris for a win of 1hr 48min 21sec over Labor's Maurice De Waele. The following year Desgrange opted to keep the same format and with both André Leducq, fourth the previous year, and De Waele now signed up as teammates of Frantz's at Alcyon, the result was never seriously in doubt. Frantz and Alcyon literally rode away with the 1928 Tour.

It meant for a relatively dull race despite *L'Auto*'s attempts to liven proceedings with hyperbolic prose – this an example after Julien Moineau won the stage to Evian:

> I cannot help but think of the energy of this brave little Moineau leading his dance alone for 150km, and against what coalitions! Consider that behind him, in more or less compact groups, there is a Fontan who slaughters his kilometres to more than forty an hour; there is a Tailleu, the Tailleu of the good days, the one who moves forward like a locomotive; and there is the group of Frantz ... and I beg you to believe that when Leducq punctures, Frantz rushes furiously towards the finish to increase his lead even further.[18]

The only real threat to Frantz's dominance came on stage 19 to Charleville when his forks broke causing great consternation among the Alcyon team management. There was talk of driving to the nearest Alcyon outlet for a replacement but there wasn't time. Eventually Frantz jumped on a spectator's bike to ride the 100km to the finish, but it wasn't exactly a perfect fit. The next day Desgrange reported:

> The frame is a girl's frame. There are two mudguards and behind the saddle, a red light, like they put on the trains. My Frantz looks like a horseman standing on his stirrups ... But you know him. He remains calm, and when he punctures, between Sedan and Charleville, he simply says: 'It's life!'[19]

Frantz had turned professional in 1923 with the Thomann-Dunlop team, securing a top-ten placing in the Tour of Flanders and twelfth in Paris–Tours, a race he would later win, within his first five months of professional riding. In the June of his debut professional season he won the first of twelve straight Luxembourg national titles, an incredible haul that remains a record to this day (at the time of writing the next best tally is six, shared by Charly Gaul, Edy Schütz and Bob Jungels). Frantz signed for Alcyon the following year and remained there until he retired.

Frantz had a reputation for thorough preparation – for the 1927 Tour he reportedly packed twenty-four sets of jerseys, shorts, socks and underwear – one for every day of the race. Early in his career he focused solely on the Tour, training specifically for its unique demands, unconcerned about other races. The result was of course the utter dominance Tour spectators witnessed during 1927 and 1928.

'We do not imagine with what care of the slightest detail, what application the great Luxembourger disputes the Tour de France,' reported Huttier after the 1928 edition. 'Throughout the year, Frantz prepares only for this event, believing that it is the one that brings him the most profit, directly or through subsequent engagements.'[20]

He wore yellow again in 1929 but shared it with two other riders with time-keepers unable to separate the three leading riders in Bordeaux: 'Frantz, Leducq and Fontan together at the top of the general classification, all three will wear the yellow jersey today,' ran the headline in *L'Auto*.[21] He would finish fifth in Paris on that occasion. He rode the Tour again in 1932 but could only manage forty-fifth. In 1931 he finished seventh in Paris–Brest–Paris, a 1200km single-stage race so demanding it was only held once a decade from 1891 until 1951. He fell asleep on his bike and crashed into a grass verge despite eventual winner Hubert Opperman shouting at him to try to keep him awake.

Frantz retired in 1934 going on to become a national selector. He died in 1985.

MAJOR WINS
Tour de France: 1927, 1928
National Champion: 1923–1934 inclusive

Froome, Chris

GBR

BORN: 20 MAY 1985, NAIROBI, KENYA

Alongside announcements regarding the costs of a coastal trip for Year 6 and the week-long absence of the headteacher due to their required attendance at a conference, a boxed notice towards the top of the 16 September 2011 Banda School newsletter sought to draw briefly the reader's attention away from immediate school matters. 'Dear Parents, it is always good to share Banda successes from around the world,' ran the notice. 'Christopher Froome left The Banda in the late 90s and has gone on to fantastic things in the cycling world. Anyone interested, both parents and children, should look up this link: http://www.teamsky.com/article/0,27290,22762_7 155978,00.html'[22]

That link is long since dead but anyone who had clicked on it back in 2011 would have been almost certainly taken to a story that detailed the emergence of Froome as a Grand Tour contender. Five days earlier the Kenyan born and raised rider had finished second at the Vuelta, a remarkable result for a rider who until then had been regarded as a *domestique*. Froome, whose parents are both British, had been trailing his Team Sky teammate Bradley Wiggins by a handful of seconds before the stage to the Alto de l'Angliru. But with Wiggins fading on the 20%+ gradients, Froome was given the nod to ride for himself. As Wiggins lost the race lead Froome maintained his second place and in Madrid he finished only thirteen seconds behind race winner Juan José Cobo.

It had been a stunning ride by the Sky rider. Previously his best result had been fourth at the 2008 Herald Sun Tour while his best Grand Tour ride had been thirty-fifth at the 2009 Giro. Now he was on the podium in Spain. And it should have been even better. Some eight years later, Froome's second place would be upgraded to first after Cobo was stripped of the win due to irregularities in his biological passport dating from 2009 and 2011. It means that today the 2011 Vuelta stands as the first of Froome's many Grand Tour titles. 'The Vuelta in 2011 was in many ways my breakthrough race, so this red jersey is special for me,' Froome said in a statement after being awarded the win. 'I guess it's extra special too, because – even though it's eight years on – it was Britain's first Grand Tour win.'[23]

Froome had honed his cycling legs in Africa, after being introduced to Kenyan cyclist David Kinjah by his mother, Jane. Froome and his mother had watched Kinjah win a race in Nairobi and approached the rider as he celebrated his win. Jane asked Kinjah if he would coach her boy and Kinjah told her to bring him to Muguga, his home village, the following week. Kinjah told *Forbes* in 2013:

> The mother was a bit unsure and afraid about bringing Chris to the village. Chris was shy and not such a strong rider. But he loved bikes and soon opened up and enjoyed the village life. With time, the mother was now a bit more comfortable with him coming to the village.[24]

Kinjah had a cycling project called Safari Simbaz that sought to teach Kenyans about bikes and cycling (Safari Simbaz would be established as a non-profit trust in 2008). 'He'd come by the compound on his little BMX,' Kinjah said in a 2017 interview with *Cyclist*. 'His main friend was his bicycle.'[25] Kinjah recalled a skinny and shy boy who they didn't really take seriously as a potential racer, but who had a lot of discipline.

Froome left Kenya for a school in South Africa but continued to ride. He got his first road bike aged 17 and by 2006 he had won the Tour de Maurice and was regarded as Kenya's finest racer. After much wrangling he was selected to ride for Kenya at the 2006 Commonwealth Games – 'the Kenyan Federation didn't want to send him. They thought Kenya should be represented just by black athletes,' Kinjah told *Cyclist*.[26] Froome finished twenty-fifth.

Later that year, aware he needed experience of racing in Europe to catch the attention of professional teams, he entered himself in the world championship road race, using the email address of the head of Kenya's cycling federation to do so. Froome had memorised the login details when he'd been asked for help with some emails that needed writing in English. 'Posing as Julius Mwangi, I wrote a short letter to the UCI, informing them that I would like to enter Christopher Froome, one of my country's most promising under-23 riders, into the world championships at that grade in the autumn. Thank you,' Froome recalled in his 2014 book *The Climb*.[27]

Despite being his federation's sole representative and being entirely unsupported, Froome finished thirty-sixth in the time trial and forty-fifth in the road race. While not earth-shattering results, it was enough to earn him a ride with the South African outfit Konica-Minolta for 2007. The following year would prove to be a pivotal one for Froome. In April he swapped his

Kenyan racing licence for a British one and three months later he was at the Tour, riding alongside Geraint Thomas as a member of the Barloworld team and finishing eighty-first. After years of hard work and knockbacks he had finally made it to the grandest race in cycling. Sadly, his mother, the woman who had taken him to his first race all those years before, hadn't lived to see her son there, having died of cancer just five weeks before the race started. Froome said after his debut Tour:

> It is difficult, but it gave me a lot of motivation and it gave me a lot of comfort ... It is something she would have killed to have seen and it made me very happy that I was actually able to fulfil that ... I had that in mind ... I had to stick in there and fight.[28]

Froome's first Tour win came in 2013 having already stood on the podium one year earlier as part of Bradley Wiggins' support team (see Wiggins entry for more). With Wiggins focused on the Giro, Froome entered the 2013 Tour as Sky's protected rider. He won three stages, including the stage to Mont Ventoux, and wore yellow for fourteen days. Afterwards he paid an emotional tribute to his mother:

> She's been a really big motivation for me and I'd like to think she was there alongside me every step of the way ... When I decided to stop my studies and spend six months cycling in Europe, she was behind me 100 per cent, saying, 'Do what makes you happy, there's nothing worse than being in a job that you're miserable in and you'll be forever asking yourself what if?'[29]

Under the direction of the all-powerful Team Sky, Froome developed into the finest Grand Tour rider of his generation. More Tour titles followed in 2015, 2016 and 2017, along with the Vuelta in 2017 – the first time a rider had won both the Tour and Vuelta in the same year since the Spanish race moved from early spring to late summer in 1995. In May 2018 he claimed his first Giro win after a stunning attack on the Colle delle Finestre turned a 3min 22sec deficit into a forty-second lead. 'I don't think I've ever attacked like that from 80km from the line all on my own and gone all the way to the finish,' Froome said.[30] That result meant that Froome held all three Grand Tour titles, the first time any rider had done that since Bernard Hinault in 1982/83.

The result was all the more remarkable for the fact that some felt Froome shouldn't have been at the race at all. In December 2017 *The Guardian* revealed he had returned an adverse analytical finding for salbutamol, a drug used to relieve symptoms of asthma, during the 2017 Vuelta. Froome, an asthmatic who maintained his innocence, rode the Giro while the resultant investigation was ongoing, meaning he faced a barrage of questions and had to contend with people dressed as giant inhalers running alongside him. In July 2018 he was cleared by the World Anti-Doping Agency of any wrongdoing, WADA accepting that the test result 'which identified the prohibited substance salbutamol at a concentration in excess of the decision limit of 1,200 ng/mL, did not constitute an Adverse Analytical Finding (AAF).[31]

With four Tour victories to his name at the time of writing, Froome's efforts to equal the record haul of five titles, currently shared by Jacques Anquetil, Eddy Merckx, Bernard Hinault and Miguel Induráin, were thwarted in 2019 after a bad training crash left him with multiple injuries a month or so before the race started. Froome underwent eight hours of surgery and remained in intensive care for a number of days. He has since confirmed his intention to return to the race in 2020. At 34 years old it will be a tough road back but if successful, it would surely represent his most remarkable achievement yet.

MAJOR WINS
Tour de France: 2013, 2015, 2016, 2017
Giro d'Italia: 2018
Vuelta a España: 2011, 2017

Garin, Maurice

FRA

BORN: 3 MARCH 1871, ARVIER, ITALY

At 8.56 a.m. on 2 July 1903 Géo Lefèvre alighted from his train in Lyon. *L'Auto*'s reporter-in-chief for the Tour, and the man responsible for its organisation on the road, had arrived to witness the finish of the very first Tour stage. There was just one problem: he was late.

The train had been on time, but the pace of the leading riders had far exceeded expectations. On the morning of 1 July, the opening day of the Tour's inaugural edition, *L'Auto* had printed a *Horaire probable* (probable schedule) for the stage, which had the first riders arriving in Lyon at 9.40 a.m. Plenty of time, in other words, for Lefèvre to leave his train and make his way to the finish. But the leading pair of Maurice Garin and Émile Pagie had blown those timings away. Garin covered the 467km from the Café

Réveil Matin, Montgeron, on the southern fringes of Paris, to Lyon in 17hr 45min 13sec. Pagie came in fifty-five seconds behind. Both were riding La Française bicycles. The next rider came in just under thirty-five minutes later. Lefèvre wrote:

> The arrival? Well, I missed it! Garin and Pagie, who I had seen eating quickly at Moulins and plunge into the night, beat me to Lyon on their simple bicycles, while I was riding the express train! When I realised for myself the incredible state of freshness of these two demons of the road, calculated their advance on a schedule which had seemed to me very optimistic when I had established it, I had thought that I would miss them ... I jumped in a car and arrived on the Quai de Vaise, I saw a thousand people from afar move, shout, applaud and surround two men covered in white dust. It was them![1]

Garin, who had been Desgrange's pick of the riders before the start because of strong past performances in Paris–Brest–Paris and Bordeaux–Paris, duly entered history as the winner of the very first Tour stage. Lefèvre shouldn't have been surprised by Garin's ride. He had a history of beating expected timings – in Bordeaux–Paris he had arrived at the Parc des Princes finish only minutes after it had opened its doors to spectators.

Nineteen days after sixty riders had set out from Paris bound for Lyon, twenty-one returned to the capital, crossing the finish line in the western Parisian suburb, Ville-d'Avray, and then riding before thousands who lined the streets to the Parc des Princes for the victory ceremonials. Top of the classification was Garin who had never relinquished the race lead he had taken in Lyon. His winning margin was 2hr 59min 2sec over Lucien Pothier. 'I had trouble on the road,' Garin said afterwards. 'I was hungry, I was thirsty, I was sleepy, I suffered. I cried between Lyon and Marseilles.' He recalled that the race had felt like 'a long grey line, monotone'.[2] Garin won 6,125 francs from the organisers and a 'magnificent object of art'[3] donated by the journal *La Vie au Grand Air*. He would race the Tour again in 1904, a race in which he initially claimed victory before he was stripped of the title for cheating (see Cornet entry for more). While he denied the accusations at the time, cycling author Les Woodland writes in his book *The Unknown Tour de France* that in old age Garin admitted the offences to locals in his adopted hometown of Lens. 'He admitted it. He was amused about it, certainly not embarrassed, not after all those years,'[4] Woodland quotes a local grave-digger who knew Garin and worked in the cemetery where the Tour's first champion is now buried.

Garin was born in Arvier, in the Aosta valley of north-west Italy, to a farm labourer and a hotel worker. Maurice Clement and his wife, Maria Teresa, had a large family – four daughters and five sons. Maurice was the eldest of the boys. Life was tough and in 1885 the couple decided to make the move over the border into France.

The exact nature of this move is the subject of some conjecture – did the Garins make the journey as a family, individually or in a bigger group? Did they use the Petit-St-Bernard pass, or a less well-known route, higher up in the mountains? Some claim that the young Maurice was exchanged for a wheel of cheese by his father, probably to a French recruiter of chimney sweeps, who then took the youngster to northern France. This may sound implausible, but it's known that there were concerns in the Aosta valley about the activities of unscrupulous outsiders who were trafficking child labourers at the time, with circulars advising officials to: 'absolutely refuse or, at least, to grant only with the most diligent precautions, the certificate prescribed by law necessary to obtain the passport for the foreigner,' alongside warnings of 'greedy speculators [who], under the pretext of teaching a trade to young children, in particular chimney sweeping, are looking to seduce parents with promises and false hopes, and [who] compel the children ... to make a great profit for them, exploiting fatigue, misery and sometimes even life.'[5]

By 1892 Garin was a regular sight as he rode around the French town of Maubeuge, close to the Belgian border, in his work as a chimney sweep. In 1893 he won his first race, Dinant–Namur–Dinant, despite puncturing and taking the bike of a rival's *soigneur* despite his protests. One year later he turned up at a race at Avesnes-sur-Helpe, near to his home, only to be denied entry because of his non-professional status. Showing the sort of bloody-mindedness that would serve him well later in his career, Garin simply waited for the professionals to start and then chased after them, catching and passing every one of them on the way to the finish. When the organisers refused to pay him any prize money the spectators had a whip round. Garin went home that night with 300 francs in his pockets, double what the organisers were offering. He would soon turn professional.

Garin came third in the inaugural Paris–Roubaix, held in 1896, a race that also featured eventual Tour founder Henri Desgrange, who abandoned. The following year Garin would claim the first of back-to-back wins in Roubaix.

In 1901 he won the second edition of Paris–Brest–Paris, beating previous winner Charles Terront's time by more than twenty hours.

Following his 1904 Tour disqualification Garin was banned for two years. He bought a garage in Lens which he retained until his death and wouldn't ride again until 1911, when he claimed tenth in Paris–Brest–Paris, greeted by a 'monstrous ovation'[6] as he rode through Montmartre. He also sold bicycles from a shop in Lens. For a while after the Second World War professionals such as Wim Van Est rode Garin-branded bicycles, claiming a number of important victories.

Garin was 85 when he died in 1957. Until 2004 it had been thought that he had adopted French nationality in 1892, upon reaching the age of 21. However, after studying his life, the Italian author Franco Cuaz wrote that he had uncovered the document that certified Garin's naturalisation. It was dated 1901, nine years later than thought. Though not affecting his Tour win, it does mean that he won his first races, including Paris–Roubaix, when he was still an Italian, not a Frenchman as first thought.

MAJOR WINS
Tour de France: 1903
Paris–Roubaix: 1897, 1898
Bordeaux–Paris: 1902

Garrigou, Gustave

FRA

BORN: 24 SEPTEMBER 1884, VABRE-TIZAC, FRANCE

In 1907 France's Gustave Garrigou turned professional with the Peugeot team after a successful amateur career. It is safe to say he didn't hang around making his mark on the professional scene.

In late March he came fourth in Paris–Roubaix. Two weeks later he was classified second at Milan–Sanremo having 'represented the French colours with dignity',[7] and despite actually crossing the line in third place – Italy's Giovanni Gerbi had pulled Garrigou back in the sprint with the unintended result of the way being left clear for Garrigou's Peugeot teammate Lucien Petit-Breton to take the win. Gerbi was relegated to third with Garrigou promoted to second. The Frenchman then took his first professional win in early May at the inaugural French national championships, beating Alcyon's Henri Lignon by three seconds in the 100km road race from Versailles to Ablis and back.

Just over a fortnight later Garrigou placed third in Bordeaux–Paris and followed that with second overall and two stage wins at the Tour. Garrigou had only been a pro for eight months but he had well and truly arrived. And still it got better. Towards the end of the season he was awarded the Tour of Lombardy after Gerbi – yes, him again – had employed more dirty deeds, this time involving a blockaded level-crossing, nails, tacks and illegal pacing from training partners. Peugeot's manager, Leopold Alibert, said: '… it is vital that this criminal is removed from the cycling scene.'[8] The authorities listened and Gerbi, who had crossed the line first, was relegated to last place and given a two-year ban – later reduced to six months.

Described in 1934 as 'taciturn' and a true 'great of the road',[9] by the journalist Robert Coquelle, Garrigou forged a reputation for consistency. He rode every Tour throughout his professional career, from 1907 until 1914, and finished each one in the top five in Paris. 'If there was a points classification, over the whole of five or six seasons, Garrigou would win!' wrote Coquelle. '[But as] modest as taciturn, he would not have been very much in favour with current journalists for whom the first quality of a champion is to be talkative.'[10]

Garrigou's Tour win came in 1911. By then he had twice placed second and once third in France's biggest race – he also claimed a *primes* of 100 francs in the form of five gold sovereigns for being the only rider not to succumb to walking up the Tourmalet in 1910, the first time the high Pyrenees had been included in the race (see Lapize entry for more). Now riding for Alcyon, arguably cycling's strongest team at the time, he claimed two stage wins and an eighteen-point win to secure the 1911 race over La Française's Paul Duboc. But still, his victory had a whiff of good fortune about it.

First, Lucien Petit-Breton was taken out of the race on the very first stage after colliding with a drunken sailor who 'literally flung himself on to the riders'.[11] Then, in the Pyrenees, a strange incident of poisoning hit the second-placed Duboc, harming his chances of truly challenging the race leader.

Duboc had just won back-to-back stages to eat into on Garrigou's lead and on the stage to Bayonne he set off quickly and led over the Peyresourde and the Aspin. By the time he soared over the Tourmalet all was looking good for the stage win and further progress towards the top spot of the overall classification.

At the Argelès-Gazost control station he grabbed a bottle and continued on his way towards the Aubisque, the day's final major climb. Suddenly he collapsed. Bent double, Duboc started to vomit violently. Weak and feverish, he remained curled at the side of the road as riders he had cruised by a few hours ago began to pass. In 1937 Paul Ruinart, a 'spiritual advisor' to Duboc's La Française team at the 1911 Tour, told *Le Miroir des Sports*, what happened next:

> Obviously, a criminal hand had poured into the container taken to the control some harmful drug. I rushed to help him, but a draconian and, it must be said, excessive regulation forbade me even to treat him, for fear of immediate disqualification.
>
> Taking advantage of a moment of inattention [by the commissaires] I managed to pass to the unfortunate Duboc, who continued to moan with pain, an antidote that I happily found in my pharmacy case. After vomiting several times, a dreadful blackish liquid, Duboc, who was extraordinarily brave, was able to get back on his feet and managed the feat of arriving at Bayonne only an hour and a half after the first rider.[12]

That first rider was Maurice Brocco who himself was engaged in a fierce row with Henri Desgrange over whether he had breached race regulations by selling supporting services to other riders. Brocco who was derided by Desgrange as nothing more than a servant or *domestique*, went on his Pyrenean raid to prove his worth only for Desgrange to decide that if he could ride like that then he definitely had been selling support services on other stages and promptly threw him off the race. Meanwhile the chief beneficiary of the Duboc's poisoning was Garrigou and so suspicion centred on Alcyon's manager, a Monsieur Calais, who had left Luchon the night before and spent the night in Argelès-Gazost. Duboc supporters were outraged and Garrigou had to ride in disguise and on a blacked-out bike to avoid repercussions on the road.

'I remain convinced that Calais was not at fault,' Ruinart said in 1937. 'Besides, it is claimed that a soigneur, whose name I will not say although he has been dead for some years, had confessed, before his death, of having dealt the blow.'[13] Pierre Chany writes that 'this "soigneur" was a former rider called François Lafourcade'.[14] Lafourcade died in 1917.

Garrigou's win came the year that the high Alps were introduced for the first time, most notably the Galibier, Desgrange's favourite and where a monument to the Tour's founder now stands on its southern flank. Émile Georget was the first to scale the Alpine giant, going on to win the stage in Grenoble. The introduction of the climb did not sit well with the riders and Garrigou spoke of the 'tasteless prank of slipping mountains under the roads of our beautiful country', and saying, somewhat tongue in cheek it must be said, that during the Galibier stage he had considered Desgrange a 'real assassin to force us to spend our holidays like this'.[15]

Garrigou didn't ride again after the outbreak of the First World War. After his retirement from cycling he ran a shop in Paris. He died of pulmonary congestion in 1963 aged 78.

MAJOR WINS
Tour de France: 1911
Tour of Lombardy: 1907
Milan-Sanremo: 1911
National Champion: 1907, 1908

Gaul, Charly

LUX

BORN: 8 DECEMBER 1932, PFAFFENTHAL, LUXEMBOURG

One of the greatest climbers in cycling history, Charly Gaul came to life in the rarefied air of the peaks of France and Italy. Former Tour director Jean-Marie LeBlanc once said that he recalled Gaul as 'a graceful silhouette that turned the legs incredibly quickly and was able to dig huge gaps in the mountains'.[16] Like many riders of his era Gaul was bestowed with nicknames. For his exploits in the mountains he was known as L'Ange de Montagne (the

Angel of the Mountains), while for his exploits in the bushes during the 1957 Giro he was dubbed Chéri Pi-pi (Dear Wee-wee). More on that later.

Gaul turned professional in 1953, quitting his job as a slaughter-man at the age of 20 and signing for the Terrot-Hutchinson team. Second place at the Dauphiné Libéré swiftly followed behind his teammate Lucien Teisseire, an immediate demonstration of his talent. Raphaël Géminiani, French national champion in 1953 and the man who would have the 1958 Tour ripped away from him by French infighting, to the benefit of Gaul, described the Luxembourger as '... a murderous climber ... turning his legs at a speed that would break your heart, tick tock, tick tock, tick tock'.[17] Indeed, Gaul's legend was forged principally by two incredible displays in the mountains during terrible weather that secured him two of his greatest wins – the 1956 Giro and that 1958 Tour.

By 1956 Gaul had already secured his reputation as one of the finest climbers in the peloton. He was now riding for Faema, a team formed in 1955 to publicise the coffee-machine manufacturer on the roads of Italy and beyond. Gaul had a string of victories behind him as well as third place overall and the mountains prize at the 1955 Tour, during which he took his first Tour stage win, leading over the climbs of the Aravis, Télégraphe and Galibier to record a 13min 47sec win in Briançon. After signing for Faema he rode the Giro for the first time in May 1956, opening his account by winning the seventh stage, from Pescara to Campobasso, and then claiming a short hill climb to Bologna the following week.

But as the Giro peloton prepared for the 242km stage from Merano to Monte Bondone, Gaul remained outside of the top ten. There were only three stages remaining and the Luxembourger was more than sixteen minutes behind race leader Pasquale Fornara. No one could ever have considered him a realistic contender for the title, even though there were four long climbs that day. What happened next has entered Giro lore.

More than nine hours after the peloton rolled out from Merano a photograph was taken of Gaul on the summit of Monte Bondone. It shows the Angel of the Mountains in some distress. Dead eyed and on the verge of hypothermia, Gaul is pictured being carried from his bike by two policemen. Concerned team officials surround him, hot flasks at the ready. He has the look of a man that is about to abandon, not of one who has just torched the rest of the Giro field during a stage of unimaginable torture, but that was exactly what Gaul had done.

As the stage had progressed the heavy rain that had been falling all day turned to snow. On the descent of the penultimate climb conditions worsened still, brakes iced up and riders, on the verge of hypothermia, were forced from their bikes. Despite wearing pink, Fornara gave up and sought refuge in the sanctuary of a farmer's kitchen. But Gaul was at his best in the cold and the wet. With the weather deteriorating with every passing minute he rode the steep slopes of the Bondone in his red and white short-sleeved Faema jersey. The crowds, huddled under umbrellas, watched him weave his way up the mountain in defiance of the apocalyptic conditions, crossing the line 7min 44sec ahead of second-placed Giuseppe Fantini and more than twelve minutes before the third-placed rider Fiorenzo Magni – although Magni's own performance was perhaps even more spectacular, given that he was riding with a shattered collarbone.

On a day when over half the field abandoned, Gaul seized the pink jersey, easily keeping it until the finish in Milan just two days later. The following year, again on a stage to Monte Bondone, Gaul stopped for a 'natural break' in the bushes. As the peloton passed, he made a gesture to his rival Louison Bobet who, incensed, promptly told his team to raise the pace – somewhat against the unwritten code of the sport. Gaul's attempt to regain the group was in vain. He lost ten minutes but gained a second, more unflattering nickname in the process: Chéri Pi-pi. Although Gaul gained some measure of vengeance by helping Gastone Nencini win that Giro, guiding him through the mountains to ensure Bobet wouldn't win, he would have to wait another year to exact his full revenge.

Going into the 1958 Tour the French team had too much talent to fit easily into one team. The defending champion, Jacques Anquetil, informed the team manager, Marcel Bidot, that he would ride only with one of either Louison Bobet or Raphaël Géminiani, not both. That left a furious Géminiani to ride with the Centre-Midi regional team, but not before he had posed for photographs alongside a donkey that he'd just happened to call Marcel.

Gaul was riding on the joint Netherlands/Luxembourg team. As the race progressed he won two time-trial stages, including one on Mont Ventoux in front of 100,000 fans. 'He really looked like an angel, pedalling his tiny gear at an amazing rate on the punishing slopes, encouraged by a chorus of praise,' reported Jock Wadley.[18] But once again Gaul didn't seem to be in the mix for the overall classification. As the riders started stage 21, 219km from Briançon to Aix-les-Bains that included the Lautaret and the Luitel before three climbs in the Chartreuse, Géminiani, who had been making a point by riding aggressively all race, was in yellow by nearly four minutes while Gaul was 16min 3sec back.

At the start line, Gaul was happy. It was raining. He found his rival Bobet, who himself was four minutes behind Gaul, and taunted him. He told him he was going to attack on the Luitel. He even told him on which hairpin.

Sure enough, on that very hairpin Gaul attacked. In the cold and rain, he turned the Tour upside down. By the time he crossed the summit of the Porte, the first of the Chartreuse climbs, Gaul had nearly six minutes over Géminiani. At the top of the Cucheron it was nearly eight, at the Granier it was over twelve. Gaul was riding a different race to everyone else. Géminiani was frantically trying to muster support, asking his fellow Frenchmen for assistance. None came to his aid. Gaul rolled into Aix-les-Bains more than fourteen minutes ahead of Géminiani who rounded on his countrymen, branding them Judases.

Gaul was not yet in yellow, the race lead having been taken by Vito Favero. But Favero was only 1min 7sec ahead and Gaul was a fine rider against the clock and the favourite for the final time trial. He took yellow one day from Paris and claimed the Tour by a little over three minutes.

Gaul liked to ride low gears, remaining seated and spinning his legs at high cadences while others drove larger gears, standing on the pedals. The reporter René de Latour once wrote:

> Gaul's easy action makes you think he is not really trying. He does not seem to be paying so very much attention to the job, or to realise the importance of the occasion ... When eventually you go by him in the car he will give you a playful wink. And sometimes race followers have been startled to hear him whistling a tune.[19]

He retired from cycling in 1965, becoming a recluse and living as a hermit in a forest until he emerged some twenty years later. He returned to the Tour in 2002, bearded and full-bellied, vest visible through his shirt and with braces holding up his trousers, looking far more like a retired farmer than a former angel of the mountains. He died three years later of a pulmonary embolism.

MAJOR WINS
Tour de France: 1958
Giro d'Italia: 1956, 1959
National Champion: 1956, 1957, 1959–1962 inclusive

Gimondi, Felice

ITA

BORN: 29 SEPTEMBER 1942, SEDRINA, ITALY

When he retired from cycling, five Grand Tours, four Monuments, one world championship and two national titles to his name, Felice Gimondi entered the insurance business. In his office in Bergamo, north-east of Milan, he hung a photograph of himself with Eddy Merckx, the man against whom he so often raced and who in many ways helped Gimondi define his career. Just outside the door to that office, hung on a hallway wall, was a frame that displayed a very special article of cycling memorabilia: the yellow jersey that Gimondi won in 1965, when he was just six months into his professional career.

Gimondi only got the call to ride the Tour in 1965, five days before it started in Cologne, Germany. The 22-year-old's professional career had started well. He had just finished his debut Giro in third place while helping his Salvarani team leader, Vittorio Adorni, claim the pink jersey in Florence. He was in Forlì, northern Italy, for a 77km time trial when the phone rang telling him he was needed for the Tour because teammates Bruno Fantinato and Battista Babini couldn't ride due to an injured knee and a fever respectively. Gimondi finished second in Forlì and then dashed home to Sedrina, just north of Bergamo, and packed a bag. Three days later he was on a plane to Frankfurt with nine other Salvarani riders, all bound for Cologne.

While that call would transform his life, at first Gimondi didn't really want to ride the Tour. He was a neo-pro and had just come off a hard Giro. The Tour's route that year was 4,188km in total and featured nine mountain stages, including a summit finish on Mont Ventoux and a mountain time trial on Mont Revard. Surely it would be too tough on his young legs, even if the previous year he had impressed in France, winning the Tour de l'Avenir – essentially the amateur Tour. Still, the call had come and so off he went, ready to work again for Adorni who was aiming to emulate both Fausto Coppi (1949/1952) and Jacques Anquetil (1964) by securing the Giro/Tour double.

Gimondi won the third stage sprint into Rouen and briefly held the race lead, wearing yellow for five days early on. As the Tour reached the Pyrenees he was lying fourth, nearly three minutes ahead of Adorni and perfectly placed to help his team leader in the mountains.

Then, on the Aubisque, Adorni collapsed with stomach cramps and abandoned. He wasn't the only one. No fewer than eleven riders left the race that day including the race leader at the time, Bernard Van de Kerckhove. The mass withdrawals raised eyebrows with allegations of increased doping in cycling – during the 1965 Tour de l'Avenir two riders were taken ill in similar circumstances, prompting the Tour's chief medical officer, Dr Dumas, to say: 'As far as I am concerned, the joke has gone on long enough. It is up to the federation to now take its responsibilities [seriously].'[20]

With Adorni out of the race and Van de Kerckhove also gone, it fell to the young Gimondi to both assume the Salvarani leadership role and again take his place in the yellow jersey. There remained two weeks to go and he came under repeated attacks, principally from Raymond Poulidor who had his eyes on the race in the absence of his great rival Jacques Anquetil. Gimondi held tough, although sometimes only just – on the stage to Mont Ventoux the Italian was so exhausted he ground to a halt and could only remain upright by quickly grabbing a parked car. He lost more than a minute and a half to Poulidor that day but retained the jersey. He won the Mont Revard time trial and the final time trial into Paris to record a 2min 40sec win over Poulidor. Gigi Boccacini reported in *La Stampa*:

> Today, the Tour de France has definitively graduated a great champion. Little by little, he has taken flight, day by day becoming the great protagonist of the event ... And the crowd, without losing themselves in foolish nationalism, said: 'He looks like Coppi,' in 1952, another day like this. The crowd that had then cried: 'Ale Fosto,' today shouted: 'Bravò Gimondi.' ... It is an exceptional result obtained by an exceptional athlete.[21]

He'd only been a professional six months, and already Gimondi had secured the biggest prize in cycling.

A stylish rider who was nicknamed the Phoenix, Gimondi won his first Monument the following season, claiming Paris–Roubaix with a 40km solo escape to win by 4min 8sec, a victory that again drew comparisons with Coppi's greatest exploits. Later that year he took the first of two Tour of Lombardy titles, emerging victorious from a small breakaway that included the likes of Poulidor, Anquetil and Merckx. Six months later he won the first of an eventual three Giro titles.

Like many riders of his era Gimondi defined his career through the prism of the dominant Merckx, arriving at races and immediately looking at the

Belgian's legs. 'I did that my whole career,' Gimondi once said. 'Not only during the race but also at the start. I would look at Eddy's legs at the start and sometimes I would already know that today there is no way [I could win].'[22]

Of course, Gimondi did sometimes beat Merckx, most notably at the 1973 world championships in Barcelona. By then Gimondi had won all three Grand Tours as well as the Tour of Lombardy and a brace of national titles. The rainbow jersey, along with Milan-Sanremo, were the two races missing from his palmarès before he could be considered a true Italian great.

On Barcelona's famous Montjuïc circuit he claimed his world title, part of a four-man breakaway alongside the Spaniard Luis Ocaña and two Belgians – a youthful Freddy Maertens and Merckx himself. Maertens went to lead Merckx out and as the Cannibal came off his teammate's wheel so Gimondi came around Merckx. Maertens saw Merckx was spent and tried to catch the Italian but Gimondi was not to be beaten. Ocaña took third ahead of an aghast Merckx. 'The single biggest day of my life,' Gimondi said at the time. 'When one is 31-years-old and wins the title in the last ten metres it is something that you cannot explain. In in those last ten metres my entire career passed.'[23] In 2016 Gimondi reflected:

> My plan was to stay close to Merckx. I stayed there all the time. At most there was only ever one other rider between me and Merckx. No more. I had Eddy constantly under control because I was expecting Eddy to go … His strongest attack was on the penultimate lap but at that moment I realised that this Merckx was not the strongest Merckx. Once he tried this very strong attack it showed he was not so powerful because I lost no more than 20 metres and then made contact again. At that moment, at that key moment, I realised that today Merckx is very good, but he is not the perfect Merckx … Honestly, the best Merckx could have won everywhere but he was not in his best condition that day – if Maertens had had the opportunity to do the sprint for himself he could have been the winner, no doubt.[24]

The following year Gimondi finally claimed his Milan-Sanremo win, riding alone to victory while wearing the rainbow jersey. He retired in 1979 and remains one of only three riders to have won the Tour, the Giro, the Vuelta, the Worlds and Paris-Roubaix – Merckx and Bernard Hinault are the other two. His last major victory came at the 1976 Giro, when he was 33 years old. In 2016 he added:

I have a special evaluation of my career. Of course, these kind of victories show the most complete riders but what I think is more important for me is how I was able to get a Grand Tour win when I was a new professional and then again when I was at the end of my career. For me to win the Tour in 1965 and then my third Giro in 1976 ... that is really meaningful. That means that your career has been long and consistent.[25]

Gimondi died in 2019, aged 76, after suffering a heart attack while on holiday in Sicily.

MAJOR WINS
Tour de France: 1965
Giro d'Italia: 1967, 1969, 1976
Vuelta a España: 1968
Paris–Roubaix: 1966
Tour of Lombardy: 1966, 1973
Milan–Sanremo: 1974
World Champion: 1973
National Champion: 1968, 1972

Hinault, Bernard

FRA

BORN: 14 NOVEMBER 1954, YFFINIAC, FRANCE

How best to summarise France's Bernard Hinault? The saying goes that a picture paints a thousand words, so let's take a single frame from the 1978 Tour. It is 12 July and a split-stage day, a format that was *en vogue* at the time but has long since fallen out of fashion. In the morning the peloton faced 158km from Tarbes to Valence-d'Agen, in the afternoon 96km onwards to Toulouse. It was the second such split-stage of the race and the riders, who also had numerous transfers between the various finishes and starts to contend with, were fed up. They wanted to make a point to the race organisers and so, towards the end of the morning's racing, with the finish line approaching, they simply stopped and got off their bikes.

Study the photograph that captured this moment of protest for prosperity and you see riders that appear a little nervous. They are fiddling with their caps and jerseys, looking around, hands on hips, seemingly unsure of themselves. Yet one man is stood firm. Chest proud, head held high, hands behind his back, a look of complete certainty on his face; a picture of defiance. Rock solid. That man is Bernard Hinault.

Hinault was wearing the jersey of national champion that day, the title he had claimed just three weeks earlier by embarking on a 55km solo escape to record a six-minute win, despite suffering severe hypoglycaemia in the closing moments of the race. In the pages of *L'Équipe* Jean-Marie Leblanc wrote that a fully-drained winner made for the most appealing of spectacles – a rider who had to battle blurred vision and lifeless legs as well as 'adversaries and the elements'.[1] He had also won the Vuelta earlier in the season, the first time he had ridden a three-week Grand Tour and a race he was riding only to ready himself for his first attempt at his own national tour. He won the Vuelta with five stages to his name and an overall margin of just over three minutes. 'He won as he wanted and when he wanted,' reported *ABC*. 'His presence in the Spanish race was undertaken with a view to his preparation for the Tour, where things will not be as easy as they have been in Spain.'[2]

With wins at Liège–Bastogne–Liège, Gent–Wevelgem, the Dauphiné Libéré and the GP des Nations already in the bag from the previous season, Hinault entered the Tour as a rider to watch. But could he climb well enough and last long enough to be a real match for the best riders in the world's greatest race? This was a definite step up for the 23-year-old Renault man; could he cope?

The answer was emphatically yes. Hinault rode well in the key stages, winning stage 8's time trial and performing impressively in the Pyrenees. He won the sprint into St-Étienne and in the Alps placed second on l'Alpe d'Huez to lift himself into second place overall, just 14 seconds behind Joop Zoetemelk. Then, on stage 20, he destroyed the Dutchman in the final time trial, taking over four minutes out of the then race leader and claiming the yellow jersey for the first time in his career. There remained just two days to go to Paris and Hinault held the jersey with some ease. His final margin on the Champs-Élysées was 3min 56sec. 'I feel so good I could race another three months like that,'[3] he said on the eve of his win. The peloton had been warned.

Born in Brittany, on the Côtes d'Armor, Hinault was a gifted athlete at a young age and in 1972 won the junior national championship. He turned professional three years later with the Gitane team, which later morphed into Renault. Although Hinault would later deny he was the ringleader during that 1978 Tour protest, it was the first demonstration of what was to become an absolute authority at the Tour – a new patron of the peloton had arrived.

Nicknamed 'The Badger' for his tenacious spirit, Hinault would spend a total of seventy-five days[4] in yellow over the course of his career, collecting five Tour victories in total. Add to that three Giro titles and a brace of Vuelta wins and you have the first rider in history to record more than one win in all three Grand Tours. His best year at the Tour was 1981, when, after having to retire from the 1980 edition with a knee injury, he returned with a vengeance, winning the opening time trial, briefly relinquishing the race lead for five days when his team was beaten in the team time trial, before grabbing it back on stage 7. He then held it for the final eighteen days in a row, winning every individual time trial as well as the stage from Bourg d'Oisans to Le Pleynet, over five categorised alpine climbs. His overall winning margin over Lucien Van Impe was 14min 34sec.

Hinault also put in some legend-making performances during the Classics, his 1980 win at Liège–Bastogne–Liège just one example. With over 100km of that race to go Renault's sports director, Cyrille Guimard, drove alongside Hinault, wound down the car window, and told his team leader to take off his jacket. 'The race is starting now,' he said.

Hinault must have thought Guimard was crazy. It was mid-April but snow had been falling since the race's start and the roads were drenched with slush. So bad were the conditions that more than 100 riders abandoned without even reaching the turnaround at Bastogne – in fact Gilbert Duclos-Lassalle told *L'Équipe* that some had collected their start numbers only to return to their hotels without ever turning a pedal. 'My cape was made of waxed fabric and I was very warm inside it,' Hinault later reflected. 'But I took it off as instructed ... I decided the only thing to do was ride as hard as I could to keep myself warm.'[5]

So Hinault set off on what would become one of cycle sport's most storied rides. Ahead, Rudy Pevenage was being chased by a small group of other riders. Hinault accelerated up the Stockeu, caught those chasing Pevenage, towed them to the Belgian, and then attacked again. No one went with him. There was still 80km to go and Hinault was alone in some of the toughest conditions ever faced in a bike race. So he did what he always did. He put his head down and got on with it.

Hinault survived the perilously icy roads to win by over nine minutes and claim his third Monument, reportedly saluting his teammates who were watching from a nearby hotel as he approached the finish. Only twenty-one riders finished the race.

A little over four months later Hinault won the world championship title on a brutal course in the French Alps. Just six days before he had abandoned the Tour du Limousin with abdominal pain and as the Worlds started no one was sure of his condition, maybe even Hinault himself. On the thirteenth lap he split the field in the climb of the Domancy. Next time round he did it again, resulting in a five-man breakaway. One by one his breakaway companions fell away until only the Italian Gianbattista Baronchelli remained.

'*Et voilà!* Now he attacks! Attack! Bernard Hinault!' yelled the TV commentator as the Frenchman pulled decisively away on the final climb of the Domancy. Baronchelli had no response. Soon Hinault was alone, left to ride himself into history. 'Hinault! Hinault! Hinault!' the crowds cried as he sped to the finish. 'Animated by the spirit which so characterises him, anxious to silence the rumours circulating concerning his possible decline ... he struck strongly and gave us the image of a timely champion, one whose effort is meticulously planned,'[6] reported *Le Monde*. It was the first time in eighteen years that a Frenchman had won the Worlds. On a day when only fifteen riders finished, Hinault's performance was Merckx-like, predictably prompting comparisons between the two champions with *La Stampa* running the headline 'Hinault: a champion the old way'.[7]

The following year Hinault wore the rainbow jersey as he won Paris–Roubaix, a race with which he had a famously difficult relationship, claiming the win despite crashing seven times and branding the race 'bullshit'. That was pure Hinault, a man who, to put it mildly, developed a reputation as an outspoken rider with a no-nonsense approach. In 1984, during Paris–Nice, he threw a hay-maker of a punch at an unlucky shipbuilder who had been participating in a protest that had forced the stage to stop. The previous year he'd reacted furiously as fans booed when he abandoned Paris–Roubaix. 'He lifted his bike,' reported the Dutch daily, *Leidsch Dagblad*, 'threw it at the feet of a spectator and shouted wildly: "Please, just try it for yourself."'[8] In 2008, while working for ASO, the organisers of the Tour, he literally threw an interloper off the podium before calmly carrying on with introducing stage winner Samuel Dumoulin to the great and the good of Nantes.

Hinault won his fifth and final Tour title in 1985 but, with the emergence of his teammate Greg LeMond as a genuine Tour threat, his win was clouded by claims of infighting within the team. The team turmoil continued the following year until he eventually turned *domestique*, helping LeMond to his first Tour win (see LeMond entry for more). Hinault retired later that season to work his farm in Brittany.

So just how good was Bernard Hinault? Hinault's old mentor, Cyrille Guimard has claimed he was the best, telling author Richard Moore that Hinault had by far the 'greatest athletic potential,' of all riders, including Merckx.[9]

The Badger greater than the Cannibal? That may be a little tough to swallow for most, but it is undeniable that Hinault's exploits and uncompromising style set him apart from nearly everyone who has ever thrown a leg over a racing bike.

MAJOR WINS
Tour de France: 1978, 1979, 1981, 1982, 1985
Giro d'Italia: 1980, 1982, 1985
Vuelta a España: 1978, 1983
Paris-Roubaix: 1981
Tour of Lombardy: 1979, 1984
Liège-Bastogne-Liège: 1977, 1980
World Champion: 1980
National Champion: 1978

Induráin, Miguel

ESP

BORN: 16 JULY 1964, VILLAVA, SPAIN

An exceptional time trial rider who could defend his lead in the mountains, Miguel Induráin, or Big Mig as he was known, is the only rider with five consecutive Tours to his name. During that time he also won the Giro twice in a row, meaning he is also the only rider to have completed the fabled Giro/Tour double back-to-back. Given that, at the time of writing, no rider has done that particular double even once for more than twenty years (Marco Pantani was the last rider, in 1998), such an achievement should inspire wistful acclaim. But it is not so. The perceived manner of his victories – always controlled and never with panache – gave rise to grudging respect rather than provoking passion.

Induráin ruled the Tour from 1991 to 1995. No one ever really came close to challenging him. His tactics could be summed up thus: win the time trials, don't lose time in the mountains, win the Tour.

And that is what Induráin did. For five straight years. Always in complete control, he was accused of never riding on instinct, never with aggression. He was the antithesis of those champions from a bygone era, the romantic ages of Coppi, Bobet and Merckx, riders so often remembered though sepia-tinted glasses. Where Hinault rode with undimmed fury and passion, so Induráin kept on keeping on, biding his time, not reacting to anything, waiting for his turn against the clock where he knew he would prove unbeatable. To watch Induráin ride a time-trial bike was to watch a man at one with his machine. True, during his five-year Tour reign he never won a stage that wasn't a time trial, but there was more to Induráin than just being a ruthless metronome.

Induráin started cycling aged ten and took to the sport quickly. There is a popular story that describes the young Miguel, distraught at the theft of his cherished second-hand bike, going to work the fields alongside his father in order to save enough money to buy a replacement. The reality would seem slightly different. In 1995 the writer Stuart Stevens travelled to Induráin's home town, keen to find out more about the man and the foundation of his dominance of cycling's biggest race. In Villava he spoke to Aitor David, the man who ran Induráin's official fan club. David told Stevens that when that bike was stolen Induráin's father simply bought another one. 'People like to say Miguel was a poor farm boy,' David said. 'Farm, yes. Poor, no.'[1]

By the time he was 18 Induráin had won the amateur national championship and in 1984, he turned professional with the Reynolds team, claiming stage wins at the 1984 and 1985 Tour de l'Avenir and the overall in 1986 – the former amateur-only event having been opened to professionals by the 1980s.

The Spaniard took to the Tour's start line for the first of twelve straight appearances in 1985, lasting only four stages. Early on in his career he worked for his various team leaders, including the 1988 winner Pedro Delgado, and recorded unspectacular results. However, by the end of the 1980s Induráin had been transformed from also-ran to Tour team leader. He claimed summit-finish wins in the Pyrenees in 1989 and 1990 on his way to respective seventeenth- and tenth-place finishes in Paris.

Those two mountain-top wins, at Cauterets and Luz-Ardiden respectively, showed a glimpse of what Induráin was capable of when the road tilted skywards. The following years brought often equally impressive, if more defensive, performances in the mountains as he went in search of yellow. And it was the same at the Giro: his definitive climb into pink for his second win in Milan came after a 245km slog over the passes of the Costalunga, the Pordoi (twice), Marmolada and Campolongo, where he finished just one second behind Claudio Chiappucci, a rider whose mountain exploits have in the past been hailed to high heaven.

Induráin's first Tour win arrived in 1991. He took yellow in the Pyrenees after a difficult 232km stage from Jaca, in Spain, over the climbs of the Pourtalet, Aubisque, Tourmalet and Aspin and up to Val Louron. Induráin had been more than four minutes behind Luc Leblanc at the start of that stage and more than two minutes behind the defending champion Greg LeMond, but, after countering LeMond's initial attack at the foot of the Tourmalet, Induráin moved away towards the top of the climb. On the Aspin he waited for the chasing Chiappucci to get across and then worked with him to build a greater lead over the chasing main contenders. Up the Aspin, down the Aspin, along the valley and up to Val Louron they rode together. Behind, LeMond was labouring, hitting the deck after having his rear wheel clipped by a rival team's car. The American lost more than seven minutes as Chiappucci took the stage and Induráin the race lead. The Spaniard defended his jersey through the Alps and then won the final 57km time trial to claim his first Tour.

Devastating displays against the clock were occasionally matched by rip-roaring rides in the mountains, not least his incredible ascent of Hautacam in 1994 when he led the pursuit of Marco Pantani, an expert climber who was threatening Induráin's lead, heading a group of around twenty riders before leaving them scattered on the mountain as his speed devastated the group. Only Festina's Luc Leblanc could stay with the Spaniard as the pair caught the Italian. Leblanc went on to get the stage win while Induráin kept hold of his yellow jersey.

Other riders have won five Tours – Anquetil, Merckx and Hinault – but none claimed those wins in succession. The only other rider to have matched Induráin's five-straight haul at the Tour was Lance Armstrong who took seven but no longer has those wins to his name. Induráin dominated the Tour like no one before. 'Every year the same song. By now, we don't have to spend much time practising it,'[2] the leader of the band charged with playing the national anthems in Paris jokingly told the NY Times in 1995.

Stuart Stevens' trip to Spain to try to understand Induráin had come before that 1995 race. He writes of growing frustrated as the real Induráin remained elusive, a flurry of aloofness and polite answers that said very little: 'I begin to understand, however, why Pedro Delgado, the only other Spaniard to win the Tour in the last two decades once said, "I was his roommate for years, and even I don't know him,"[3] Stevens reported. He asked other riders of their take, why was Big Mig so successful? What was his secret? Was he an extra-terrestrial like Gianni Bugno had once said after a Tour time trial? Was it his placid temperament? Or his slow-beating heart and expansive lung capacity? Was it that he had lost weight but maintained the power in those huge thighs? Did he train differently? Do more speed work? Ride longer distances? 'Why do you think he keeps winning the Tour de France?' an exasperated Stevens asked Induráin's domestique Vicente Aparicio. Aparicio just shrugged with a look that said you really don't understand before offering this simple explanation: 'He is Miguel, of course.'[4]

Induráin's final race was the 1996 Vuelta. Two months earlier he'd had his Tour reign ended by Bjarne Riis. On the Vuelta stage to the Lagos de Covadonga he climbed off his bike outside his team's hotel, the ride to the lakes too much to bear. After thirteen years as a pro he was done. Three months later he confirmed his retirement. 'My family are waiting,' he said.[5]

MAJOR WINS
Tour de France: 1991, 1992, 1993, 1994, 1995
Giro d'Italia: 1992, 1993
National Champion: 1992

Janssen, Jan

BORN: 19 MAY 1940, NOOTDORP, NETHERLANDS

On the morning of 29 June 1963, Jan Janssen and his Pelforth teammate, Dick Enthoven, were in Angers along with the rest of the Tour peloton. The day before had been a split stage, a 118km race from Rennes into Angers in the morning followed by 24.5km time trial around the town in the afternoon. After their night's rest, Janssen and Enthoven went to where they thought the day's start line was located but when they arrived there was no one there. 'People were telling us, "They've already gone! They've already gone!"', Janssen said in a 2011 interview. The two men, frantic with worry, rushed to find the arrows they knew would guide them to the start and finally got on their way. 'We rode for three hours, 80km,' Janssen recalled. 'In the distance, we could see something happening. It was the Tour.'[1]

Eventually, after those 80km spent chasing, Janssen and Enthoven got back to the peloton where they received 'a jolly greeting', with everyone laughing at them. But it was Janssen who would have the last laugh. He might not have known exactly where the start was but he knew the finish, remembering that there was a stiff climb a couple of kilometres from the cinder track in Limoges. 'I could ride on that, there is a cinder track where I lived. I had trained on a horserace track. I was at home there,' he said.[2]

And so Janssen attacked on the climb, got a gap, and raced onto the track with a slender lead that he held to the finish despite a fierce chase going on behind. The Dutchman, in his first year on the Pelforth team, claimed a four-second win over probably the greatest sprinter in the race – Belgium's Rik Van Looy. All on a day when, six hours earlier, he had missed the start.

Fast forward five years and as the 1968 Tour was about to start, Janssen was in the midst of a successful career and riding his sixth Tour in a row. He had developed from a talented sprinter into a tenacious all-rounder with a string of first-rate wins behind him, including the 1964 world championship when 65,000 people lined the Sallanches road circuit in the French Alps expecting to see a French victory, but instead watched the 24-year-old Janssen profit from the inability of France to work as a team, with Jacques Anquetil and Raymond Poulidor paralysed by their rivalry. Janssen crossed the line that day with both hands raised, looking dapper in dark sunglasses despite the rain that had fallen on the race. He had also claimed the points classification at the Tour three times, the overall at the 1967 Vuelta and the 1966 edition of Bordeaux–Paris. In 1967 he won Paris–Roubaix, again beating Van Looy in the final sprint. 'I won Bordeaux–Paris, that was great,' Janssen said after winning in Roubaix. 'I've finished second in the Tour and have worn the green jersey into Paris. That was fine. But this? [To win] Paris–Roubaix is really something. Then you are a great rider.'[3] But as the 1968 Tour rolled out from Vittel, things were about to get even better for Janssen.

Two years previously the Dutchman had finished second in Paris behind Lucien Aimar. He had worn yellow for just one day that year before losing it. At the 1968 race he would again wear the famous jersey only once, but this time there was no way anyone could snatch it from him, because Janssen only claimed the jersey at the end of the final day – right when it mattered most.

As the race had entered its final third, so Janssen had begun his ascent through the rankings, from being outside the top ten after stage 15, to lying third, just sixteen seconds off the race leader, Herman Van Springel, with one stage to go. That stage was a 55km time trial from Melun into the Cipale velodrome in the Bois de Vincennes, south-east Paris. In a precursor of the famous 1989 Tour's final-day time trial (see LeMond entry for more) Janssen powered to victory, winning the stage and taking fifty-four seconds out of Van Springel, stealing the jersey off the Belgian's back at the very last moment having never once worn it during the race. Janssen's margin of victory in Paris was just thirty-eight seconds, which remained the record for the narrowest Tour win until 1989. 'I gave everything, I fought ... I was so empty,'4 Janssen said afterwards as he became the first Dutch rider to win cycling's biggest prize.

It would turn out to be his final major win. He retired in 1972, immediately setting up his own bicycle business, which remains operational today.

MAJOR WINS
Tour de France: 1968
Vuelta a España: 1967
Paris–Roubaix: 1967
World Champion: 1964
Bordeaux–Paris: 1966

Koblet, Hugo

SUI

BORN: 21 MARCH 1925, ZURICH, SWITZERLAND

There is a photograph, taken on 2 November 1964 along the road that leads from Zurich to the Swiss village of Esslingen, that shows a crumpled white Alfa Romeo car that has crashed headlong into a tree. Leaves are scattered on the car's roof, the bonnet is completely caved in. The driver-side front door lies twisted, torn from its hinges. Where there should be a steering wheel there is only a mass of mangled and destroyed engine components. On the ground lies a single hubcap. Behind, a man dressed in a hat and coat, wearing a black tie and carrying a camera is reaching into his coat pocket while looking into the distance, it seems like he is trying to figure out exactly what has happened here, perhaps all the more so because this car belonged to one of Switzerland's greatest ever sportsmen – Hugo Koblet.

By the time that photograph was taken Koblet was in hospital in Zurich. He had multiple injuries, including a fractured skull. He underwent a four-hour operation but two days after the incident the *Gazette de Lausanne* reported that 'only a miracle'[1] could now save Koblet. That miracle never came and on 6 November, Hugo Koblet died. He was 39 years old.

Nicknamed the '*pédaleur de charme*' by the French singer and actor Jacques Grello, Koblet earned a reputation as an elegant rider and one popular with both fans and fellow riders. He was said to carry a comb, a damp sponge and a bottle of cologne in his back pocket and there is many a photograph of him slicking his hair back in front of a mirror. Legend has it that if he was at the front of a race and confident of victory he would sit up, get out the comb and cologne, and set about making himself presentable for the finish-line victory salute.

Koblet's first win of note came at the 1950 Giro, where he benefitted from the absence of Fausto Coppi after the Italian champion crashed and quit the race with a broken pelvis. Koblet had taken the pink jersey the day before, after winning the stage into Venezia. With Coppi out of the race Koblet went up against the Campionissimo's great rival, Gino Bartali, for the overall win. With Coppi's Bianchi team fully onside with preventing a Bartali win and apparently standing to benefit financially if the Swiss man triumphed, Koblet gained from their work. Thirteen days after first wearing pink he rode into Rome with a 5min 12sec cushion over Bartali to become the first non-Italian winner of the Giro. 'We see that Swiss gold was worth more than [the] love of [our] country,' Bartali said.[2] Koblet, who was Protestant, not Catholic, was nevertheless received by the Pope at the Vatican along with the rest of the riders. 'Koblet will bend his knee with all the others before the Vicar of Christ,' reported *La Stampa*. 'And this act of humility will make him even closer and dearer to Italian sportsmen.'[3] Two weeks after his Giro victory he won on home roads, securing the first of an eventual three Tour de Suisse titles.

In July 1951 Koblet lined up at the start of the Tour in Metz as the leader of the Swiss team. He won the first time trial before staging one of the great Tour breakaways during the stage from Brive-la-Gaillarde to Agen, escaping some 135km before the finish and staying away despite a full-paced chase involving the likes of Coppi and Bartali as well as Louison Bobet, Fiorenzo Magni, Raphaël Géminiani and Stan Ockers. Koblet crossed the line, got out his stopwatch, and ran a comb through his hair as he waited. Koblet's stopwatch would have counted to 2min 25sec before Marcel Michel led the best of the rest in. 'It's not possible, a rider like that,' said Géminiani afterwards. 'If there were two of Koblet, I would change occupations immediately.'[4]

Koblet received a one-minute bonus for the win which was enough to propel the Swiss rider into third place overall. Three days later he won the mountain stage into Luchon over the Tourmalet, Aspin and Peyresourde to assume the race lead. With two mountain stages to go Koblet's nearest challenger was Géminiani, 1min 32sec back. After climbing the Vars and Izoard *en route* to Briançon that gap was over nine minutes. By Paris, after Koblet had won the final time trial two days before by nearly five minutes, the margin of overall victory had grown to twenty-two minutes. It was an absolute masterclass of riding.

A talented track rider – he had worked in the Oerlikon velodrome as a 17 year old and went on to hold national pursuit titles and win a number of six-day races – Koblet never again finished the Tour. He crashed out in 1953 and 1954 after which he suffered badly with injuries which hindered the rest of his career. 'I have had a lot of trouble with my back,' Koblet said in 1956. 'So much so that instead of being a very good hill climber, I am now just an ordinary one. The back is very important for climbers and sprinters. It got so bad that during the summer I could not even stand upright for more than a few seconds and could not even dance with my wife.'[5]

Koblet retired in 1958. Bad investments cost him, and his debts mounted. On 2 November 1964 Koblet was driving along the Esslingen to Zurich road when he passed a large pear tree. He stopped, turned around and drove back, passing the tree again. He drove past the tree once more before turning a final time and driving straight into it at 120km/h.

His fellow Swiss rider Ferdi Kübler was at his funeral, as were Bobet and Bartali. 'The Swiss star was a wonderful man to watch on the bicycle,' wrote Jock Wadley in *Sporting Cyclist*. 'He was, as so many people have lately testified, always the complete gentleman, ever ready to help.'[6]

MAJOR WINS
Tour de France: 1951
Giro d'Italia: 1950
National Champion: 1955

Kübler, Ferdi

SUI

BORN: 24 JULY 1919, MARTHALEN, SWITZERLAND

In stark contrast to Hugo Koblet, his elegant countryman and rival, Ferdinand Kübler was a seething mass of energy when he rode, to the point that occasionally he seemed deranged, talking to anyone who would listen and referring to himself in the third person. The results of this idiosyncratic style were sometimes spectacular, sometimes catastrophic.

Born into a poor family, the young Kübler found his racing legs by making deliveries for a baker. In 1940, with the world at war, he turned professional, riding mainly in Switzerland – though he also raced in unoccupied France, most notably at the GP des Nations in 1941 and 1942 finishing third and seventh respectively. He took five wins in six years during the war at the Dwars Door Lausanne and also claimed the Tour de Suisse in 1942, a race he would win again in 1948 and 1951.

He rose to international prominence in 1947, the year that the Tour returned following the end of the Second World War. Billed the Tour of the Liberation, Kübler won the first stage from Paris to Lille, bridging up to the lead rider Camille Danguillaume, who had poured all his energy into a big effort as Lille approached unaware that there remained a 25km traverse of the city before the finish, and then breaking away with André Mahé on his wheel before beating the Frenchman in the sprint. It meant that Kübler claimed the first yellow jersey of the post-Second World War era. He would win another stage four days later but retired with Paris still more than two weeks away.

Two years later and Kübler would find himself more than four minutes ahead of eventual winner Fausto Coppi as the Tour entered the Alps for its crescendo. Kübler broke away early on the stage but Coppi and his rival-turned-temporary-teammate-for-once, Gino Bartali, came back and soared away on the Izoard as Kübler punctured three times and lost fifteen minutes. A photograph taken on the final climb shows a hugely distressed Kübler brandishing a bicycle pump, his face full of despair. The next day he lost more than forty minutes to Coppi who was now leading the race.

The next day the Tour visited Switzerland with a stage finish to Lausanne but Kübler didn't make it. He packed up just outside Saint Rhemy before the race crossed into his homeland. While there were some raised eyebrows in France the Swiss press merely put his abandonment down to him being thoroughly demoralised having suffered incredible bad luck. 'The Tour for Kübler is coming,' reported the *Gazette de Lausanne*. 'Perhaps.'[7]

Kübler erased that 'perhaps' the following year, although it came in controversial circumstances. Such was the strength of the Italian nation that they entered two teams into the 1950 Tour. By the time the race entered the Pyrenees they had claimed half of all the stages and were poised to make a move on the overall standings. But with Italy winning the past two editions of the race (Bartali in 1948 and Coppi in 1949) the French were getting fed up of Italian domination and on the stage from Pau to Saint-Gaudens, with Bartali and his teammate Fiorenzo Magni in the leading group, the restless spectators started shouting abuse at the riders. Near the top of the Aspin, with the crowds swarming all over the roads, Bartali and France's Jean Robic touched wheels. Both riders went down, with Robic suffering damage to his front wheel. Some of the crowd went to their aid, others took the opportunity to beat and swear at Bartali, throwing stones. It took the intervention of Jacques Goddet, the race director, to allow Bartali and Robic to continue. Bartali flew down the other side of the Aspin to the stage win while Magni took yellow. Then a furious Bartali promptly announced 'We have been victims of aggression; no Italian will ride tomorrow.'[8]

And no Italian did ride. With Magni in yellow that meant the race lead passed to the best-placed non-Italian. Step forward Kübler who by this point had claimed one stage. He went on to win another two stages and wore yellow into Paris to become the first Swiss rider to win the Tour.

The following year Kübler sat out the Tour, preferring instead to concentrate on the world championships which were being held in Varese, Italy. It had been a main focus of his season but, with the kilometres counting down on a tough and hilly course, Kübler had a problem – he was in the lead group, but he was also outnumbered by three Italians racing on home roads.

But Kübler's preparation had been perfect and he knew the course better than anyone. He controlled the closing moments, chased down any attacks, and then launched his own sprint from 300 metres out. He won by three lengths from Magni to claim the rainbow jersey for Switzerland. The *Journal de Genève* gushed:

Undeniably our champion yesterday was stronger, his performance proves it irrefutably ... It was a good escape; He controlled it without exhausting his strength, he mastered his impulses and he had sufficient resources to contest the final 'rush' without error, that is, taking the lead and not letting it go! The best has won and all the athletes will congratulate Ferdinand Kübler for this exploit which crowns his career and brings our riders to the pinnacle.[9]

Other performances of note included a double-double at the Ardennes Weekend (winning La Flèche Wallonne and Liège-Bastogne-Liège on the same weekend) in 1951 and 1952.

By 1955 Kübler's career was on the slide. In a story that has passed into cycling lore, at the Tour he set off up Mont Ventoux like a rocket despite the warnings of other riders. 'Careful Ferdi, the Ventoux is a climb like no other,' Raphaël Géminiani is said to have told him. In response Kübler is supposed to have shouted back: 'And Ferdi is a champion like no other.'[10] This story has passed through the years, though in a 2007 interview with the French magazine *Vélo*, Kübler denied ever saying it. 'It's not true,' he said. 'I never said that. Géminiani is a great storyteller. In the peloton his nickname was Telephone. We're good friends but this story, it isn't true.'[11] What is undeniably true is that Kübler had seriously underestimated the Ventoux. He was soon weaving all over the road, in a state of delirium, sweat dripping from his brow, eyes haunted. He stopped to rest, then promptly tried to set off in the wrong direction before a spectator endured his wrath to set him right. 'Ferdi going to explode!' he yelled. Amazingly, given his state, he fell into Avignon just 26min 19sec down on stage-winner Louison Bobet, but he had paid a heavy price. He abandoned that night and never rode again at the Tour. 'Ferdi killed himself on the Ventoux,' he said later.[12]

Kübler carried on riding for a couple of years before retiring, later running a flower shop in Zurich. He died in 2016 aged 97. 'I became a champion because I was poor,' he said in a 2013 interview with *L'Équipe*. 'I struggled to eat, to have a better life. I won the Tour de France because I dreamed, because I knew that afterwards I would never be poor again.'[13]

MAJOR WINS
Tour de France: 1950
Liège-Bastogne-Liège: 1951, 1952
World Champion: 1951
National Champion: 1948, 1949, 1950, 1951, 1954
Bordeaux-Paris: 1953

Maurice Garin, Tour de France 1903. Garin was the winner of the very first Tour that year.

Henri Cornet, the Tour's youngest winner at 19 years old, *c*.1905.

Lucien Petit-Breton and Henri Cornet at the finish of the Tour in 1908.

Lucien Petit-Breton, the Tour's first back-to-back winner in 1908. Picture c.1912.

Henri Pélissier in 1913. Pélissier suffered an unfortunate end to life, shot dead by his lover.

Philippe Thys, Tour de France 1914. Thys was the first three-time winner.

Ottavio Bottecchia, Tour de France 1923. Bottecchia won the Tour in 1924 and 1925. He was found unconscious at the roadside while out training in 1927 and later died from his injuries. His death remains unexplained. (Agence Rol / Bilblioteque National de France, CC SA 4.0 via WikimediaCommons)

Nicolas Frantz, Ottavio Bottecchia and Omer Huysse, Tour de France 1924.

Louison Bobet, Tour de France 1954. Bobet was the first rider to win the Tour three times in a row. (Noske, J.D./Anefo CC SA 3.0 Netherlands via WikimediaCommons)

Opposite: Gino Bartali, c.1945. Bartali won the Tour in 1938 and 1948. The ten-year gap between first and second victories, partly explained by the Second World War, remains a record.

Jacques Anquetil, 1966. Anquetil was the first five-time winner of the Tour. (Eric Koch/Anefo, CC SA 3.0 Netherlands via Wikimedia Commons)

The Belgian cyclist Eddy Merckx has just finished a time trial stage of the Giro d'Italia. San Marino, 6 June 1968. The dominant Merckx counts five Tour wins amongst his incredible haul of race victories.

Luis Ocaña during the 1976 Tour. Ocaña won the Tour in 1973 and was one of the few riders to truly challenge Eddy Merckx at the race. (BastienM, CC SA 3.0 via WikimediaCommons)

Bernard Hinault, 1978. Hinault was a force at the Tour between 1978 and 1985, claiming five wins. He remains the last Frenchman to stand on the top step of the podium in Paris. (CC SA 3.0 Netherlands via WikimediaCommons)

Greg LeMond, the first US winner of the Tour, riding on the lower slopes of Alpe D'Huez during the Tour De France, July 1991. (Steve Selwood, CC SA 3.0 via WikimediaCommons)

Miguel Induráin, 1996. Induráin was the first rider to win five Tours in succession, claiming every edition between 1991 and 1995. (Darz Mol, CC SA 3.0 via WikimediaCommons)

Geraint Thomas leads the Tour de France 2018, with teammate Chris Froome in his wake. (Konstantine Kleine, CC BY-SA 4.0 via WikimediaCommons)

Bradley Wiggins and Mark Cavendish during the 2012 Tour de France. The sight of Wiggins in yellow and Cavendish in the rainbow jersey of World Champion truly announced Britain's arrival at the top of road cycling. (Josh Hallett from Winter Haven, FL, USA, CC SA 2.0 via WikimediaCommons)

Bradley Wiggins, the first British winner, Tour de France 2012. (Sapin88, CC SA 3.0 via WikimediaCommons)

Chris Froome, Tour de France 2017. Froome is a quadruple winner of the Tour. (Hoebele, CC SA 4.0 via WikimediaCommons)

Lambot, Firmin

BEL

BORN: 14 MARCH 1886, FLORENNES, BELGIUM

Tour history recognises that the yellow jersey was officially introduced as the means of identifying the race's leading rider in 1919, first presented without much fanfare to France's Eugène Christophe in Grenoble. That moment was captured by a photograph, taken outside race control at the Café de l'Ascenseur, that shows Christophe, tubulars wrapped around his shoulders, goggles perched on his forehead, hands on hips, looking not exactly overjoyed to be wearing his new jersey. 'I handed this morning to valiant Christophe a superb yellow jersey,' reported *L'Auto*'s correspondent. 'You already know that our director has decided that the lead man of the overall classification would wear a jersey in the colours of *L'Auto*. The fight will be passionate for possession of the jersey!'[1]

While there is some conjecture as to whether this really was the first time the race leader had worn a yellow jersey – in a 1953 interview with *Champions et Vedettes*, three-time Tour winner Philippe Thys said that he had worn a 'golden coloured jersey' as leader of the Tour in 1913 and in 1914 (see Thys entry for more). Pierre Chany later wrote that perhaps after experimenting sporadically with the idea for a couple of years Desgrange finally resolved to formalise it during the next race which, as things turned out, was in 1919, though he admitted this was just a theory. What is certain is that in 1919 the jersey did not bring Christophe any luck. A little under a week after he first pulled on yellow, and with a lead of 28min 5sec just two days from Paris, Christophe's front fork collapsed on the cobblestones of northern France. It took him more than an hour to repair his machine as Firmin Lambot inherited the race lead.

While Christophe was proclaimed the race's moral winner it was Lambot who entered history as the first man to take the official yellow jersey into Paris. It was far from an empty victory in a race that took the riders through a country that had been devastated by war. On the penultimate stage, where Christophe had suffered his ill-fortune, Lambot rode into Dunkirk after spending more than twenty-one hours on the road. In an edition of the Tour where only eleven riders made it to Paris (Paul Duboc was later disqualified for taking a car to a repair shop to mend his bike meaning there were only ten classified finishers), Lambot's winning margin was 1hr 42min 54sec. 'I was good, I was fresh,' he said in Paris. 'I am really happy to have won. However, tell Christophe that I consider him a tough man and a fellow who deserved to attach his name to the Tour de France this year.'[2]

A former saddle-maker, Lambot signed for Le Globe in 1911. He rode his first Tour that year, finishing eleventh overall and claimed his first stage win two years later having moved to Griffon. He claimed a second stage win in 1914 before war brought a five-year hiatus to the race.

A naturally cautious rider who reportedly 'always had 600 francs [on him] just in case he needed another bicycle along the way because of an emergency',[3] Lambot focused his efforts exclusively on the Tour. He wasn't interested in any other race (beyond the Tour his most notable result being fifth in the 1920 edition of Liège-Bastogne-Liège).

Lambot won the Tour again in 1922. Again, he benefitted from the bad luck of others. First, race leader Christophe endured a broken fork, yes, again – this time in the Pyrenees, the third time that broken forks had derailed his efforts. Jean Alavoine assumed the lead, held it for five days but then punctured and lost time which robbed him of the jersey. The lead passed to Hector Heusghem who then rode his bike into a pothole on the stage to Metz and instead of stopping to repair it, simply took a bike belonging to a teammate. That was against the rules and the day after the stage the *commissaires* imposed a one-hour penalty. That dropped Heusghem down to fifth meaning the second-placed rider was promoted into the race lead. That rider was Lambot and he held the lead into Paris to become the first rider to win the Tour without claiming a stage. All that good fortune fell to Lambot despite him wearing 'unlucky' 13 during throughout the race. He was 36 years old and, at the time of writing, remains the oldest winner of the race.

Lambot never made it to Paris again. He rode two more editions of the race but finished neither. He retired from cycling to run his bike shop in Antwerp, building bikes under his own name. He died in 1964.

MAJOR WINS
Tour de France: 1919, 1922

Lapébie, Roger
FRA

BORN: 16 JANUARY 1911, BAYONNE, FRANCE

Incredible as it may seem today, when the thrust for new and cutting-edge technology is at the forefront of the cycling industry, elements of the cycling world were at first stubbornly resistant to the introduction of the derailleur, arguably the one invention that transformed cycling most during the twentieth century. Henri Desgrange mocked the innovation, saying: 'Isn't it better to triumph by the strength of your muscles than by the artifice of a derailleur,' before deriding it as something only needed by grandparents.

Desgrange held firm against the use of the derailleur in his race, but in 1936 he was forced to leave the Tour early for health reasons. Jacques Goddet took over as race director and the following year the universal use of derailleurs was permitted. 'How many will use it in the mountains?' pondered two-time winner André Leducq on the eve of the 1937 race. 'Really, this novelty can bring us big surprises.'[5]

The first surprise for some was the inclusion of Roger Lapébie in the French team. While he had placed third and grabbed five stage wins at the 1934 Tour, Lapébie's greatest victories had been at the national championships in 1933 and Paris–Nice, which he had claimed a little more than three months prior to the start of the 1937 Tour. If that suggested a rider in form, Lapébie had actually been suffering with a hernia and opinion was divided over whether he should be selected for the Tour or instead check himself into hospital for an operation. As it turned out he headed to Paris for the start of the Tour and just under one month later returned to the capital with three stage wins and the yellow jersey on his back.

Not that his win was uneventful. His handlebars were sabotaged in the Pyrenees with the blame apportioned to 'someone close to the Belgians';[6] he was warned by the organisers for receiving assistance from spectators who were pushing him up the mountains despite his claims that he had asked them not to; and he was accused of grabbing cars and getting tows during long mountain stages. After the stage from Luchon to Pau he was hit with a ninety-second penalty and promptly threatened to quit and take all the French team with him.

But Lapébie was still second behind Belgium's Sylvère Maes, the defending champion, and so decided against acting on his fit of pique. On the next stage, as Lapébie went on the attack, Maes punctured and was held up in his pursuit by a closed level-crossing which forced him to push his bike under the barrier. Maes was booed and jostled by crowds in Bordeaux and then penalised fifteen seconds for accepting the assistance of two Belgian riders who were not part of his team. All of which meant that his lead was cut to twenty-five seconds. The Belgium team were furious and promptly abandoned *en masse*, saying they could not continue in such conditions. Desgrange countered in the pages of *L'Auto*, admitting the Belgian riders had suffered at the hands of a minority of spectators but stating the penalty was justified and was no reason to leave the race, writing:

> The day before yesterday, a similar penalty fell on Lapébie, precisely that which will provoke the incidents of the following day. But the next day, from Pau, Lapébie is at the start, with all his French team. Moreover, the morale of the team has never been better and all have sworn to make up for Lapébie the minute and a half which he was penalised. Which of these two attitudes do you prefer, dear readers?[7]

For his part Lapébie bemoaned the loss of the opportunity to beat Maes 'normally'. 'He had absolutely nothing to fear from the crowd,' he said. 'I think he was afraid of being beaten ... The best proof of that is that Belgian journalists are still searching for the real reason Sylvère left.'[8] Four days later Lapébie rode into Paris with a 7min 17sec lead to become the first rider to win the Tour using a derailleur for the entire race.

The son of a railway worker in Bayonne, Lapébie was one of three children (his younger brother Guy would also ride professionally). He started riding after his family had moved to Talence, near Bordeaux, later joining the famous Parisian amateur club Vélo Club de Levallois. He turned professional in 1932 with La Française, winning a Tour stage in his debut season. Two years later he crossed the finish line first at Paris–Roubaix but was disqualified having switched machines twice on the road – first grabbing a woman's bike out of a ditch after he had a mechanical problem and then later swapping it for a man's racing bike he'd spotted at the side of the road. Francis Pélissier, director of the Mercier team, appealed to race officials pointing out that Lapébie had contravened race regulations by not finishing the race with the machine on which he had started. The appeal was upheld. 'In a few seconds, the photographers took me crying with joy, then with sorrow,' Lapébie recalled in a 1994 interview. 'That night, in the car that brought me back to Paris, I cried all the way.'[9]

Lapébie reportedly endured a difficult relationship with Desgrange, falling out regularly. The rows meant that despite his third place in the 1934 Tour he wasn't selected for the French national team the following year (though his relatively poor results that year didn't help his cause). '[A] team is good, certainly,' he said, 'but there is no better way than to do things your own way, not to depend on anyone, to ride without thinking I have to help Peter or Paul at a particular time.'[10] Lapébie didn't make it to Paris, abandoning during the stage to Marseilles. He didn't ride at all in 1936, his relationship with the Tour organiser still broken. Then came his 1937 win.

Two years later his career was over after he crashed during Bordeaux–Paris and broke his kneecap. He later reflected on the conditions riders endured during the 1930s: 'There were potholes as big as birds' nests, pebbles, dust, gravel,' he said. 'We got lots of saddle sores because of the dirt, the cow dung. It was easy to get infected.'[11]

Lapébie died in 1996 aged 85.

MAJOR WINS
Tour de France: 1937
National Champion: 1933

Lapize, Octave

FRA

BORN: 24 OCTOBER 1887, PARIS, FRANCE

Between 1909 and 1914 Octave Lapize started six Tours but only finished one, leading the way back to Paris with four stage wins and the overall title in 1910. That was year that Henri Desgrange introduced high mountains into his race route, with the Pyrenees featuring on the *parcours* for the first time.

Lapize was a multi-talented rider, at home on the road, in the velodrome and on the mud (he rode on the track in the 1908 Olympics, contested six-day races in the winter and was a national cyclo-cross champion early in his career). Predicted to be 'the best rider of his generation',[12] after an amateur career in and around Paris – his first win, the Grand Prix de Villiers, was reported in the pages of *L'Auto* in 1906 – he turned professional in 1909. He quickly won Paris-Roubaix, beating Louis Trousselier in the final sprint in front of thousands who packed out the velodrome in Roubaix. If the professional cycling world didn't know much about him before that race, they certainly did afterwards, with him being described as 'the revelation of an unforgettable day'.[13] 'I'm first, I won!' was Lapize's own succinct report on the race. 'It is the most beautiful day of my life! But, good God – the dust, the crowd.'[14]

Lapize rode his first Tour three months later but only lasted a handful of stages until abandoning with a broken bike. Twelve months later he returned to the Tour, with a second Paris-Roubaix win in the bag, ready to take on cycling's greatest challenge again.

The idea of introducing the Pyrenees into the Tour's route came from Desgrange's assistant at *L'Auto*, Alphonse Steinès. Desgrange wasn't sure that taking riders over mountains of such a scale was a good idea, so Steinès famously set out to prove his boss wrong by traversing a proposed stage over the Tourmalet. With snowdrifts making car travel impossible he was forced to tackle the final kilometres on foot, asking the driver to drive back through the valleys and meet him in Barèges, on the other side of the pass. Steinès was eventually found stumbling towards the lights of Barèges, on the brink of hypothermia. After a bath and some sleep he had recovered enough to send a telegram to Desgrange. It said simply: 'Crossed Tourmalet. Stop. Very Good Road. Stop. Perfectly Passable. Stop.' And so it was that stage 10 of the 1910 Tour de France was designed as 326km from Luchon to Bayonne.

Lapize was placed second overall as the stage started, engaged in a battle for the top spot with François Faber. Fifty-nine riders set out from Luchon at 3.30 a.m. heading for the four huge climbs that collectively would become known as the 'Circle of Death'. Lapize and Gustave Garrigou quickly became engaged in a battle at the front of the race with Lapize leading over the Peyresourde, Aspin and Tourmalet. With an uncertain Desgrange opting to stay away just in case the whole thing turned into a disaster, it was left to Steinès and his colleague Victor Breyer to record proceedings and they waited on the top of the last climb, the Aubisque. The clock ticked on, minutes became hours, and their concern grew. What had happened? Had there been a terrible accident? Then, at long last, the shape of a rider and his bicycle appeared in the distance.

Recounting the story years later in *Sport et Vie*, the writer François Brigneau wrote that the emerging rider came by in a daze, 'his eyes out of his head, mouth open'. But it wasn't Lapize and neither was it Garrigou. Brigneau continued: '"Who are you? Where are the others?" cried Breyer, running by his side. But the rider heard nothing. He said nothing. He just moaned and shook his legs. His number half hanging off. "It is Lafourcade" said Steinès, "an *isolé* [amateur] from Bayonne."'[15]

Lapize appeared fifteen minutes later. Eyes wide with pain he turned towards Steinès and Breyer and, according to cycling lore, uttered the now immortal words *'Vous êtes des assassins. Oui, des assassins.'*[16] Lapize would go on to win the stage in Bayonne which, incredibly, after more than fourteen hours of racing came down to a sprint, with the Frenchman just pipping Pierino Albini to the line. Somewhat surprisingly, for the toughest stage in the Tour's short history, only thirteen men abandoned. The last to finish was Georges Cauvry. He arrived more than seven and a half hours down.

Lapize, nicknamed Frisé because of his curly hair and who was once described by Desgrange as having the 'hands of a rider who could destroy any handlebar in the world when he pulls hard on them on the hills',[17] took over the race lead three stages later and maintained it until Paris, recording his finest victory.

It would be the only Tour he ever finished and he would complain that riders ganged up on him, riding together to neutralise his efforts. Such tactics couldn't prevent him claiming three Paris–Roubaix titles, three national championships and three Paris–Brussels wins, all in succession. He also claimed Paris–Tours in 1911.

With the outbreak of war in 1914 Lapize signed up to fight for his country. After being wounded on the ground he joined the French air force. In 1917 he was shot down, reportedly while battling several enemy planes, and taken to hospital in Toul, 25km west of Nancy, where he was pronounced dead. The plane was recovered and taken to the Parc de l'Armee where his friends and fellow pilots wrote a moving inscription to him on the cabin: 'This Old No 4 was piloted by our dear and poor comrade, O. Lapize,' the inscription read. 'Whoever you are, do not climb in without a thought for this brilliant pilot, who fell gloriously.'[18]

MAJOR WINS
Tour de France: 1910
Paris–Roubaix: 1909, 1910, 1911
National Champion: 1911, 1912, 1913

Leducq, André
FRA

BORN: 27 FEBRUARY 1904, SAINT-OUEN, FRANCE

Shortly before 5 p.m. on Sunday 31 July 1938 André Leducq rode onto the Parc des Princes track in Paris. It was the final stage of Leducq's final Tour and the Frenchman wanted to bow out in style. With him was fellow two-time Tour winner, Antonin Magne. Both men were beloved by the French public, between them responsible for four of France's six Tour wins during the 1930s. So often they had been teammates on the France national team, riding together in the colours of their country. This time, however, as they entered the famous velodrome for the final act of the 1938 Tour, they wore

different jerseys – Magne wore the colours of France while Leducq was riding
for the Cadets team. Both were riding their final Tours and had escaped from
the pack some 55km from the finish. Together they rode around the Parc des
Princes track and together they crossed the line, arms around each other's
shoulders, inseparable in the country's affections and inseparable on their
final Tour stage. 'They knew, magnificently, these two of the old guard, how
to finish their careers as Tour de France riders,' wrote Robert Perrier the
following day. 'We had tears in our eyes.'[19] Shared though it might have been,
it went into the books as the twenty-fifth stage win of Leducq's illustrious
Tour career, a record haul that stood until Eddy Merckx surpassed it more
than thirty years later.

Born into a cycling family, Leducq turned professional in 1926, at the age
of 22, two years after he had claimed the amateur world title in Versailles.
While his first season in the pro-ranks, riding for Thomann-Dunlop while still
enlisted in the military, brought no significant results, in 1927, still riding for
Thomann, he started his first Tour.

A little under one month after the race left Paris, Leducq led the gallop
back into France's capital city. It was his third stage win as he claimed fourth
overall, the best-placed Frenchman. Hailed as the 'French revelation of the
race,'[20] the result propelled Leducq into the public's gaze. 'He returns to Paris,
a darling of the public', wrote Jean Routier in Le Miroir des Sports. 'We can
easily see it in his mail. Every morning, he receives a heap of letters, most
of them signed by admirers ... Leducq laughs heartily when he is asked to
marry two or three times a day on average.'[21] One month later and Le Joyeux
Dédé had signed for arguably the most powerful outfit in France – Alcyon.

Three stage wins and fourth at the Tour in 1927 became four stage wins
and second in 1928, alongside a Paris–Roubaix win that would remain
Leducq's only Monument. He wore the yellow jersey for the first time in 1929,
though he shared it with two others when time-keepers were unable to
separate the leading three riders in Bordeaux – 'Frantz, Leducq and Fontan
together at the top of the general classification, all three will wear the yellow
jersey today',[22] reported L'Auto – and one year later claimed his first Tour.

The 1930 Tour was the first run in national teams as Desgrange once again
changed the format of his race and how Leducq needed the support of his
compatriots. After assuming the race lead in the Pyrenees, going into stage
16, 331km from Grenoble to Évian over the Lauteret, Galibier and Aravis,
Leducq had 16min 13sec over Italy's Learco Guerra. All was looking good, but
then disaster befell the Frenchman on the descent of the Galibier when he

was knocked unconscious after losing control and 'somersaulting off [his] bike'.[23] He came around, his body battered, bloodied and bruised, his machine seemingly beyond repair with a bent pedal. Leducq was distraught and wanted to abandon but his teammates arrived on the scene, forced his pedal back into shape and convinced him to continue. Shortly after he remounted, his brakes failed. Another hasty repair completed, and Leducq was again on his way. Then his pedal snapped clean off. Another stop. Another repair job.

By now Leducq had five teammates around him. At first, they rode tentatively as *Dédé* found his racing legs again, then in the valley they launched a furious pursuit of Guerra who was up the road having gained nearly twenty minutes in all the commotion. For the next 75km the French train worked seamlessly and without pause, relentlessly reeling the Italian rider in. Astonishingly, they caught Guerra and the leading group with 140km still to ride. But Leducq, with adrenaline surely now coursing through his veins, was not done. As the finish line approached so he went to work, claiming the sprint ahead of twenty-nine other riders. Despite a day of high drama the general classification remained essentially unchanged. *Le Miroir des Sports* reported:

> Rarely have we seen, in the Tour de France, a hunt as fantastic ... We felt that all the teammates of Leducq were animated by the same flame and that they would go to the limit of their forces to try to save the prestige of the French cycling [team]. We have here one of the most beautiful demonstrations of the moral power of team spirit that can be found.[24]

Six days later Leducq's winning margin in Paris was 14min 13sec as he claimed his first Tour title. 'You can rest assured, Dédé will not stop there,' reported *L'Auto*.[25]

Indeed, he did not. After seeing his compatriot and teammate Magne triumph in 1931, Leducq won again in 1932, claiming six stages along the way and benefitting from a rule that gave four-minute time bonuses for stage winners as he beat Germany's Kurt Stoepel by 24min 3sec. It was to prove to be the last of his major wins and one which would apparently go some way to saving his life during the Second World War when a German soldier who had captured Leducq recognised him from following his race against Stoepel and released him.

'You see,' Leducq is quoted as saying later to Raymond Poulidor, the French rider who famously made the final Tour podium eight times but never once stood on the top step, 'sometimes it helps to have won the Tour.'[26]

Leducq retired in 1939, moving on to work in the media, for the Mercier bicycle company, as a team director and as a café owner. He died in 1980 aged 76.

> ## MAJOR WINS
> Tour de France: 1930, 1932
> Paris-Roubaix: 1928

LeMond, Greg

USA

BORN: 26 JUNE 1961, LAKEWOOD, USA

When America's Greg LeMond arrived at the start for stage five of the 1989 Tour, he knew that all eyes would soon be on him. Ahead was a 73km time trial, from Dinard to Rennes, and LeMond had something new to unveil that would get tongues wagging.

Earlier that day José De Cauwer, LeMond's sports director at the ADR team, had wheeled the American's bike through the corridors of a hotel in search of the head of the Tour's race jury, Claude Jacquat. It was early and Jacquat was still blurry eyed when De Cauwer showed him the new aerobars he had bolted on to LeMond's handlebars and asked if they were acceptable under the regulations. 'I know the rule is that a handlebar must be in one piece,' De Cauwer reflected thirty years later. He continued:

> [Jacquat] opens the door in his white fluffy bathrobe from the nice hotel, white slippers on. 'What are you doing here? Are you crazy or something? You've woken me up.' 'Monsieur Jacquat, I'm sorry, excuse me, but I have here the bike for Greg LeMond ... we have to put this thing on the front, he has a problem with his back ...' 'Ah, go on, for me it's OK. Go, go. You are crazy.' I backed out of there like a stupid dog ... 'Sorry, sorry, sorry.' Then I go back to our hotel ... 'Yes! It's OK. We can use it.' ... He was never at that moment thinking that it could [have the impact it did].[27]

And so when LeMond rolled down the start ramp it was with his aerobars fitted. The result was remarkable. He caught riders that had started minutes in front of him and won the stage, taking 24sec and 56sec out of Pedro Delgado and Laurent Fignon respectively, claiming the yellow jersey by five seconds over Fignon. Fignon's team considered a protest but ultimately never lodged a complaint. And so commenced a battle royale between LeMond and Fignon that would last the remainder of the race. According to De Cauwer, 'nobody at that moment believed that Greg LeMond could stay [at that level] for three weeks. They didn't believe in the quality of Greg LeMond – at that moment.'[28]

The lead switched four times between the pair from stage 5 until the end of the race. As the race left the Alps with only three stages remaining Fignon looked to have taken hold of the jersey definitively, holding on to a fifty-second lead into the final stage, a 24.5km time trial from Versailles to the Champs-Élysées.

It was of course conceivable that LeMond would gain enough time, but few expected it. LeMond, again using his aerobars rode wearing a streamlined helmet; Fignon had his blond ponytail flapping in the wind and looked decidedly old-fashioned in comparison. The television pictures captured the clock counting down as Fignon laboured to the line, LeMond looking on, surrounded by reporters, wide-eyed in disbelief. The end result was a win of eight seconds for the American, the closest finish in Tour history. 'I just went all out,' LeMond said afterwards. 'I thought I could win, but I knew I needed something special ... I just rode.'[29]

LeMond's 1989 Tour win was the second of an eventual three wins. It was also his most remarkable. During the spring of 1987, just eight months after claiming his first Tour title and when a period of LeMond dominance seemed as certain as anything ever can be in sport, the American was accidently shot during a hunting trip. He lost a lot of blood and suffered a collapsed lung and broken ribs. He was operated on for over two hours. At the time his surgeon reported that the Tour champion would need a couple of months to get back to normal. In the end it took two years.

LeMond signed with ADR for the 1989 season, nobody certain of how well he could come back. A month or so before the Tour he rode the Giro and suffered hugely. He flirted with the idea of quitting the sport there and then but was convinced to carry on riding. As the Giro neared its end, he started to find his racing legs, riding a very good final time trial on the last day. 'From that moment on you could see that he would come back,' remembered De Cauwer.[30]

Born in California, LeMond grew up a freestyle skier, discovering cycling only as a way of training in the summer. His talent was obvious as soon as he entered his first race, beating well-hardened club cyclists while still in his early teens. By 1979 he was a junior world champion, awarded the win when Kenny De Maerteleire, the Belgian rider who actually crossed the line first, was relegated after coming off his line and forcing the American into a wall of tyres. Two years later LeMond turned professional after the legendary director Cyrille Guimard had travelled to Reno, Nevada, to recruit him for his Renault team.

While his first two seasons as a pro returned decent enough results, his first major wins came in 1983 when he followed a win at the Dauphiné Libéré with the world championships, escaping on the final lap in Switzerland and soloing to a famous win to become the first American male to claim the professional world title. 'You've got to take risks,' he later reflected. 'In this sport, anybody who doesn't take them is certainly making a mistake.'[31]

Initially recruited as a *domestique* for Bernard Hinault, by the time LeMond rode his first Tour, in 1984, Hinault had left Renault and was riding for La Vie Claire. Instead Renault was led by Fignon who would claim his second Tour win, ahead of the former Renault leader, Hinault. LeMond claimed a very creditable third overall and the young rider's classification, showing his abilities could stretch to a three-week race. He then went and joined Hinault at La Vie Claire, a decision that would cost him a fair crack at the 1985 Tour. He spent that race in the service of Hinault when arguably the American was the stronger rider, eventually finishing second behind the French legend who claimed his fifth title. The following year Hinault eventually assumed a supporting role as LeMond won his, and America's, first Tour title. The pair rode the ramps of l'Alpe d'Huez together as the race reached its crescendo, LeMond wearing yellow and Hinault claiming the stage. With Hinault about to retire the stage seemed set for LeMond to dominate the Tour for years to come. But then came that hunting accident

With blonde hair and blue eyes, LeMond was the very picture of the all-American hero. Once described by *Sports Illustrated* as 'a Huck Finn with steel thighs',[32] he helped popularise road cycling in America. When he rode his first Tour in 1984, LeMond was one of only two Americans in the race (the other was Jonathan Boyer); two years later, as LeMond was busy claiming his first win, there were no fewer than nine of his compatriots on the start line with him, including an American-registered team. The headlines and column inches he was getting back home were clearly having an effect.

He also developed a reputation for innovation – from those aerobars to being an early adopter of carbon-fibre bikes.

A little over one month after his comeback Tour win in 1989, LeMond added a second world title in another face-off with Fignon. The result in Chambéry on a day when thunder roared across the French Alps, would be the same: an exciting finale featuring both Fignon and LeMond, both attacking and countering each other during the final instalment of the race, with LeMond ultimately taking the jersey and Fignon missing out by seconds. The Frenchman, who had attacked on the final climb in a desperate bid to avoid a sprint finish, could only manage sixth while LeMond held off a strong effort from Ireland's Sean Kelly as the line approached. LeMond's win meant he became only the fourth rider in history to win the Tour and the world championships in the same year, an achievement that no rider has since matched. 'This Greg is my Bête Noire,' Fignon said afterwards.[33]

A third Tour title in 1990 was LeMond's final major victory. With no wins for two years he retired in 1994 having been diagnosed with mitochondrial myopathy – 'I can't spell it,' he joked when announcing his decision. 'My energy-delivery system has been off whack. It's a mild state that affects my performance at a high level but not my day-to-day living.'[34]

Still involved in the cycling industry, today he leads LeMond Composites, a company working to develop and commercialise carbon-fibre technology.

> ## MAJOR WINS
> Tour de France: 1986, 1989, 1990
> World Champion: 1983, 1989

Maes, Romain

BEL

BORN: 10 AUGUST 1912, ZERKEGEM, BELGIUM

Possessing a level of strength and power that belied his small stature, Belgium's Romain Maes rode professionally from 1933 until the outbreak of the Second World War effectively ended his career.

Maes started four Tours in that time but only once made it back to Paris, in 1935, when he stunned the cycling world by carrying the yellow jersey he had claimed by winning the opening stage into Lille all the way around France. At the time only four other men had led the race from start to finish – Maurice Garin in 1903; Philippe Thys in 1914, Ottavio Bottecchia in 1924 and Nicolas Frantz in 1928. No one has managed it since (although Jacques Anquetil came very close in 1961 when he led from the end of the first, split-stage, day. André Darrigade won that Tour's first stage in the morning and wore yellow, if only for the afternoon).

Maes had done little before the 1935 edition to show that he could contend with the best riders in the world. True, he had a top-ten finish at Paris–Roubaix and claimed a stage of Paris–Nice in 1934, decent enough results, but he had also failed to finish the Tour that year, abandoning on stage 10 after a crash.

One year later, however, and it was a different story. During the Tour's opening stage he escaped and made a solo bid for victory, benefitting from getting to a level crossing that was about to close before the chasing pack. He rode onto the velodrome in Lille some fifty-three seconds ahead of second-placed Edgard De Caluwé, claiming the yellow jersey in front of 20,000 spectators. With time bonuses awarded to the stage winner his lead was increased to over two minutes. 'As soon as I left, I felt that I would win,' Maes said afterwards. 'Two months ago, I won Paris–Lille by escaping five kilometres from the finish line … this time, I escaped 70 kilometres away. It was so successful. Tomorrow, I will take on the yellow jersey. Will I have it a long time? I hope so.'[1]

Described by Desgrange as a 'compact ball of muscle',[2] Maes set to defending the jersey, surviving a second-day scare when thousands of nails were poured onto the race route and two punctures threatened the Belgian's lead – for 150km it looked like Maes would have only one day in the jersey – before his team worked to pace him back into the race, salvaging the situation. A sprinter rather than a climber, most people expected him to falter in the mountains. Not so. He emerged from the Alps with a 4min 31sec advantage, then won a second stage in Cannes and retained a two-minute gap after the Pyrenees. In the final week he got even stronger, increasing his lead and winning the final stage in Paris. His overall margin was 17min 52sec come the end as he benefitted from a unified Belgian squad in contrast to a disappointing Spanish team and a French outfit that were all riding for themselves after Antonin Magne had been forced to abandon in the Alps.

Maes hailed from a large family – he had fourteen siblings – and in Paris he was pictured with his head resting on the railings of Parc des Princes in front of his mother who had travelled to France to watch the race finish. 'The young Belgian, Romain Maes, rushed to the stands where his mother was waiting for the arrival of her glorious son,' ran one report. 'Emotion embraced the champion who, with his face on his arms, cried tears of joy.'[3]

Maes never again finished the Tour. He was robbed of a Paris–Roubaix victory in 1936 when race commissaires controversially judged Georges Speicher to have crossed the line ahead of the Belgian, before retiring from cycling in 1939. He later opened a café he called Le Maillot Jaune. Maes died in 1983, aged 70.

> **MAJOR WINS**
> Tour de France: 1935

Maes, Sylvére
BEL

BORN: 27 AUGUST 1909, ZEVEKOTE, BELGIUM

No relation to fellow Tour winner Romain, Sylvère Maes followed his namesake's surprise 1935 Tour win with his own victory the following year, the first time Belgium had secured back-to-back wins since the early 1920s.

Maes, who apparently had a taste for pickled herrings, reportedly eating the head of one every day, had turned professional in 1932, signing for the French team Alcyon the following year. He was soon proving his worth, taking a top-ten finish at the Tour of Flanders in early April before winning Paris–Roubaix two weeks later. Maes had ridden at the head of the race with three more experienced riders for 160km, helping to hold off the marauding peloton behind, before beating Julien Vervaecke in the final sprint. It was a wholly unexpected victory, prompting sports writers to already declare him 'the [cycling] revelation of 1933', despite the year being only four months' old. Lucien Avocat wrote:

> A few months ago, in Belgium, several road cycling technicians told me that they were pinning very high hopes on young Sylvère. Never has confidence been so well placed. Maes proved to us today that he is truly a superb champion … To win a different race, even Bordeaux–Paris or the Tour de France, is good; winning Paris–Roubaix is better, because we know that Paris–Roubaix can only be won by a real champion. There is not, in cycling sport, a safer criterion.[4]

Three years later Maes confirmed his champion credentials when he claimed his first Tour win. It was a race hit by torrential rain, the riders forced to navigate flooded roads and endure terrible conditions. Maes had already proved he could ride in the high mountains in 1935, winning a stage into Luchon and then leading the race over Tourmalet the following day. Twelve months on he took the first yellow jersey of his career after the eighth stage to Briançon and held it until Paris.

It was in the Pyrenees that Maes cemented that win with a stunning ride over the Peyresourde, Aspin, Tourmalet and Aubisque, leading the race over the final two climbs, before descending into Pau with a lead of 8min 39sec. '[He] jumped at the opportunity to attack,' wrote Jacques Goddet. 'He finished in a masterful flight, with magnificent strength and health, under a shell of mud he had accumulated for 200 kilometres.'[5] The 1934 winner, Antonin Magne, trailing by more than eight minutes at the start of the day, had long planned to launch an offensive during the stage but punctured and trailed in 8min 39sec behind Maes before then being docked a further five minutes for taking an illegal feed from the former racer Victor Fontan. It all meant that exiting the Pyrenees, Maes had the Tour all but won. His final margin of victory over Magne was 26min 55sec. 'You are a great rider. You are loyal, and I am happy to be beaten by you,' Magne said in Paris.[6]

The following year Maes' defence of the jersey ended when he abandoned in a protest against his treatment in Bordeaux, taking the entire Belgian team with him (see Lapébie entry for more).

He returned in 1938, only managing fourteenth and finishing well over one hour adrift of Gino Bartali. One year on he rediscovered his form, beating France's great hope, René Vietto by 30min 38sec to claim his second Tour title. With war in the air there were no Italian riders in the race, which meant no Bartali. Vietto, a talented climber but suffering with bronchitis, held yellow until the Alps where a brace of stellar rides from Maes took the Belgian definitively into the race lead. First, he destroyed the rest of the race on the Izoard, riding away from Vietto as the road steepened. Then he won the Tour's first mountain time trial, over the Iseran, putting yet more time into his French rival. 'All has disappeared for Vietto,' exclaimed a radio reporter after the Izoard stage. 'For Sylvère Maes the yellow jersey and the Tour de France.'[7] It would be the last Tour until its post-war return in 1947.

Maes used to phone home during races to ask about the condition of his beloved racing pigeons, and he owned a café in Gistel that he called Tourmalet, in a nod to his exploits over the Pyrenean giant. He returned to racing after the war, claiming fifth at the Giro in 1947, before retiring from cycling the following year. He died in 1966 at the age of 57.

> ## MAJOR WINS
> Tour de France: 1936, 1939
> Paris-Roubaix: 1933

Magne, Antonin
FRA

BORN: 15 FEBRUARY 1904, YTRAC, FRANCE

'So it's true. I'm a world champion. The rainbow jersey is in the suitcase. There is no doubt.' So wrote Antonin Magne in the pages of *Paris-Soir* on 8 September 1936. 'Of course, I went to Bern with the hope of defending myself, but I knew that to win, one would have to be very strong and have a little luck. I had that luck.'[8]

The luck that the ever-honest Magne referred to was to not suffer a single puncture on a day when heavy rain fell on the roads of Switzerland, loosening the stones and grit that forced many of his rivals into unplanned stops due to deflated tyres. But luck was just one part of his win. Magne made sure he was well placed through the whole race, first joining a three-rider breakaway and then powering on alone over the final three laps when his companions had fallen away. He crossed the line more than nine minutes ahead of the second-placed Aldo Bini. 'What a beautiful thing, what a Champion,'[9] commented the Italian national coach, the great Costante Girardengo.

That 1936 world title, only the second time a French rider had won road racing's professional world championship, would be Magne's last major win of a cycling career that had captured France's imagination.

He had ridden his first race in 1920, at the age of 16. Six years later he entered the professional ranks, sponsored as an individual by Alleluia-Wolber. The following year Alleluia-Wolber sponsored a team of seven and

Magne rode the Tour for the first time, finishing a creditable sixth overall and winning a stage, a result which propelled him into the limelight.

More strong performances in the Tour and other major races followed – including third at both Paris-Roubaix and the Tour itself in 1930 – without a major race win coming. Magne was beginning to form a reputation as a talented rider who could fare well against the best in the biggest races, without actually winning.

That changed in 1931 when Magne won the Tour for the first time. The Frenchman, who reportedly forced himself as a teenager to move a heavy rock he kept in the garden every day to build his strength and who was regarded to be decades ahead of his time in terms of dietary and training techniques,[10] prepared for the race by training in the Pyrenees with Victor Fontan. And it was on the slopes of the Tourmalet that he mounted his challenge, winning the often-pivotal stage into Luchon and securing a lead of 9min 32sec over the Italian Antonio Pesenti.

With the French national team united behind Magne, the Frenchman successfully fought off repeated attacks from the Italian squad. As the Tour reached Charleville, with only two stages remaining, Magne had a lead of more than five minutes over Pesenti and nearly thirteen minutes over Belgium's Joseph Demuysere.

In Charleville, Magne was relaxing in the room he was sharing with André Leducq, eyeing the pile of letters that had been sent to him. Normally he only opened those he knew were from family, opting to read the others after the race, but this time one caught his eye. 'He never revealed the reason why: intuition, chance, luck?' writes Pierre Chany. 'Call it whatever you like, but it was certainly good fortune.'[11]

The letter was written anonymously but the correspondent warned of a potential threat to Magne's lead. The letter-writer told Magne that they had just returned from visiting Menin, where the parents of the Belgian rider Gaston Rebry had a café. Rebry's parents had claimed that their son had written to them detailing a plan for him and Demuysere to attack Magne on the cobblestones of the penultimate stage – 271km from Charleville to Malo-les-Bains. Magne was bemused but took the warning seriously, resolving not to let the two Belgians out of his sight the following day.

Sure enough, the attack came some 170km from the finish. Magne, aided by Leducq, went with Rebry and Demuysere, sitting on their wheels much to their annoyance. They repeatedly tried to get away, resorting to threatening to push him off if he didn't at least take a turn at the front.

Wave after wave of attacks came but Magne wouldn't be distanced, holding on for 170km despite crashing. The three men arrived at the finish together, Rebry took the stage but Magne retained his lead. The next day he stood in Paris as the winner of the Tour by 12min 56sec. In Paris, Magne said that if he had to suffer the psychological pain he'd just endured, he wouldn't start again for all the money in the world.

Three years later Magne secured his second Tour title. This was a Tour when Magne's teammate, René Vietto, captured French hearts with a stunning Tour debut, claiming four stages and finishing fifth overall. Perhaps more importantly, Vietto twice sacrificed his own chances to help Magne win. First, on the descent of the Puymorens where Magne crashed and buckled a wheel, Vietto offered his leader a wheel from his own bike, leaving Magne able to carry on his race. Vietto was photographed that day sat on a wall, his face a picture of anguish, forlornly looking up the road and willing the service van to finally appear, his wheel-less bike propped beside him. The next day, at the summit of the Portet d'Aspet, Vietto was over two minutes ahead of his leader when Magne's back wheel locked up and his chain seized. Giuseppe Martano, lying second overall, couldn't believe his fortune. Here was his chance to seize the race lead – Magne couldn't repair his bike and he was alone with no teammates and no service van.

Then Vietto suddenly appeared before the yellow jersey. Told of his leader's troubles he had turned around and ridden back up the mountain to find Magne and hand over his bike. Magne gratefully took it and, helped by other teammates, started his frantic pursuit, catching Martano before the finish. Vietto trailed in over eight minutes back. He may have been kind with his actions but Vietto was anything but sympathetic: 'That Antonin, he doesn't know how to ride a bike,' he said. 'I'm not going to play the slave forever, you know.'

'I really thought it was all over,'[12] Magne would admit later.

Magne won his last race in 1939. After retiring he entered the world of team management, guiding the Mercier team for twenty-five years, unmistakable in the white coat and Basque beret that he wore to every race. Such was his success as a team manager at Mercier that his exploits as a rider were sometimes forgotten.

Regarded as taciturn but genuine, Magne's own motto was 'glory is never where virtue is not'.[13] In 1962 he was made a Chevalier de la Légion d'Honneur. He died in 1983 at the age of 79.

Merckx, Eddy

BEL

BORN: 17 JUNE 1945, MEENSEL-KIEZEGEM

Inside of Chicago's United Center, home of the Chicago Bulls, there is a bronze statue of the peerless basketball player Michael Jordan. Jordan is depicted soaring into the sky, ball gripped tightly by his right hand. His entire being is rising with majesty and power, to heights far above the lesser mortals cowering beneath him. It was his signature move, cast for evermore. Below the statue, engraved on the plinth that supports this perfect depiction of basketball's brightest star, are eleven simple words: 'The best there ever was. The best there ever will be.' For Michael Jordan and basketball, read Eddy Merckx and cycling.

Édouard Louis Joseph Merckx turned professional in 1965 and retired thirteen years and 525 wins later.[14] During that period he dominated the sport with such ruthlessness that the record of every other rider of that time should come with a disclaimer that draws attention to the fact that their achievements need to be taken into some sort of context: that they had the misfortune to be riding during the era of Eddy. Italy's Felice Gimondi once said that when he won the world championship road race in 1973, his daughter was at home in Bergamo watching the race on TV while wearing an Eddy Merckx t-shirt.[15]

Merckx won everything that mattered. And then he won it again. And again. He is the only rider to have claimed all three Grand Tours and all five Monuments. He is the only rider to have won both the Tour and the Giro five times. He is the only rider to have won every Monument more than once. He holds the record for stage wins in the Tour (thirty-four) and the most days in yellow (ninety-six); at the Giro he holds the record for the most days in pink (seventy-eight). Quite simply, in cycling history Eddy Merckx stands alone, head and shoulders above the rest.

Merckx's first major win came in 1966 when he claimed the first of seven Milan–Sanremo titles, winning the race from a small bunch-sprint on the Via Roma. He secured his second Sanremo win the following year, again prevailing in a four-man sprint despite, or perhaps because of, the presence of three Italians alongside him – none of whom were prepared to gamble by leading the sprint. Two months later Merckx turned his attention to the Giro in his first Grand Tour appearance.

Stage 12 of the 1967 Giro was 220km from Caserta, taking in climbs of the Macerone, Rionero Sannitico and Roccaraso before a summit finish on Blockhaus. It was a brutal examination of Merckx's abilities to climb against the best mountain men in the business, deep into the second week of a punishing three-week schedule. Up until this stage, despite finishing sixth on Mount Etna five days earlier, Merckx had never shown what he was truly capable of during a Grand Tour mountain stage.

On the early slopes of Blockhaus the peloton splintered but Merckx stayed with the front group. Then, with 2km left to ride, Italy's Italo Zilioli attacked and rode away from the remnants of the leading group. Only one man was able to match the move – Merckx. The Belgian stuck with Zilioli before then riding away from the Italian with 1km to go. It was an explosive move and Zilioli would later say that it seemed one second Merckx was behind him and the next he had disappeared up the road. Merckx won the stage by ten seconds ahead of the disbelieving and distraught Italian. The Belgian had issued a huge statement of intent. He had stayed with and beaten the best climbers the Giro had to offer during one of the race's toughest climbs. The Italian media couldn't believe it. They were getting used to Merckx winning one-day races on a rolling route in the spring, but this was something else entirely. *La Gazzetta dello Sport* ran the headline: 'Italian disappointment: Belgian sprinter wins in the mountains.'[16] As if to make things worse, Merckx would win again two days later in Lido degli Estensi. On the flat. In a sprint.

Later that year he secured his first professional world championship title in a race he had spent much of the season focused on. Some described his targeting of the event as a gamble that happened to pay off, and if the notion today of anything that Merckx tried or targeted being deemed a gamble seems slightly absurd given his complete domination of the sport, it should be remembered that at the time the Cannibal had not yet completed two complete seasons as a pro.

Merckx had taken the amateur world title three years earlier when he won a race in which he would not have competed without the intervention of his mother. When subjected to medical checks before the final squad selection he had been told that there was a problem with his heart and that he wouldn't be considered for the team. His mother, Jenny, didn't believe it. She questioned the chief selector and talked to the family doctor. He told her there was no problem with her son's heart. So Merckx rode and Merckx won. A pattern that would soon become familiar.

Three years on Merckx became just the third amateur champion to go on to take the professional title. His win was crafted in the style to which the cycling world would soon become accustomed – in short, he was at the head of the race from the first moment until the last.

When Gianni Motta attacked just 5km into the 265km race in the Dutch town of Heerlen, a small group of riders went with him. The circuit had one significant climb and Motta had long planned this attack, with the Italian under instruction to strike out early whether or not anyone went with him. As it happened Merckx went with Motta, as did Jos van der Vleuten of the Netherlands, Ramón Sáez of Spain and Bob Addy of Great Britain. The race had only just started and yet it was in many ways already over. Only one man would later infiltrate this leading group, Van der Vleuten's teammate Jan Janssen, the 1964 champion, who put in a huge effort to claw back two and a half minutes to join the leaders.

Merckx took the final sprint ahead of Janssen and Sáez. Motta, whose aggressive race plan had prompted the whole thing, finished fourth. The reign of the Cannibal had definitively begun. The next year he won Paris–Roubaix and then the Giro for the first time, winning three stages on the way to a 5min 1sec win. He would claim the Giro again in 1970 before taking three in a row between 1972 and 1974.

Merckx remains a case apart from all other riders not only because of the sheer volume and quality of the races he won but also because of how he won them, which is to say often in a display of such unforgiving power and superiority as to crush all that tried to challenge him.

The 1969 Tour remains the perfect example of Merckx's might. By the eve of that race he had proved himself in classics and stage races; on the flat, against the clock and in the mountains. But he had yet to tackle the Tour. Now, at 25 years old, Merckx was finally ready to tackle cycling's greatest race.

It took the Belgian all of two days to get his hands on the yellow jersey. Merckx in yellow – it would soon become a familiar sight on the roads of France in July. Despite losing it for a few days, by the time the Tour hit the Pyrenees, Merckx had a very comfortable 8min 3sec lead with just five days to go. All he had to do was sit in the pack, mark the attacks and get ready to stand on the top step in Paris. But no, that wasn't Eddy's style.

Instead, on stage 17, 214km from Luchon to Mourenx, over the Peyresourde, Aspin, Tourmalet and Aubisque, that notorious set of mountains, Merckx struck out alone. He attacked near the top of the Tourmalet, got a gap and never looked back. He rode fearlessly on the descent and then tirelessly in the valley towards the foot of the Soulor, the climb that leads to the eastern slopes of the Aubisque. At the top of the Aubisque his lead was nearly seven minutes. And still on he went. In the end his winning margin that day was just shy of eight minutes. For over 130km the yellow jersey had ploughed a lonely and furious furrow through the Pyrenees. It was the sort of display rarely seen before or since, particularly from someone already firmly in place at the top of the GC. His margin over second-placed Roger Pingeon was now 16min 18sec. Merckx's all-conquering ride sent the Tour's wordsmiths into overdrive. 'Merckxissimo!' wrote Jacques Goddet, 'Never again will we be able to say that the Tour is not won until Paris.' Merckx, pursued 'the destiny prescribed by the natural play of his uncommon gifts', typed Antoine Blondin. Whilst for Pierre Chany the Belgian was 'like those matadors thirsty for blood who provoke the bull simply to feel the thrill of excitement'.[17] For his part Merckx reflected: 'Over the last 20 kilometres I hurt all over. My tongue was shredded, my throat was on fire. I was drooling. But I was happy to have achieved something that will go down in history.'[18]

Five days later Merckx stood in Paris in yellow. The first Belgian to do so for thirty years. He also won the points jersey and the mountains prize, something that had never been done before nor repeated since. He would go on to stand on the top step in Paris on another four occasions. Merckx also won the Vuelta in 1973, completing a clean sweep of all three Grand Tours.

If Merckx dominated three-week stage racing, one-day classics were no different. As well as those seven Milan-Sanremo wins, Merckx claimed five Liège-Bastogne-Liège titles, three Paris-Roubaix wins and the Tour of Flanders and Tour of Lombardy twice each, to become the most successful classics rider of all. He also added a further brace of world championship titles to his 1967 win and secured the hour world record in 1972. The list goes on and on. That the majority of these wins come after he suffered a terrible crash in 1969 that inflicted serious injury on him and killed his Derny-riding pacer, makes his story all the more incredible.

Stories of Merckx's daring escapes and solo escapades are legion. For him it didn't matter what the head said; if his heart and legs told him to go, he went. One of his most legendary wins came in the 1969 Tour of Flanders when, in gales and downpours he destroyed the peloton on the Muur van Geraardsbergen and, with 70km still to go, disobeyed his team director's orders to wait and soloed into a headwind to win by over five minutes. 'I thought to myself that if I was going to do all the work on the front, I may just as well ride off alone,' he later reflected.[19]

The Cannibal's insatiable hunger for success and thirst for ruthless domination has been the topic of much debate, although a couple of incidents can be offered to portray him in a different light. First was his refusal to wear yellow in 1971 the day after he inherited the race lead from Luis Ocaña after the Spaniard, one of the few to truly challenge Merckx's dominance at the Tour, suffered a sickening crash in the Pyrenees that ruled him out of the race (see Ocaña entry for more); the second was his presenting the 1972 green jersey to Cyrille Guimard in Paris that he had again inherited when Guimard was forced to leave the race just two days before the finish – though it should be noted that Guimard said in 2012 that Merckx had been encouraged to do so by the race organisers (something the Belgian has reportedly acknowledged). 'Merckx had no charisma despite his five victories in the Tour,' Guimard said. 'I respect the great champion he was; he made our legs ache enough. On the other hand, ... he conveyed no sympathy. We did not call him the Cannibal for nothing.'[20]

Merckx's final win came in September 1977 in Ruien (Kluisbergen).[21] He retired the following year with those incredible 525 victories to his name.

The Cannibal: The best there ever was. The best there ever will be.

MAJOR WINS

Tour de France: 1969, 1970, 1971, 1972, 1974
Giro d'Italia: 1968, 1970, 1972, 1973, 1974
Vuelta a España: 1973
Paris-Roubaix: 1968, 1970, 1973
Tour of Flanders: 1969, 1975
Tour of Lombardy: 1971, 1972
Milan-Sanremo: 1966, 1967, 1969, 1971, 1972, 1975, 1976
Liège-Bastogne-Liège: 1969, 1971, 1972, 1973, 1975
World Champion: 1967, 1971, 1974
National Champion: 1970

Nencini, Gastone

ITA

BORN: 1 MARCH 1930, BILANCINO, ITALY

On the penultimate stage of the 1960 Tour, 229km from Besançon to Troyes, the peloton passed through the village of Colombey-les-Deux-Églises, location of Charles de Gaulle's family home, La Boisserie.

At the gates of La Boisserie the race paused so that the President of the French Republic could meet the riders. There, at the head of the race, resplendent in his yellow jersey was Gastone Nencini. Introduced as Italian, Nencini pointed out that he was actually a Florentine. 'Bravo,' the President said. 'Paris is now yours. You'll win the Tour because you fought every day. Good luck for the future.'[1]

Twenty-four hours later Nencini entered Paris. 'I have never experienced a stronger emotion,' Nencini said after the finish in front of 40,000 people at the Parc des Princes. 'After the time trial I was almost sure of success, but now I can only breathe a sigh of relief. I have won thanks to a team that, from [Ercole] Baldini to the last of the wingmen, has done his best to guarantee my success.'[2]

As well as strong team support within the Italian squad Nencini, who hadn't won a stage during the race, had also benefitted from some instability within the French outfit and the misfortune of one of France's most fancied riders.

French riders claimed ten stage wins during the race, but such was the strength in the national squad that some began scrabbling for status. On stage 6, with France's Henry Anglade in yellow, his 'teammate' Roger Rivière launched a fierce attack more than 100km from the stage finish in Lorient. Only three riders could go with the Frenchman, one of them being Nencini. Rivière won the stage but France lost the jersey as Anglade trailed in nearly fifteen minutes back.

During the stage it was reported that Anglade had asked Marc Bidot, France's sports director, to order Rivière to stop riding so aggressively. When questioned afterwards Rivière said that Anglade was just moaning and that he had done him a favour by removing from his shoulders the 'weight of the race'. Anglade had a somewhat different take. 'Have you seen Roger?' he asked journalists after the stage. 'What's he saying? No doubt that he did me a favour? By relegating me by a quarter of an hour! He was not allowed to do that. I am convinced that we have just lost the Tour de France.'[3]

While the immediate 'weight of the race' went to Belgium's Jan Adriaenssens, the result propelled Nencini, a good climber and a daredevil descender with nerves of steel, into second overall with Rivière just over one minute behind. 'There are only four possible winners left,' said Anglade. 'The four that escaped. In reality, the fight is over before it has begun because Rivière will make mistakes. What I fear for him is worse. He will try to follow Nencini on the descents and one day it will go wrong.'[4]

Four days later Nencini took over the race lead from Adriaenssens in Pau, again arriving at the stage finish alongside Rivière who again won the stage. Nencini, who had pulled on yellow for two days early in the race, was once more at the head of affairs, with Rivière second overall. Then, with one week left until Paris, came the day Anglade had feared. On the stage to Avignon, Nencini attacked on the descent of the Perjuret. Rivière set off after him. But the Italian's pace was too hot and during his pursuit Rivière lost control of his bike, somersaulting over a low wall. Rivière's teammate, Louis Rostollan, saw·the crash and rode back up the climb to tell people what had happened. Rivière was found lying prostrate in a ravine, his face covered in leaves, unable to move. The Frenchman was gently lifted on to a stretcher and taken to hospital. He had broken his back, his cycling career over. In Paris, Nencini asked that his winner's bouquet be taken to Rivière's wife who was at the bedside of her husband.

Born in rural Tuscany, Nencini, nicknamed the Lion of Mugello, worked in a quarry in order to earn enough money to buy his first bike. He soon moved to Florence, joining a cycling club in the city. His performances as an amateur, including second at the 1953 amateur world championship ahead of Belgium's Rik Van Looy, caught the eye and in October 1953 he signed as a professional with the Legnano team.

Just two years later Nencini came agonisingly close to winning his national tour. Two days from Milan he was in the pink jersey with forty-three seconds over Raphaël Géminiani and just under one and a half minutes over compatriot Fiorenzo Magni.

The penultimate stage was 216km to San Pellegrino. This was Magni country. The then two-time Giro winner knew the flinty roads well and knew that punctures would be a problem. He arranged for heavy-duty tyres to be fitted to his own bike and then set about plotting a move to wrest the pink jersey from Nencini. That included getting Fausto Coppi involved. Coppi had been angered by Nencini taking mountain points he considered rightfully his and so, with the promise of the stage win should he help in the move that Magni was convinced would bring him pink, Coppi didn't need much convincing to come onboard.

With other riders recruited to the cause Magni made his move, taking Coppi with him. As two of Italy's most successful ever cyclists rode away, no one other than Nencini made any effort to react to the move. Nencini punctured. He fell. His Giro was as good as over. Coppi took the stage and Magni the pink jersey as Nencini trailed in, tears dampening his face, more than five minutes behind. Anna Maria Ortese reported:

He is no longer wearing the pink jersey, no longer a champion, he is no longer the revelation of this 38th Giro. He is nothing. ... Nencini's innocence, his breathless face which tried hard to contain his surprise, his joy, which had been acclaimed by everyone only 12 hours earlier, that face is now beaten, hard, unhappy, covered with sun and tears.[5]

'Nencini, with tears in his eyes, saw his beautiful dream vanish,' reported *La Stampa* who found the former race leader lying in bed in a darkened hotel room, 'the portrait of disappointment, of pain', with crowds outside chanting his name. True to his nature he had fought for 150km to keep hold of his lead. 'Four tyres I punctured – four. And few of my little group helped me chase,'[6] he said from his hotel room before walking on to the balcony to acknowledge those in the street below.

In 2010 Nencini's daughter, Elisabetta, reflected in an interview with *Rouleur* that her father had the 'character of a wild horse. He didn't like that someone imposed rules on him, didn't like to be harnessed.' He was also fond of a cigarette and a drink. 'Ever since he was a young man, he liked to have a glass of wine on the table. It did him good, lifted the tension. Although his directeur sportifs prohibited it, my father did not listen. Those glasses of wine stayed on the table.'[7]

Two years after losing the Giro to Magni, Nencini would finally wear the pink jersey in Milan. He benefitted from the feud between Charly Gaul and Louison Bobet to win over the Frenchman by nineteen seconds after Gaul, his own chances of victory long gone, had helped the Italian bridge up to Bobet on the final climb of the race. Gaul took the stage as Nencini saved his Giro to claim his first major victory.

Nencini came close to winning a second Giro three years later, only to be beaten by Jacques Anquetil. Anquetil's winning margin was just twenty-eight seconds and there was talk of a conspiracy, with Anquetil said to have paid two Italian riders – Tino Coletto and Guido Carlesi – to ride for him after Nencini had attacked the Frenchman, again on a descent. In *Maglia Rosa*, Coletto tells author Herbie Sykes that Anquetil was angry because Nencini – 'the best descender I ever saw, without question'– had been pushed up a climb by partisan Tuscans. But there was no payment and no collaboration against Nencini, Coletto said, 'that's absolutely invented and absolutely false.'[8]

Nencini was reportedly found by the Tour's doctor with drips in both arms in 1960[9] and was involved in the infamous 'bad fish' incident at the 1962 Tour when a number of riders, including Nencini, all abandoned on the same day blaming food poisoning with doping suspected as the real cause. He retired from racing in 1965, later opening a bike shop and working as a sports director. He died in 1980 aged 49.

> ## MAJOR WINS
> Tour de France: 1960
> Giro d'Italia: 1957

Nibali, Vincenzo

`ITA`

BORN: 14 NOVEMBER 1984, MESSINA, ITALY

With 7km to go of the 2018 edition of Milan–Sanremo, on the final climb of the day – the famous Poggio – Italy's 'one genuine superstar'[10] of the current era, Vincenzo Nibali, made his definitive move, following an attack made by Krists Neilands before quickly disappearing up the road alone.

Nibali had made this move on the Poggio before in past editions, three times in fact, and not once had it paid off with a win in Sanremo. But the Sicilian is nothing if not a determined figure and his Bahrain-Merida team had worked hard to position him well. A gifted climber and descender, Nibali knew that if a bunch sprint finish was to be avoided, he had to do something on the Poggio. And so once again he rolled the dice. Fourth time lucky, perhaps.

Over the top of the climb Nibali had eleven seconds, at the bottom it was seven. Behind, the pace picked up as the sprinters' teams went to work, ready to lead their fast-men into the apparently inevitable sprint. But the gap wasn't falling quickly enough and Nibali showed no signs of slowing. With 100m to go the Italian looked over his shoulder to see a marauding peloton finally sprinting at full tilt. But he knew that for them it was too late. Nibali had time to sit up and raise his hands in celebration before crossing the line ahead of Australia's Caleb Ewan. Reflecting on the race, Nibali said:

> I told myself it is now or never. So I tried a solo attack and it turned out spectacular. I tried to be as rational as possible, not going full-gas on the descent because I knew the most important part was the flat. From the where the Poggio finishes to the finish it is really short but the road goes up a little bit on the Via Roma so it feels like you will never arrive at the

finish. The ride I did there, to hold on to the finish, was more important than the descent.[11]

The win meant that Nibali became only the second Italian after Felice Gimondi to have won all three Grand Tours alongside both Italian Monuments – the Tour of Lombardy and Milan–Sanremo. Belgium's Eddy Merckx is the only other rider of any nationality to have achieved the same feat. At the end of the season Nibali only narrowly missed out on a third Lombardy win despite having undergone surgery just months earlier after fracturing a vertebra when he collided with a spectator on l'Alpe d'Huez during the Tour. It was a remarkable ride but still earned him a rebuke from an elderly woman after the race who complained he had only come second. 'For us Italians, it is never enough,' Nibali later told *Procycling*.[12]

Born in the Sicilian city of Messina, Nibali was obsessed with cycling from an early age. Always on his bike, he rode with his father before going out on his own. He soon developed a reputation as a rider that shone when the roads tipped upwards. He came second in the first race he entered and by the time he was 16 he had moved to Tuscany to ride for the development team Mastromarco, living in the home of Carlo Franceschi, the outfit's sports director. 'Carlo really believed in Vincenzo,' Nibali's mother, Giovanna, said in 2017. 'In fact, he transformed the team from a junior team to an elite team just so that Vincenzo could get into the bigger races as he matured.'[13] His father said:

> The thing about him and the bike was that he always wanted more than the others. Different handlebars, a particular type of tyre, a special headset, the good things. Every time we changed something for him, it gave him a charge. You could say to him, 'Vincenzo, do me a favour and I'll get you a new saddle,' and he'd do it right away.[14]

The young Vincenzo didn't always do as he was told, however, often getting into scrapes. 'When he was about 10, one day his father was so frustrated that he took Vincenzo's bike and actually cut it in half with a saw,' Giovanna recalled. 'Oh, Vincenzo cried. He was devastated. But his father just said: "When you learn to behave, I will get you a new bike." That changed him!'[15]

After decent performances in world championships in the junior and under-23 categories, Nibali turned professional in 2005 with the Fassa Bortolo team. Two years later, and now riding for Liquigas, he took his first notable victory – the Giro di Toscane – and claimed a top-twenty finish in his first Giro. The signs were promising and by 2010 he was a Grand Tour winner, claiming the Vuelta, the first Italian to win in Spain for two decades. Nibali said:

> I've become part of an elite group of riders who can win Grand Tours but I don't want to change as a person. It's a promise I've made myself ... People are saying that I can be a big rival to [Alberto] Contador because I can time trial and climb. But he's won every Grand Tour he's ridden [sic] and I've only won one. It will be incredibly difficult to beat him and other riders have been trying it for several years, but perhaps one day, perhaps at the Tour de France, we'll go head to head for victory.[16]

To his 2010 Vuelta win he then added the 2013 Giro, a race he had dominated for his new Astana team, wearing pink for the final two weeks. That Giro was a race blighted by rain and cold and, having already twice stood on the lower steps of the race's final podium, Nibali was squarely in Italy's public gaze as a true hope. He didn't falter, impressively winning by more than four minutes. *ESPN* reported:

> Only Vincenzo Nibali seemed immune to the wind, cold, rain, and snow that pelted the pack from Napoli to Brescia ... Italy found the new superstar it needed in the form of the 28-year-old Sicilian. The 'Shark of Messina' took a bite out of the peloton early, snagging the pink jersey in stage 8, and rode it all the way to Brescia ... The hype is already building in Italy that he could be the first Italian winner of the Tour de France since Marco Pantani in 1998.[17]

And how Nibali responded to the hype. The following year he sat out the defence of his Giro title, eyes fully fixed on cycling's greatest prize. The defending champion, Chris Froome, and two-time winner Contador, were considered the pre-race favourites, but Nibali was also fancied. As it happened both Froome and Contador crashed out of the race before the first rest day. By then Nibali had already worn yellow for seven days, claiming the jersey on the second day, later only briefly losing it to Tony Gallopin. The Italian then held the jersey all the way to Paris having claimed a total of four stages *en route*.

Rightly or not Nibali has a reputation as a fragile rider, a man that needs to feel the confidence of his managers and the support of the team in order to perform at his best. That fragility came to the fore at the 2016 Giro, a race he entered as a major favourite. Nibali endured a terrible first two weeks, losing minutes as the race progressed, unable to perform even in the mountains. In Italy there was an inquest. What was wrong with their main man? Everything was questioned: his form, his mental state, his tactics, his race programme, his choice of equipment, the team environment. Nibali spoke to the press only grudgingly – 'Why do you want to wound my pride even more? I'm already in pieces,' he said. His team, seeking answers, ordered medical tests. 'If these are the results I can achieve, then they've got to be accepted and understood,' Nibali said. 'Some have even suggested that I'm suffering mentally, but it's just not true. I'm fine.'[18]

Then, with three days of the race left, the Shark swam into life. He launched a flurry of attacks in the final 10km of stage 19 to Risoul, taking a stage win that reduced him to tears just as the pink jersey, Steven Kruijswijk, was somersaulting into a snowbank and losing his race lead to Esteban Chaves. On the penultimate stage Nibali attacked again, putting Chaves into trouble. By the end of the day he had the pink jersey by fifty-two seconds. One of the great comebacks of the modern era was complete. 'I didn't even believe it myself that we would manage it,' Nibali said as he claimed his second Giro title. 'But thanks to some great teamwork, we defied a lot of predictions.'[19]

Considered by some the finest rider of his generation for his ability to perform in both three-week races as well as one-day Classics, Nibali continues to ride and continues to feature at the sharp end of races. Reflecting in 2017, he said:

Success comes in different ways. Perhaps the success of a victory has the most flavour, but to always be there, always competitive, that's also success, and it has its own value, because it shows the quality of the rider, year after year. You have to take all of these different elements together.[20]

MAJOR WINS

Tour de France: 2014
Giro d'Italia: 2013, 2016
Vuelta a España: 2010
Tour of Lombardy: 2015, 2017
Milan–Sanremo: 2018
National Champion: 2014, 2015

Ocaña, Luis

ESP

BORN: 9 JUNE 1945, PRIEGO, SPAIN

If his luck had been different, the career of Spain's Luis Ocaña could have turned out very differently. A hugely talented rider, Ocaña still managed to amass a list of results that would be the envy of many a professional cyclist, including wins at the Tour and the Vuelta. Yet he could have finished his career with more major titles to his name had his life – a life that would be cut short by his own hand when he was just 48 years old – not been beset by poor luck and tragedy.

Born in arid central Spain to a poor family, Ocaña's mother and father sometimes struggled to put food on the table for the young Luis and his three siblings. The family moved to Catalonia in search of better times when Ocaña was just 6, not that things improved much. His sister Amparo once recalled: 'It was a complicity of misery. Life was hell in the Aran valley. At teatime my mother would lock us inside the house so we wouldn't see the other kids eating.'[1]

After discovering the bicycle Ocaña realised that a life spent racing was his best chance of escaping poverty. His father disapproved and refused to sign the racing licence the teenaged Ocaña presented to him. No matter, the young Spaniard wasn't going to let that stop him, he simply forged the signature. He applied to join Stade Montois, a renowned amateur club where Pierre Cescutti, president of the club and a figure who would guide Ocaña throughout his career, found him a room and job in Mont-de-Marsan, the club's home town.

Ocaña forged a reputation as a good climber and a strong time-trial rider, recording a string of good results, both regionally and nationally, including the amateur version of the Grand Prix des Nations. By 1967 his results had attracted the attention of professional teams and, after accepting an offer from the Spanish outfit Fagor for the 1968 season, Ocaña had achieved what he had always dreamt of – he was a fully fledged professional cyclist. The first of two national championship titles came later that same year. In 1970, now riding for the Bic team, he took the overall win at the Vuelta as well as the prestigious Dauphiné Libéré.

Ocaña was one of the few riders that cycling's colossus, Eddy Merckx, genuinely feared. The Spaniard took it upon himself to challenge to the all-conquering Merckx, even naming his dog after the great champion so he could order 'Merckx' about and call him to heel. He took his first Tour stage in 1970, winning the 190km stage into Saint-Gaudens. Ocaña finished thirty-first in Paris that year, the first time he had completed the race, as Merckx ran away with the lead to claim his second Tour.

One year on and Spain's great hope was ready to take the fight to the Belgian during the 1971 race. On the stage to Puy de Dôme, Ocaña escaped to win by seven seconds over Joop Zoetemelk. More importantly Merckx had not been able to react. The defending champion lost only a handful of seconds and retained the yellow jersey he'd already held for nine days, but Ocaña thought he saw a weakness. That evening the ten members of the Bic team sat around the dinner table at their hotel in high spirits. 'The time has come, guys,' Ocaña told his team. 'The Cannibal is ripe for the picking.'[2]

Three days later, on the 134km stage from Grenoble to Orcières Merlette, Ocaña attacked some 60km from the finish after he had broken away earlier with a small group of favourites. Merckx hadn't reacted to the breakaway and the Spaniard took 8min 42sec from the Belgian and claimed the yellow jersey. It was an incredible ride. 'Never will things be like before,'[3] wrote Jacques Goddet in an editorial which Merckx later said made him doubt himself.

Merckx reacted how only Merckx could react: by attacking right from the gun of the next stage and clawing back nearly two minutes as the Spaniard was left behind. Two days later, came a day that has entered Tour legend.

Stage 14 was from Revel to Luchon, taking in the climbs of the Portet d'Aspet, Mente and Portillon. Ocaña was still in yellow by 7min 23sec but felt apprehensive for reasons he couldn't quite fathom and went to pray before the stage.

Merckx again went on the attack but this time Ocaña easily matched the Belgian as the skies darkened and a fierce storm hit the mountains. Quickly the road became little more than a river of sludge as rain and hailstones fell heavily. Braking soon became useless with the riders forced to use their feet to slow down as lightning bounced around the peaks of the Pyrenees. When Merckx skidded around a corner the following Ocaña couldn't stop and careered off the road. When the sports director of the Bic team, Maurice de Muer, arrived he found his star rider in agony. 'Ocaña was screaming in pain as he lay there amid the stones and mud like Christ taken down from the cross,' L'Équipe later reported. 'One hand clutching his chest and his yellow jersey torn and spattered with a mixture of blood and earth.'[4]

It later emerged that as Ocaña had tried to remount Zoetemelk and Joaquim Agostinho had smashed into the fallen Bic leader as they too lost control in the terrible conditions. Rumours swirled – Ocaña had died; Ocaña had been paralysed. Neither was true but his race was over. Merckx assumed the race lead but refused to wear yellow the next day out of respect for his rival. The Belgian rode on to a third Tour win in a row.

A little more than two months after the accident Ocaña was back racing, winning the GP Diessenhofen at the start of a remarkable run of results that included wins at the Volta a Catalunya, the Trofeo Baracchi and the GP des Nations. Ocaña carried that form into the following season and entered the 1972 Tour having just taken his second Dauphiné Libéré win. Merckx meanwhile was also powering along having won his third Giro. Both were eager to resume the battle they had started the previous year but once again, the Spaniard wouldn't get to Paris due to a fall in the Pyrenees. Trailing Merckx by under a minute on GC, Ocaña fell on the descent of the Soulor. It was nowhere near as severe as his 1971 accident but still it took its toll. He trailed in 2min 40sec behind Merckx. In theory the Spaniard was still in contention with seven more mountain stages to come, but he had contracted a lung infection and steadily began to lose time. Finally worn down by tackling the world's biggest race while ill, and now trailing Merckx by more than twelve minutes, Ocaña abandoned.

Ocaña's fortune finally changed for the better in 1973 when he at last claimed the Tour win he had long seemed destined to take. He started his assault on the jersey early, joining a breakaway on the cobblestoned flatlands of northern France to unexpectedly gain more than two minutes on his rivals. After the first day of climbing Ocaña assumed control of the race and then, during the second day in the Alps he tightened his grip, more than trebling his 2min 51sec lead on a stage that went over climbs of the Madeleine, Télégraphe, Galibier and Izoard before a summit finish at Les Orres. Only five riders finished the stage within fifteen minutes of the climbing supremo.

Merckx, having won the Vuelta and the Giro already that year, beating Ocaña in the former by over three minutes, had opted to miss the 1973 Tour. In his absence Ocaña claimed six stages and an overall win of 15min 51sec. It was a devastating display, with more than a hint of Merckx about it.

Ocaña never again won a major race. In 1977 he retired to his farm with his wife Josiane. He suffered poor health and was diagnosed with hepatitis C, then with cancer. He drank heavily and he argued with his wife. 'They fought, they screamed at each other and then they made up; then they hated each other forever and almost within the same breath loved each other for all eternity,'[5] Juan Hortelano, a close friend of the family, told the writer Carlos Arribas.

On 19 May 1994, with certain death from his illnesses not far away and having just had another row, Ocaña went into his office. He called Hortelano, wanting to speak to his friend one last time and to explain what he was about to do. Then he shot himself. He was 48 years old.

MAJOR WINS
Tour de France: 1973
Vuelta a España: 1970
National Champion: 1968, 1972

Pantani, Marco

ITA

BORN: 13 JANUARY 1970, CESENA, ITALY

Italy's Marco Pantani won the Tour in 1998 and he did so by escaping the clutches of the leading group on the grimmest mountain the Tour could throw at him, in terrible rain and cold. On stage 15, 189km from Grenoble to Les Deux Alpes, Pantani, at the time lying fourth some 3min 1sec behind race leader Jan Ullrich, had decided it was time to make his move. The stage took the peloton over the Croix de Fer, the Télégraphe and the Galibier, before the final climb to the ski resort. It was the first time that Les Deux Alpes had featured on the Tour route and it would turn into a classic.

On the mighty Galibier, Pantani went to work. In no time he distanced Ullrich. The German watched the Italian disappear, had a chat with his sports director, and then did nothing. After all, they were still around 55km from the stage finish, with a technical descent and a final climb to go once they had crested the Galibier. But Pantani, who was a special climber, had other ideas. Standing on the pedals in his unique, crouched way, the diminutive Italian tamed the Galibier. At the summit he had an advantage of more than two minutes over Ullrich. It had been a devastating attack but still he needed more time in order to end the day in yellow.

Pantani dropped like a stone from the Galibier, flew down the Lauteret, hung a left by the Lac du Chambon and waltzed skywards towards Les Deux Alpes. Clad in soaking wet and lurid Lycra, his shaven head covered with a bandana, his face grim with pain, Pantani found a total of 8min 57sec on Ullrich, taking over the race lead. That sodden day in the Alps, Pantani was untouchable as he soared towards Tour glory on a classic day in the mountains.

If any edition of the Tour had needed a classic stage, 1998 was it. The race had been plagued by scandal from before a single rider had turned a pedal when a car driven by Willy Voet, a *soigneur* on the Festina team, was stopped and found to be full of banned drugs of almost every sort. Voet was arrested but the Festina team still took to the start line. As the race progressed team hotels and buses were raided, entire squads were taken in for questioning. Riders threatened to go on strike and staged sit-ins over what they saw as invasions of privacy. The Tour was descending into bedlam. For a while it looked like the race might not even get to Paris. It was farcical, a mess, an embarrassment to sport. And it was against this background that Pantani's ride to Les Deux Alpes provided one of the great stories of the modern Tour, billed as the ride that saved the Tour from oblivion.

In Paris, Pantani stood on the final podium wearing yellow and becoming just the seventh rider to complete the fabled Giro/Tour double in the same year, adding his name to the likes of Eddy Merckx, Bernard Hinault, Fausto Coppi, Jacques Anquetil, Miguel Induráin and Stephen Roche. It is a feat that, at the time of writing more than twenty years later, no other rider has since matched.

Pantani had risen steadily through the Italian amateur ranks. Third in the 1990 Baby Giro became second in 1991 and first in 1992. He signed professional forms with Carrera in 1992 and while he had to wait for nearly two years before his first professional wins, when they finally arrived, what wins they were.

Pantani would devote his career to just two races: the Giro and the Tour. He was a Grand Tour rider and that was it. The classics were not for him, nor week-long stage races. He needed three weeks and the long and high climbs of the Alps and the Pyrenees to shine; those mountains were his playground.

He claimed his first Giro stages in 1994 on his second start at the race, securing back-to-back wins on two unbelievably tough days in the Dolomites. The first was a 235km stage from Lienz to Merano, taking in four climbs. It was on the final climb of the day that Pantani showed for the first time what he was really capable of. On the Passo Monte Giovo, a 20km ascent with stretches upwards of 9 per cent, Pantani flew away, overhauling the stage leader, Pascal Richard, to solo to the win.

The following day was even tougher, featuring the feared passes of both the Stelvio and the Mortirolo. Pantani launched his attack on the early slopes of the Mortirolo where the first 3km average a thigh-burning 11 per cent. Through dappled shade the Carrera rider left the pink-jersey group in his wake. He ploughed through the leftovers of an earlier escape group, now splintered over the mountain road, overhauled Franco Vona, the rider who had been leading the stage, and then rode on to conquer the Mortirolo alone in front of enormous crowds.

Caught on the descent by Miguel Induráin, the pair rode to the final climb of the day, the Santa Cristina, where Pantani lit the afterburners once more. There was no holding him back as he scaled the day's final peak in solitude. It had been a virtuoso display. In Aprica, Pantani won his second Giro stage by just under three minutes and climbed to second overall. And there he would stay. In the space of two days Pantani had announced himself not only as a fine climber but also as a serious Grand Tour contender. 'A 24-year-old boy, born in Cesena, is perhaps the great climber that Italian cycling was waiting for,' wrote Gianni Ranieri in *La Stampa*.[1]

One month later he rode his first Tour, placing high on a number of mountain stages and finishing third in Paris. Surely the age of the pure climber from Italy was just around the corner.

Fragile of mind and of body, Pantani was dogged by controversy and accidents throughout his career. After his explosive 1994, hopes were high for a successful 1995 but a collision with a car early in the year ruled him out of the Giro. He made the start line of the Tour though, winning stages on l'Alpe d'Huez and Guzet-Neige and finishing thirteenth overall. Then, towards the end of the season came a sickening accident during the Milan–Turin semi-classic when he collided with a 4x4 that was on the course.

After nearly twenty months of recuperation, Pantani returned to the Giro in 1997. This time a cat ran out in front of him on stage 8 causing him to crash again and abandon. Again, he rose at the Tour, claiming another two stage wins and another podium spot in Paris.

Pantani's greatest year was 1998. He entered the Giro with no real expectation of a win but after some stunning rides in the mountains he assumed the race lead as the end of the race approached. He cemented his overall win on the final climb of the entire race, to Plan di Montecampione, cracking Pavel Tonkov who had eyes for sticking with the Italian and overturning his lead in the final time trial. As it turned out Pantani took fifty-seven seconds out of the Russian on the climb and then beat him in the time trial to secure his first Grand Tour title. Just two months later he won his second as he completed the Giro/Tour double thanks to that ride to Les Deux Alpes. Il Pirata – a nickname prompted by the bandana and earring he wore while riding – was now a hero in his homeland.

Then everything came crashing down. In 1999, just two days from the end of the Giro, and while wearing the pink jersey, Pantani failed a 'health check'. His haematocrit level breached 50 per cent and he was declared 'unfit' and suspended from the race – raised haematocrit levels are one indication of EPO abuse. Pantani was humiliated and distraught. He said he wouldn't ride any more, that his sport had betrayed him. Fans held banners that implored him to continue, that told him they believed in him – 'Marco, don't give up, you're the Giro, you're the Tour, you're the world of cycling,' they read.[2] Later investigations identified a link between Pantani and Francesco Conconi, an Italian sports doctor who was charged with sporting fraud arising from alleged provision of EPO in the 1990s. Although Conconi was later formally acquitted of the charges, the judge described him as 'morally guilty'.[3]

Pantani's team convinced him to continue and he returned to both the Tour and the Giro, winning two Tour stages in 2000, including an enthralling duel on the slopes of Mont Ventoux with Lance Armstrong. But he was never truly the same rider. His last race win came in 2000 at a criterium in the Netherlands. He rode his last Giro in 2003, finishing fourteenth.

After the 1999 Giro expulsion, Pantani had descended into depression and drug abuse. He was often rambling and incoherent, struggling to cope with what he saw as his persecution. At one point it was reported no fewer than seven separate investigations into his affairs were in progress.

Pantani died on Valentine's Day 2004, alone in a cheap hotel in Rimini. Cerebral and pulmonary oedema was the official cause of death, with the coroner's report stating it had been brought on by 'acute intoxication from cocaine'.[4] He was just 34 years old.

Pélissier, Henri

FRA

BORN: 22 JANUARY 1889, PARIS, FRANCE

Wednesday 27 May 1936: the French daily *Le Petit Dauphinois* runs a photograph on its front page. It shows a solemn-looking woman staring into space, her sharply collared blouse, worn under her coat, is buttoned up to her neck. Her dark hair is scraped back under a loose-fitting hat. She looks ill at ease, though that is no wonder. The woman's name is Camille Tharault and she is sitting in the dock of the Seine-et-Oise Cour d'assises in Versailles. A policeman sits impassively to her side, another sits behind. Above the grainy image runs the headline that explains the picture: 'Murderer of her boyfriend the champion cyclist Henri Pélissier, Camille Tharault is sentenced to one year in prison.'[5]

A little more than one year earlier, on 1 May 1935, 'the champion cyclist Henri Pélissier' had been at his home in the Chevreuse Valley, south-west of Paris. With him were Tharault and her younger sister Jeanne when a furious row broke out. Such rows weren't uncommon – indeed Tharault had said not long before that if she had enough money, she would have left the former cyclist long ago. Enraged by something Jeanne had said over dinner, Pélissier furiously attacked the younger sibling, hitting and kicking her before taking a knife and slashing her face. Fearing for her life and that of her sister, Camille rushed from the kitchen into the bedroom.

In 1933 Pélissier's then-wife, Léonie, had committed suicide. The gun that Léonie had used to take her own life that terrible day was still in a bedside cabinet. Scared of what Pélissier would do next, either to herself or to her sister, Camille returned to the kitchen with the gun in her hand, turned it on her lover, and then squeezed the trigger. According to subsequent press reports five shots were fired. Four of the bullets ended up in a wall but one 'severed an artery, causing almost instantaneous death as a result of very heavy bleeding'. Such had been the reputation of Pélissier that two days later the newspaper *Paris-Soir* reported that 'The tragic end of Henri Pélissier did not surprise anyone.'[6] During the subsequent criminal trial the courts recognised the extreme circumstances of the events and suspended Tharault's one-year prison sentence. Albert Baker d'Isy wrote:

> The brutal end of Henri Pélissier was painfully felt [by those] in the sports world. He certainly did not count on them as friends, for his absolute opinions, and his clear manner of expressing them, had earned him some enmity. But everyone bowed to the prestigiousness of the great champion who was considered the greatest French cyclist after the war, the rival of the Italian [Costante] Girardengo.[7]

Pélissier was one of four brothers born into relative comfort in Paris. While one (Jean) would lose his life during the First World War, the others all found a living on the bike, with Henri's younger brothers, Charles and Francis, both joining him in the professional ranks. All three would become national champions – Charles in cyclo-cross, Francis and Henri in road cycling. Indeed, such was the strength of the three brothers in France that from 1919 until 1931 there were only three editions of France's national championship road race that didn't result in at least one Pélissier standing somewhere on the podium.

Pélissier had turned professional in 1911 after bumping into Lucien Petit-Breton at the Porte Maillot in Paris and being invited to join him for some races in Italy. He had to decide quickly – Petit-Breton told the young Frenchman he had six hours before the train left. 'I did not argue for a minute,' Pélissier recalled years later. 'I jumped home, packed my suitcase in five seconds, without even knowing what team I was going to ride for.'[8]

It turned out Pélissier was to ride for Fiat in Italy. He went on to win a number of races that same year, including Milan–Turin and the Tour of Lombardy, the first of an eventual six Monuments – including a second win in Lombardy in 1913 in hugely chaotic circumstances which included a poorly observed neutralised section of the race that enabled the Frenchman to get back on terms having trailed by some three minutes at one point. Then, over-excited spectators decided they would join in the racing on their own bikes, disrupting the finale of the race. That's not to mention the car that found its way onto the course right in front of the riders just when they were gearing up for the final sprint. As carnage ensued, with Italian favourite Costante Girardengo crashing in all the chaos, Pélissier led home a French 1-2-3. Rumours quickly circulated that Pélissier had collided with Girardengo and caused his crash. The Frenchman needed police protection at the finish and could only leave the scene in disguise.

Pélissier started the Tour eight times but only made it to Paris twice. He won his first stage in 1913 and in 1914 took another three stages while finishing second overall. After the break in racing caused by the First World War, Pélissier returned to the Tour in 1919. He had enjoyed a terrific first six months, winning Paris–Roubaix and Bordeaux–Paris within a month of each other, and by the end of the third stage of the Tour he already had a stage win in the bag and an overall lead of more than twenty minutes. Pélissier, the race seemingly in his control, likened the other racers to cart horses and himself to a thoroughbred. Sickened by the arrogance of the race leader, the 'cart horses' started to work together. When Pélissier stopped to tighten his headset and remove his jacket on the stage to Les Sables-d'Olonne, his rivals took their chance and rode away as one. Pélissier lost more than thirty minutes, declared the race as being 'a thing for convicts',[9] and promptly abandoned.

The incident caused a deterioration in an already difficult relationship with the Tour's founder Henri Desgrange who wrote that Pélissier had no one to blame but himself. The following year Pélissier abandoned again, prompting Desgrange to declare that 'this Pélissier does not know how to suffer, he will never win the Tour de France.'[10]

Desgrange was proved wrong three years later when Pélissier, who had blazed a trail by championing speedwork while out training rather than just building endurance, claimed his one and only Tour victory. Trailing his Automoto teammate and future champion, Ottavio Bottecchia, as the race entered the Alps, Pélissier blitzed through the mountains, tearing up the climbs of the Allos, Vars, Izoard on his way into Briançon. He did so again on the next stage, this time up the Galibier and Aravis. Over two dramatic stages he turned a 29min 52sec deficit into a 29min 12sec lead. After Pélissier's stage win in Briançon Desgrange gushed:

Why does this great rider, so complete in his muscles, in his class, style, and dress, why does he not give us each year, since the war, the admirable spectacle he has given us since the start in Paris. ... Why did he tell us, in 1919 and 1920, that the task of the Tour de France was too heavy for a greyhound like him ... Henri Pélissier gave us a show that is the worth of all the art shows together. His victory was a beautiful arrangement, with the classicism of the works of Racine, it had the aesthetic value of a perfect statue, a flawless canvas, a piece of music intended to remain in every memory.[11]

It was the first French victory at the race since 1911. It would also be Pélissier's final major win, though his impact on the sport was by no means done.

Twelve months on and Pélissier was back to his usual ways at the Tour. Along with his brother Francis and fellow rider Maurice Ville, Pélissier abandoned during the third stage, frustrated after being quizzed by officials over how many jerseys he had started the race with – the rules being that you had to finish with exactly the same equipment and clothing with which you had started.

Word reached the journalist Albert Londres, who had been driving ahead of the race, that the Pélissier brothers had abandoned. 'We turned the Renault around and, without mercy for the tyres, went back to Cherbourg,' Londres wrote the following day. 'The Pélissiers are worth a thousand tyres.'[12] How right he would be.

Londres found the three riders in a café where they were holding court in front of a large crowd. The writer fought his way over to the riders and asked what had happened. The brothers told him of their run-in with the race official. 'We are not dogs,' they said.

The resulting article was a revelation and lifted the lid on how riders dealt with the terrible conditions and the formidable examinations of human stamina they faced in Desgrange's race. The riders showed Londres the contents of their bags: 'That, that is cocaine for our eyes and chloroform for our gums...' Henri told Londres. 'In short we run on dynamite,' said Francis.

Splashed on the front page of the next day's *Le Petit Parisien* the story became one of the most explosive pieces of cycling journalism of the age.

Pélissier retired from professional cycling in 1927. For the first six months of 1928 the journal *Le Miroir des Sports* serialised his autobiography under the title *Le Roman de ma Vie*. Pélissier wrote:

I was much criticised. No one has been able to say that I have not lived throughout my career wisely, soberly, regularly, as a champion must live. Those who, so often, have attacked me with their clumsy little quills, sheltered behind the blackness of their inkwells, can they boast of leading an exemplary life? ... Now, I am going to my home in Dampierre to fully enjoy family life ... [Will I do something else] Maybe. I have time to think about it, and that will be another story.[13]

When he wrote those words Pélissier could have had no idea how his story would end, seven years later, in tragic circumstances at that same family home in Dampierre. 'He was a complete rider,' the 1911 Tour winner Gustave Garrigou said when reflecting on Pélissier's career. 'If he had wanted, he could have been a phenomenon.'[14]

> ## MAJOR WINS
> Tour de France: 1923
> Paris–Roubaix: 1919, 1921
> Tour of Lombardy: 1911, 1913, 1920
> Milan–Sanremo: 1912
> National Champion: 1919
> Bordeaux–Paris: 1919

Pereiro, Óscar

ESP

BORN: 3 AUGUST 1977, MOS, SPAIN

On Monday, 15 October 2007, 30-year-old Óscar Pereiro visited the offices of Spain's sports minister in Madrid. Dressed in a dark suit, white shirt and pale-blue tie, watched by a host of officials and dignitaries that included Christian Prudhomme, the director of the Tour, Pereiro was presented with a glass trophy and a yellow jersey. In front of all present, the Caisse d'Epargne rider then stripped off his jacket, shirt and tie and put on the yellow jersey. And there he stood, smiling for the cameras, finally crowned as the winner of the 2006 Tour nearly fourteen months after he had ridden into Paris in second place. 'I wasn't far from believing this would never happen,' he'd said a few days before travelling to Madrid for the ceremony. 'So much time has passed and so many things have happened since the 2006 Tour. For me, it was the longest Tour in history.'[15]

Pereiro had started cycling when he was just 9, going on to claim the under-23 national cyclo-cross championship before turning professional in

2000 with the small Portuguese team Porta da Ravessa. A move to the big league came two years later when he signed for Phonak, twice finishing in the top ten at the Tour and claiming a stage win while with the team.

After moving to Caisse d'Epargne, in the summer of 2006 Pereiro enjoyed his best-ever Tour ride. The Spanish team had entered the race with that year's Liège-Bastogne-Liège winner, Alejandro Valverde, as their leader but a crash during the third stage ruled Valverde out of the race. That gave Pereiro the freedom to ride for himself that he otherwise wouldn't have enjoyed. And how he took advantage.

On stage 13 the Spaniard got himself into the day's break. Nearly thirty minutes down on race leader Floyd Landis, the peloton was content to let him go. Big mistake. As the break pulled out more and more time so Pereiro, the best-placed of the escapees, climbed the virtual standings. Pereiro reached the finish in the same time as stage winner Jens Voigt and then the clock started counting. Five minutes became ten, became twenty, became twenty-five minutes. The clock finally showed 29min 57sec before the Australian Robbie McEwen led the main bunch over the line. Incredibly, Pereiro had grabbed the yellow jersey off the shoulders of Landis. 'I was dreaming about this, but I never thought it would happen,' Pereiro said that evening. 'I will enjoy every day I wear this yellow jersey and I will try to defend it as long as possible, but I think that the day Floyd decides to get it [back], he will.'[16]

Landis reclaimed the jersey two stages later but then cracked on the first day in the Alps. On the climb to a summit finish at La Toussuire, Landis lost ten minutes and the jersey, which went back to Pereiro. A stunning ride the next day brought the American back into contention and he reclaimed the race lead, eventually wearing the jersey into Paris. Pereiro stood on the second step of the final podium, his best-ever result in a major race. Then it was announced that Landis had tested positive (see Disqualified entry for more).

More than a year later, and once the American's appeal had been ruled on and dismissed by the US Courts in a 2-1 ruling by arbitrators, Pereiro was confirmed as the winner of the 2006 Tour. In that time Pereiro had had his own brush with controversy having twice tested positive for salbutamol at the same race, a banned substance unless supported by a therapeutic use exemption certificate.[17] In January 2007 he was cleared of all charges after France's anti-doping agency declared that Pereiro had provided the necessary paperwork. That cleared the way for the Spaniard to be announced as the Tour winner when Landis was eventually stripped of the title. 'I feel like a Tour de France winner exactly like any other winner,' Pereiro said.[18]

It was by far Pereiro's biggest win of his career though still the negative stories swirled. In 2011 Landis claimed that Pereiro was 'also doped', telling the cycling journalist Paul Kimmage, 'I knew it, I had seen it first-hand [the two riders had ridden together in 2005 at Phonak]', saying the two men had talked openly about doping during the 2006 race.[19] Pereiro furiously denied the claims, telling *Velonews* that the story was an 'absolute lie':

> I am not guilty. I'm innocent. To be honest, I am not going to enter into some bullshit game like this. All I can say is that there is a lot of envy and bad feelings involving a lot of people in this sport. It started with Lance, now with Floyd, everyone will see that they are wrong.[20]

Pereiro retired in 2010 after a year with the Astana team, trying his hand at football and rally driving before moving into the media.

MAJOR WINS
Tour de France: 2006

Petit-Breton, Lucien

FRA

BORN: 18 OCTOBER 1882, PLESSÉ, FRANCE

Find a picture of Lucien Petit-Breton and you will see a man with arched eyebrows, dark eyes, a large moustache and perfectly parted hair, more often than not perched on his bike and looking cheerlessly straight into the camera. He cut quite the sartorial figure amongst the pre-First World War professional peloton. He was also a remarkably talented cyclist, winning the inaugural edition of Milan–Sanremo and then becoming the first rider to win the Tour back to back.

Born Lucien Mazan, Petit-Breton's family moved to Argentina when Lucien was just 8 years old, his father establishing himself as a watchmaker and jeweller. In Argentina, Petit-Breton found a love of horse racing, eventually working at the Jockey Club of Buenos Aires. But if the racecourses of Argentina sparked an interest in sport, it was when he first rode a bicycle – on Bastille Day as part of a celebration organised by French expats – that he discovered his true calling.

Determined to start racing despite the disapproval of his parents who thought it would bring shame on the family in their social circles, the young Lucien hesitated when asked his name while registering to ride his first race. Hailing from Brittany, he eventually said: 'Breton, I'm a Breton.'[21] Sources vary as to whether the 'Petit' was added in Argentina or later, in France, but agree that it happened when he entered a race that already had a 'Breton' riding. Either way, he was soon beating European champions who had travelled to South America, leading the 20 year old to return to Europe, arriving in 1902 to try his luck in the velodromes of Paris.

Petit-Breton won his first race in Europe on 23 March 1902, winning the second heat of a track meeting at the Parc des Princes and for the first time attracting the attention of the press. Four months later he finished second in the prestigious Bol d'Or 24-hour track race at the Vélodrome Buffalo, showing 'great quality' in a race that L'Auto otherwise described as 'deadly boring, irrelevant'.[22] Two years later in the same race, Petit-Breton took his first win of real note, beating Léon Georget by some 42km and setting a record distance of 852km. In 1905 he claimed the prestigious hour record on the Buffalo track, riding for 41.110km and beating the mark set by America's William Hamilton seven years earlier by some 329m.

Nicknamed l'Argentin, Petit-Breton had ridden his first Tour a month before claiming that hour record, finishing an impressive fifth in Paris. One year later he moved one place up the standings before then winning Paris–Tours towards the end of the season, his first major road-race victory.

The Frenchman was clearly on an upward trajectory and in April 1907 entered the record books as the first winner of Milan–Sanremo, the one-day race that would grow into one of the most prestigious Classics in the sport. Riding for Bianchi, having accepted an offer from them to race in their colours in Italy, Petit-Breton trailed fellow Bianchi rider Giovanni Gerbi by some six minutes at one point. He then benefitted from some curious tactics employed by Gerbi. The Italian reportedly started to verbally abuse his fellow escapee Gustave Garrigou in the hope he could distract the Frenchman and enable Petit-Breton to bridge across to them at the front of the race. The unlikely approach worked and Petit-Breton joined the break with around 40km to go. But that wasn't the end of Gerbi's assistance. In the final sprint the Italian grabbed Garrigou's jersey, holding him back as Petit-Breton took the win. Gerbi then claimed it was Garrigou who had impeded the Italian's own sprint, prompting punches to be exchanged between the two. Initially Gerbi, who was nicknamed the Red Devil for good reason having form with such dodgy tactics, was listed as finishing second. Five days later he was relegated to third with Garrigou promoted one place. Petit-Breton's position as race winner was unaffected.

Petit-Breton's first Tour win came later that same year. Riding for Peugeot, the dominant team in cycling at the time, the Frenchman was trailing his teammate Émile Georget by nearly twenty points with nine stages ridden (the Tour's organisers having switched to deciding the race on points rather than time in 1905). Then the organisers uncovered that Georget had illegally switched machines after puncturing on the stage to Bayonne and relegated him to last place on the stage. That added forty-eight points to his overall tally (the winner of the race being the rider with the fewest points) effectively ruling him out of contention, although he still managed to finish third in Paris. The race lead switched to Petit-Breton who then easily defended his position through the remaining five stages.

Fast-forward twelve months and Peugeot reigned supreme at the 1908 Tour, winning every stage and taking all three places on the final podium. The best of the Peugeot riders was once again Petit-Breton who won five stages in total and enjoyed a final margin of thirty-two points over the second-placed François Faber. Petit-Breton was in terrific form having won the inaugural Tour of Belgium and the 430km Paris–Brussels by some thirty minutes in the lead-up to the race. At the Tour only once did Petit-Breton place outside the top five on a stage as he rode superbly for the entire four weeks of the race, a model of consistency. He won the stage into his adopted home town of Nantes by more than twelve minutes, falling into the arms of his then fiancée, Marie-Madeleine Macheteau, at the finish – the couple married the following November. Never before in the Tour's young history had any rider won the race more than once; now Petit-Breton had claimed two titles back to back.

Reflecting on his win in the pages of *L'Auto*, Petit-Breton wrote:

I had full confidence at the start of the race. I knew exactly what my opponents were worth, I had seen them at work in previous races. I was afraid of two or three only ... [I was] convinced at its start that this Tour de France would be mine.[23]

Petit-Breton started another five Tours but never again made Paris. In 1912 he placed second in Bordeaux–Paris, zig-zagging on the road into Paris after accepting some champagne from a friend, explaining afterwards that it had gone 'straight to my legs'.[24]

With his career interrupted with the advent of war, Petit-Breton joined the national effort. He was killed in a motoring accident in 1917 whilst on duty.

MAJOR WINS
Tour de France: 1907, 1908
Milan–Sanremo: 1907

Pingeon, Roger
FRA

BORN: 28 AUGUST 1940, HAUTEVILLE-LOMPNES, FRANCE

Frequently described by documenters of cycling history as fragile and individualistic, overly sensitive, an outsider and a hypochondriac, Roger Pingeon won the Tour in 1967 thanks to a stunning breakaway early in the race which secured him the yellow jersey and which, save for just one day, he kept all the way to Paris.

That career-defining break happened on stage 5, 172km from Roubaix to the Belgian town of Jambes. Initially Pingeon joined a twelve-rider break that included the likes of Rik Van Looy, before riding away from his fellow escapees at the summit of the Mur de Thuin. Pingeon later said that he made his move thanks to the imploring of Jean Stablinski, who was shouting 'Go on, for God's sake, go!'[25] at his teammate as the initial break went.

His wasn't a violent attack; rather he just rode the other riders off his wheel in a move that later drew comparisons with the likes of Koblet and Coppi. 'I attacked because, on the one hand, I was feeling good and, on the other hand, we were procrastinating in our group. We dragged riders who refused to do their share of work,' Pingeon reflected. His winning margin in Jambes was 1min 24 sec, but crucially he crossed the line more than six minutes ahead of the group of favourites, bringing him the yellow jersey by twenty-six seconds. 'The most fabulous thing that I have been part of at the Tour,' Pingeon's teammate and one of the pre-Tour favourites, Raymond Poulidor, said. For the French sports journalist Michel Clare it was 'one of the most breath-taking achievements in modern cycling'.[26]

By the time the Tour reached Paris, Pingeon's winning margin had grown to 3min 40sec. It was a race that had been hit hard by the death of Britain's Tom Simpson on the fierce slopes of Mont Ventoux, with Pingeon's win destined to be forever overshadowed by the tragic events of 13 July 1967.

In Paris, Pingeon stood with his children in his arms and dedicated his win to his wife Dany. It was she who had convinced him to carry on cycling when he had abandoned the Tour of Corsica the previous year and announced to the cycling writer Pierre Chany that he was done with the sport. 'It's settled, I'll never ride a bicycle again,' he had told Chany. 'Ever since last year cycling doesn't give back to me what I put in. In the end, I'm probably just not cut out for this job.'[27] How things had changed twelve months on. 'This success that is more than I could ever have dreamed of, I owe it all to my wife Dany. I dedicate it to her,' he told reporters at the Parc des Princes.[28]

The result didn't please everyone in France, however. Jacques Anquetil, still a dominant figure in the sport and the leader of the Bic team, had sat out the Tour, instead joining the media circus following the race. The Tour had been run in national teams and Anquetil was furious that Bic teammates Stablinski, Raymond Riotte and Paul Lemeteyer had spent the race working for Pingeon, a trade-team rival the rest of the year. There was a furious row between Stablinski and Anquetil at the Perroquet Vert restaurant in Montmartre where Anquetil laid into his teammates, refusing to shake hands and branding them 'sluts'.[29]

One of five brothers born in the Jura mountains, after finishing school Pingeon initially trained as a plumber. A member of his local cycling club, he was at first unable to secure a racing licence due to a cardiac arrhythmia. It took him three attempts to find a doctor prepared to sign the documents necessary. It was an early sign of the persistence that would serve him well during his career.

After completing his military service in Algeria, Pingeon returned to France, his plumbing and his cycling. After marrying and having two children, Pingeon realised that he needed to dedicate himself to cycling if he wanted to know whether there was any possibility of pursuing the sport as a full-time career. In 1964 he decided to spend three months riding as an *indépendant*, a self-employed, semi-professional status that existed at the time. It was a roll of the dice that delivered in spades.

Decent results, including victory in the Poly Lyonnaise, earned him a professional contract with the Peugeot team for 1965 – the team of Simpson and the team that would welcome Eddy Merckx into its fold the following year. It would later be said that Pingeon was one of the riders that Merckx would fear most in the Grand Tours, such was his ability to deliver the unexpected – one early example being his surprise taking of the lead at the then prestigious Midi Libre race in his first year as a professional. Such was the race organisation's dismay at a relatively unknown rider winning their race, they reportedly conspired with his own team to prevent his victory.

Pingeon rode on instinct but was said to always fear the worst. He would abandon races because of a cold or an injury that perhaps wouldn't unduly affect other, more robust riders. He complained that he had a smaller lung capacity than others, that he feared the cold more, was frailer, and that he couldn't train for as long as other riders, taking weeks to progress to riding 80km when preparing for a new season. He preferred to room alone, rarely leaving his bed during rest days – the first to go to bed and the last to appear in the hotel foyer in the morning. He once remarked that over the course of a three-week race he'd get the equivalent of one day's more sleep compared to other riders. 'People often speak of my nervousness,' he said in a television interview recorded during his career. 'My sports director often mentions it. [But] My main characteristic is the efforts I often make [to provoke the race].'[30]

He returned to the Tour in 1968, finishing fifth overall and claiming two stages that included an incredible, 193km, solo escape on the stage to Albi, recording a near three-minute win. 'It was nothing planned,' Pingeon said afterwards. 'I simply wanted to get some mountain points, but when I saw they weren't reacting behind I got caught up in the game. I put my nose on the handlebars and I rode, as if the finish was just at the end of the road.'[31] Twelve months on he took his second and final major victory, winning two stages and the overall classification at the Vuelta ahead of the Spanish favourite Luis Ocaña. Two months later he finished second at the Tour, the best of the rest behind the incomparable Merckx who was busy claiming the first of his eventual five titles.

Pingeon retired from cycling in 1974 and then spent twenty years working for Swiss television. He died of a heart attack in 2017 at the age of 76.

MAJOR WINS
Tour de France: 1967
Vuelta a España: 1969

Pottier, René

FRA

BORN: 5 JUNE 1879, MORET-SUR-LOING, FRANCE

In 1923 Eugène Christophe, the first man to wear the Tour's official yellow jersey when it was introduced in 1919, provided recollections of his career to the journal *Le Miroir des Sports*. Remembering his first Tour in 1906, Christophe wrote:

> The third stage, Nancy–Dijon (466 km), brought us for the first time into the mountains with the Ballon d'Alsace and allowed me to appreciate the value of the late René Pottier … I always remember the feat that he accomplished by distancing everyone on the Ballon d'Alsace, climbing it at such a pace … [and] continuing alone the remaining 250km to reach Dijon, still increasing his lead over a peloton launched in pursuit … René Pottier will always remain for me the man who had the courage to face this long distance alone, as [pioneering aviator] Pégoud had the audacity to attempt the first looping-the-loop, as Bleriot dared to first cross the Channel.[32]

Pottier's escape over the Ballon d'Alsace and into Dijon that July day in 1906 has remained one of the great rides in Tour history, such was its devastating effect on the peloton and the race. The Frenchman was riding only his second Tour but had already developed a reputation as a fine climber, having been the first man over the same mountain when it had been included on the race route for the first time the previous year. That day Pottier had scaled its slopes at 20km/h, finishing second on the stage and assuming the race lead. It was a stunning display, made more so by Henri Desgrange's pre-stage assertion that the new climb would reduce every rider to walking. Despite being forced to abandon the race the next day – injuries sustained on the opening stage finally proving too much to bear – thanks to his exploits on the Ballon d'Alsace in 1905 Pottier came to be regarded in Tour history as 'the first King of the Mountains'[33] despite the official classification not existing until 1933. Twelve months on from his first Tour appearance, Pottier would repeat his heroics on the Ballon d'Alsace with even greater effect.

The 1906 Tour, the race's fourth edition, brought a drastically altered route. The first Tour had been six stages and 2,428km in total, now it was thirteen stages and 4,546km. If that meant a reduced average stage distance (349km in 1906 compared to 405km in 1903) it meant a race longer in duration and with fewer rest days as the route expanded further north, further east and further west than it had done in previous years. Seventy-four of the one hundred riders who had registered to take part actually left the Vélodrome Buffalo on the opening day, and only fourteen would return to Paris.

Pottier already had the race lead going into the third stage having won the previous stage into Nancy. At the foot of the Ballon d'Alsace, Pottier turned the screws on his rivals, surging ahead as soon as the road lifted and, in the words of Victor Breyer, '[shaking] off the pack as a boar does a pack of dogs'.[34] He reached the summit of the climb in glorious solitude, more than four minutes ahead of anyone else, watched only by a hundred or so spellbound spectators. But the climbing ace had only just begun and he quickly set about descending at speed, bound for Dijon. At Montbéliard, with 172km to go, Pottier's lead was around eleven minutes; at Vesoul, with 110km to go, it was thirty-nine minutes. Untouchable, by the time he reached Dijon Pottier's lead had stretched to 47min 52sec. With the Tour settled on points calculated by a rider's stage finishing position, that dominance wasn't fully transposed into the general classification, but nevertheless Pottier had dealt a stunning blow to the rest of the peloton.

Over the course of the next two stages Pottier cemented his position at the head of the race, winning in both Grenoble and Nice. Pottier had claimed four stages in a row leading L'Auto to describe him as simply invincible. Defending his lead over the course of the following fortnight, Pottier regained that winning feeling in Paris, claiming the final stage ahead of his teammate Georges Passerieu. His final margin of victory was just eight points over Passerieu, a result that by no means reflected his superiority over the rest of the race. Pottier completed the 4,546km in a time of 173hrs 7sec, some two and a quarter hours quicker than Passerieu.[35] A little over a month later Pottier won the Bol d'Or on the Buffalo track, confirming his status as one of the most versatile and talented riders in the world.

Pottier had a reputation as a man who barely spoke and never smiled or laughed. However, wrote Christophe Penot on the website of the Ligue Nationale de Cyclisme, 'he had a huge heart, born for sport and love'.[36] A member of the famous Vélo Club de Levallois, he attracted attention for his performances on the track, getting close to the hour world record in both 1903 and 1904 while still an amateur. He would go on to claim a number of track records.

Turning professional at the back end of 1904, Pottier quickly made his mark. He took second at Paris–Roubaix behind Louis Trousselier in 1905 and then finished second again at Bordeaux–Paris, only losing the 583km race by eighteen seconds to Hippolyte Aucouturier. That result came despite getting off his bike in Versailles, just 3km from the finish, to sign a control sheet while Aucouturier simply rode on. At the finish Pottier said:

> I have suffered well. My thigh hurts, my leg is numb, and then I have suffered from the cold. I'm dead, literally dead from cold, but all that would amount to nothing if I had won as it should have been. I led the dance throughout the race ... I was ordered to get down [off the bike to sign] and I obeyed ... while Aucouturier rides away. I protest absolutely ... no, no, a thousand times no, I will not admit this defeat.[37]

If in July 1906 it had seemed that Pottier's Tour win would be the first of many major victories, it would prove not to be. In January 1907 he was found dead in the clubhouse of his team, Peugeot, having committed suicide. In 1935, Robert Coquelle wrote:

> The cause of this suicide has always remained mysterious. All the more inexplicable for your correspondent with whom Pottier had discussed that same morning contracts for several races during the season. We had agreed at noon. We had taken a 'pale ale' at midday in the velodrome bar. At half-past one, Arthur Berthelemy, director of racing equipment at Peugeot, phoned me when he returned from lunch. He had found Pottier hanging from the ceiling of his studio. He had, rightly, cut the rope, but it was already too late.[38]

André Pottier, René's brother and a fellow professional cyclist, blamed a broken heart caused by a troubled marriage, saying simply that his brother had died of 'sentimental disappointment'.[39]

MAJOR WINS
Tour de France: 1906

Riis, Bjarne

DEN

BORN: 3 APRIL 1964, HERNING, DENMARK

At 4 p.m. on Friday, 25 May 2007, a solemn Bjarne Riis sat down behind a table and microphone in a room at the headquarters of the CSC team he managed. In front of the large assembly of journalists, and as cameras continuously clicked away, the 1996 Tour winner confessed to what many had long suspected:

'I've come here to lay my cards on the table,' Riis said. 'I confess to taking performance-enhancing drugs, including EPO, during the 1990s. From around 1993 to 1998, I used drugs continuously. This was commonplace back then. I regret it, but I am still proud of my achievements.'[1]

Prompted by a series of similar confessions from former teammates, Riis, the man dubbed 'Mr 60%' during his career in a nod to his now confirmed artificially enhanced haematocrit levels, had finally come clean. His admission had come some eleven years after he had stunned the cycling world by ending the reign of five-time Tour winner Miguel Induráin. While the cycling authorities were powerless to officially act due to the eight-year statute of limitations for doping offences that was in place at the time, Riis was nevertheless asked by journalists if he should be stripped of his title given his confession. 'My yellow jersey is in a box in my garage at home,' he said. 'You can come and collect it. What matters to me are my memories.'[2] A year later Riis reflected on his confession:

> I was lying [when he denied doping during his career] – that's obvious ... It's tough that more or less everybody knows you're lying ... I don't like to tell lies – I don't think anybody does. I had to protect myself. I had no other choice ... I was ready [to tell the truth] and now I think it was the best thing I ever did. Afterwards I realised how hard it was to keep the secret. Now I feel free – they can shoot at me as much as they want, but they have nothing on me.[3]

Riis had started his amateur career in his native Denmark before moving to Luxembourg and turning professional in 1986. An unremarkable introduction to the pro ranks followed before he joined Laurent Fignon at Système U after helping the Frenchman in the Tour de la Communauté Européenne in 1988 despite them being on different teams. After signing with Système U for the 1989 season, Riis remained at Fignon's side for three years (the team changed to Castorama in 1990). In total Riis rode six Grand Tours alongside the Frenchman, helping Fignon win the Giro in 1989 and claiming a stage win for himself in the process. Riis was also part of the team that supported Fignon during his subsequent eight-second Tour loss to Greg LeMond.

In 1993, now with the Ariostea team, Riis finished fifth overall at the Tour. It was a startling result – his previous best had been ninety-fifth in 1989 and he had never won a professional stage race of any kind. Now, he was suddenly capable of riding with the very best in the world's most prestigious bike race. Two years later he finished third and the stage was truly set. Riis had transformed himself into a true Grand Tour contender, so much so that he reportedly told his teammates that he would win the 1996 Tour some eight months before it even started.

Stage 16 of the 1996 Tour ran for 199km from Agen to a summit finish at the tiny Pyrenean ski-station of Lourdes-Hautacam. True to the promise he had made his team, Riis had been in yellow since he had won a weather-affected mountain stage to Sestriere a week before (instead of the planned climbs of the Iseran and Galibier, heavy snow meant the stage was cut to just 46km). By the start of the sixteenth stage Riis held a fifty-six second lead over Abraham Olano.

The climb of Hautacam is one of the toughest in the Pyrenees, with gradients that vary wildly all the way to the summit, belying its quoted average of 7.6 per cent. But Riis made it look like child's play. With around 4km of the 13.6km climb ridden, Riis, who was in the leading bunch surrounded by rivals looking to lift the yellow jersey from his shoulders, slid back through the group. At first the television commentators thought he was in trouble, after all here he was moving backwards while his young teammate, Jan Ullrich, led the way up the climb, setting a fearsome pace. But then the truth emerged. Riis was merely checking out everybody, assessing their condition, before launching his assault on the stage in a bid to put Tour victory out of the reach of everyone else.

His first brace of attacks shed Olano and Evgeni Berzin, sitting second and third respectively on GC behind the Dane. His third got rid of reigning Tour champion Induráin, over four minutes behind but still a potential threat with a 63km time trial still to come. His fourth and final move distanced everyone else. 'Amazing to see this man go uphill,' commented the late Paul Sherwen who was covering the race for television. 'He's never a rider you thought of as a great climber but he just seems to go stronger and stronger.'[4]

Riis powered on alone. At the top of Hautacam his winning margin was forty-nine seconds over then two-time mountains prize winner Richard Virenque (Virenque would go on to claim seven mountains titles in all, two of those coming after he admitted to using EPO to a French magistrate in 2000). Riis had opened a 2min 42sec lead over Olano who would fall away over the course of the final week while Ullrich rose through the standings. In Paris, Riis stood as the first Danish winner of the Tour with an overall margin of 1min 41sec over his young German teammate who was destined to soon taste glory himself.

The 1996 Tour remained the single highpoint of Riis' riding career. After retiring he moved into team ownership and management enjoying great success as a sports director, guiding the likes of Ivan Basso, Carlos Sastre and Alberto Contador to Grand Tour victories between 2006 and 2012. He sold his stake in the team he also managed to Oleg Tinkov before being removed from his post after a fallout two years later.

Today Riis remains in cycling as a co-owner and manager of the NTT team.

> **MAJOR WINS**
> Tour de France: 1996
> National Champion: 1992, 1995, 1996

Robic, Jean

FRA

BORN: 10 JUNE 1921, CONDÉ-LÈS-VOUZIERS, FRANCE

Dubbed the Tour of Liberation, the 1947 Tour was the first to be organised since war had exploded in Europe in 1939. While a reduced programme of racing had remained in place during the war years in a bid by the occupying forces to retain some semblance of normality, in 1946 the sport embarked on its post-war renaissance. That year two five-stage candidate races – La Ronde de France and La Course du Tour de France – were held by two rival organisations to help decide which would be granted the honour of re-establishing the Tour as cycling's premier event (*L'Auto*, accused of sympathetic leanings toward the occupying Germans, had been closed following the return of peace with all of its assets, including the Tour, sequestrated by the state).

With the rights to the Tour passing to the new publication *L'Équipe*, a sports paper founded in early 1946 from the ashes of *L'Auto*, by 1947 France was preparing once again to welcome back its precious national tour. Among those taking to the start line in Paris was a 26-year-old Jean Robic.

Some eight years previously Robic, who was born in the Ardennes but raised a proud Breton after his parents – both of whom had hailed from Brittany – decided to take the family back to their home region, had joined a cycling club in Auray. After securing his first amateur victories he moved to Paris in order to further develop his cycling skills, taking a job in a bicycle dealership while recording increasingly impressive race results.

Robic was short, powerful and foul-mouthed, always ready for an argument or a scrap. He was 'a grumbler' with 'a chubby chin, a thick eyebrow, a fierce eye [and] clenched jaws'.[5] He grew into a gifted cyclist, developing into a fabulous climber who was equally comfortable on the mud and dirt of a cyclo-cross circuit as he was on the road. In 1946 he finished third in La Course du Tour de France, which ran from Monaco to Paris, claiming the stage between Briançon and Aix-les-Bains. Robic had been bitterly disappointed to have been overlooked by the French national team for the race and was instead riding for the regional Ouest outfit. That left him riding with little or no support against riders such as the 1939 Tour runner-up René Vietto, who enjoyed the backing of the French squad. Nevertheless, Robic entered Paris with a podium spot to his name. At the Parc des Princes the adopted Breton shared his feelings about the race before declaring future intentions: 'I lost alone to the French team, but I was the best. I will do that to them next year. Yes, I know they consider me amusing, but we will have the chance to talk again!'[6]

That chance came under the glare of the 1947 Tour. Once more Robic, whose face rarely seemed to fit, was destined to ride for regional Ouest team against Vietto and Co. This was meant to be the ever-popular Vietto's race and indeed for a while it looked that it would go his way, with a brace of stage wins bringing him fifteen days in yellow.

Robic, who was crash-prone and nicknamed both 'leather-head' because of the protective helmet he wore after fracturing his skull during an edition of Paris–Roubaix and 'biquet' [the kid] due to his small size (he was just under 5ft 3in), was 23min 21sec down on Vietto going into stage 15, from Luchon to Pau. Ahead of the riders were climbs of the Peyresourde, Aspin, Tourmalet and Aubisque. Despite lying sixth overall and seemingly out of the race for yellow, Robic still thought he could win the Tour, telling anyone listening that he felt unstoppable. But all was not well in his team. Robic's bluster had alienated him from his squad, 'If he's so strong, he can manage by himself,'[7] sniffed an unhappy teammate, Eloi Tassin.

And so that was what Robic did. Knowing that the stage into Pau represented one of the few remaining opportunities to make inroads into the large time gap, he rode aggressively from the start of the stage, attacking alongside Italy's Pierre Brambilla on the Peyresourde and putting Vietto into immediate problems. On the Aspin, a mountain that Robic loved – he would lead the Tour's peloton over the climb three times during his career (1947, 1948 and 1953) – Robic struck out alone. With no one able to match his pace a classic Pyrenean pursuit followed, but Robic was too strong and by the time he rode into Pau his lead was nearly eleven minutes. Robic had led the race for nearly 195km over four giant Pyrenean peaks that each earned him crucial time bonuses meaning he had actually gained over fifteen minutes in one remarkable day of racing. But it hadn't been enough to bring him the race lead. Robic was still 8min 8sec down.

Legend has it that shortly before the Tour had started Robic had told his new wife, 'I've no dowry, but I'll offer you the first prize of the Tour.'[8] Robic had also reportedly written to his mother during the race, telling her of his hopes that he could 'give you the final victory at the Parc des Princes'.[9] Inspired by promises made to the women in his life, Robic grabbed a handful of those remaining eight minutes during in a mammoth 139km time trial, coming in second, 9min 46sec ahead of Vietto who fell to fourth overall. But the yellow jersey passed to Brambilla, his initial companion on the Peyresourde. The Italian now had a lead of nearly three minutes over Robic, who had climbed to third, which he kept until the start of the final stage.

Today a truce is traditionally called on the last day of the Tour, with the race leader allowed to ride into Paris unchallenged, showing off the yellow jersey and quaffing champagne. Not so in 1947. One stage left and Robic wasn't done yet. He attacked on the only gentle rise of the final stage and got a lead over Brambilla. Édouard Fachleitner, a fellow Frenchman who was riding for the national team, tracked the move. Fachleitner was well placed himself overall but crucially was a few minutes down on Robic. The Breton convinced Fachleitner he could never beat him and so he might as well help him instead (the 100,000 francs he reportedly promised probably helped). Robic didn't win the stage but rode into Paris over thirteen minutes ahead of the yellow jersey wearing Brambilla. Robic had won the Tour of Liberation on the final day, without ever wearing the jersey on the roads of France.

Touted in 1957 by the writer René De Latour as one of finest climbers ever to have graced the Tour – 'it cannot be pretended that Robic was a pretty climber. You could read suffering all over his face, although he endured his suffering willingly and even cheerfully,'[10] wrote De Latour – Robic led over the fearsome Mont Ventoux in 1952. As the mistral wind roared over the white rock of the Ventoux, so Robic soared upwards, summiting the climb with a lead of over two minutes and winning the stage into Avignon. Five days earlier he had attacked Fausto Coppi on the lower slopes of l'Alpe d'Huez, the first time the climb had been used by the Tour, forcing the Italian master to react. Coppi did so with some aplomb, taking the stage by 1min 20secs, but even he was later moved by Robic's display on the Ventoux. 'Robic has achieved a real feat today,' Coppi said. 'I thought that the wind would have forced him to succumb.'[11]

Robic, who won the first official cyclo-cross world championship in 1950, rode his final Tour in 1959. He missed the time-cut just two days from Paris and was eliminated from the race. It was said Tour officials may have allowed many other former Tour winners to continue in such a situation but not Robic given that he had alienated so many people and created so many enemies due to his 'immoderate language',[12] and immodest tone – Robic once claimed he was so powerful, he had the equivalent of 'a [Louison] Bobet in each leg'.[13]

Plagued by failing businesses and divorce in retirement, Robic died in 1980 when the car he was driving home from a reunion of former cyclists crashed into a stationary truck during the early hours. Robic and his passenger, Lianor Sanier, the wife of a fellow former pro, died on impact. Newspapers reported that Robic had left the reunion in a rage after a row developed. Other riders reportedly implored him to go to bed instead of going home but Robic had refused to listen. He was 59 years old.

MAJOR WINS
Tour de France: 1947

Roche, Stephen

IRL

BORN: 28 NOVEMBER 1959, DUNDRUM, IRELAND

In 1987, Ireland's Stephen Roche achieved something only one man had achieved before, winning the Giro, Tour and world championship in the space of three incredible months. Pink, yellow and rainbow: the three most prized jerseys in the sport in the same season. The triple-crown of cycling. Only cycling's colossus Eddy Merckx had won this particular holy trinity in a single year before, proof enough of the scale of the achievement. On top of that Roche had also won the Tour de Romandie. In 2016 Roche said:

When I'm visiting [the tour de] Romandie the announcer will always say, 'he is only the second rider in history to win the Giro, the Tour and the Worlds in the same year' ... But he is the only man in cycling to have won Romandie, the Giro, the Tour and the Worlds in the same year![14]

Roche had started cycling in his native Ireland, becoming a good amateur and winning national titles at a junior level. He trained as a maintenance fitter, uncertain if cycling could offer him a living, while continuing to improve himself on the bike. Selected to ride for Ireland at the 1980 Olympic Games – he would come forty-fifth in the road race in Moscow – Roche went to France to prepare among the best amateurs in Europe having secured an invite from the renowned ACBB club in Paris. Decent performances soon morphed into impressive results, including victory at the amateur Paris–Roubaix. By February 1981 Roche had signed professional forms with the Peugeot team. He wasted little time making his mark, impressively winning both the Tour of Corsica and Paris-Nice just weeks after turning pro.

A first Tour stage win came four years later during a short mountain stage – 53km from Luz-Saint-Sauveur to the top of the Aubisque. Roche was now at La Redoute and his sports director, Raphaël Géminiani, had a special plan up his sleeve.

Before the stage Géminiani gave Roche a gift – a handmade silk skinsuit. Roche was less than impressed and told his director he wouldn't be seen dead wearing it during a normal road stage. But Géminiani argued his case, explaining that the stage was so short he should ride it like a time trial. Roche eventually agreed, keeping the suit hidden under his normal jersey until hitting the ramps of the Aubisque. As the Aubisque started so the jersey came off and Roche sped away. The Irishman caught and passed the lone leader on the road and sped to the stage win by over one minute.

Roche would go on to finish third in Paris that year, announcing his arrival as a Grand Tour contender. As the season drew to a close, he moved to the Italian team Carrera. He had signed as a rider who could reach the podium of the Tour, but the following season was a virtual write-off with Roche suffering with an acute knee injury. He was still able to help Roberto Visentini to Giro victory but rode few races and only managed forty-eighth at the Tour. That winter he got a call from the team director, saying they wanted to talk about his contract as he hadn't performed. Roche refused, saying they should trust him and give him time. 'If by Easter I've got no results then we can discuss and renegotiate my contract,'[15] he said.

With a doctor in Germany finally addressing his knee problem, Roche entered the 1987 season in good spirits. Training was going well and he was outperforming his Carrera teammates in training camps for the first time. In February he won his first race for Carrera – the Tour of Valencia. It was a great start but no one could imagine what was about to happen.

At the 1987 Giro, Roche did not start as Carrera's leader, but as a teammate of the defending champion Visentini. Roche wore pink early on but lost it to Visentini after a mountain time trial. The Italian's lead was 2min 42sec, with Roche in second place. Surely nothing could now stop Visentini defending his title.

Roche had been told that his and Visentini's roles would be reversed at the Tour, with the Italian riding for the Irishman. But as the Giro progressed Roche started to hear murmurings that Visentini wasn't going to ride the Tour. So, in the Dolomites, Roche got himself into a break. The Carrera team didn't know what was going on and ended up trying to chase their own man. Roche finished nearly seven minutes ahead of Visentini and grabbed back pink.

His team was furious. As were the Italian *tifosi*. In 2012 Roche told *The Guardian* he had rice and wine spat at him in the days that followed. But he held on and won the race – the first, and to date only, Irish rider to win the Giro. Roche said:

> The Giro was incredible because of the way I won it. ... The journalists were asking when I was going to go home. I said, 'Do what you want. I ain't going home.' ... I spent sixteen days being escorted back to my room every night, bodyguard on the door, my masseur making my food, my mechanic looking after my bike, being escorted down to the start line, at the finish line being escorted back to the hotel. It was amazing.[16]

A little over two weeks later Roche headed to France and went head to head with Spain's Pedro Delgado. Roche had yellow entering the Alps but lost it to Delgado on l'Alpe d'Huez. The next day took the race over the Madeleine and up to the ski station La Plagne. Roche was only behind by twenty-five seconds and with a time trial still to come he was well placed, being far better against the clock than Delgado. All he had to do was mark the Spaniard to La Plagne and wait for the 'race of truth' to take back yellow.

Instead Roche attacked early. At the foot of the Madeleine he was part of a group that had over a minute on Delgado but the race came back together on the road to La Plagne. Roche had ridden too hard too early. On the final climb Delgado sped off.

With 10km to go to the top of La Plagne, Roche was in trouble. Two minutes behind Delgado, the Tour was slipping through the Irishman's fingers. With TV coverage sporadic no one knew exactly how far away he was when Delgado finally crossed the line, but everyone thought they'd be waiting minutes to see the Irishman arrive. Wrong. In one of cycling's great race-saving rides, Roche incredibly limited his loss to just four seconds. He promptly collapsed on the finish line. Oxygen was given. Four days later he stood in yellow in Paris. Nearly thirty years later, Roche said:

> If race radio would have been there that day, and my sports director had told me when I was at thirty seconds, I would have backed off probably because I knew I could probably win by one minute in the time trial. So while I was killing myself on La Plagne I could have backed off. But because I didn't know where he was ... history was made.[17]

Three-hundred thousand people reportedly lined the streets of Dublin to welcome him home. 'The reaction of the people was unbelievable,' Roche reflected in his book commemorating his 1987 season *My Road to Victory*. 'An experience that can never be forgotten.'[18]

The icing on an already fruit-packed cake came a month and a half later in Austria. The plan had been for Roche to be near the front at the end of the race to help lead out his Ireland teammate Sean Kelly in the sprint. But after marshalling a break for Kelly, Roche found himself away in a small group with his teammate having little realistic chance of getting back to him in time. With 500m to go Roche squeezed through a tight gap to the left-hand side of the road and held off a fast-approaching group for the win. Kelly celebrated as he rolled across the line in fifth and went straight up to Roche to congratulate him. Roche later said that Kelly's immediate reaction meant a lot to him. 'Sean threw his arms up in the air,' he said. 'Sean was a friend and while certain people and journalists in Ireland would have liked to have had myself and Sean against each other because it would have made for better stories, we were always good friends. Even to this day.'[19] It was a remarkable end to remarkable season.

With his career continuing to be blighted by injuries, Roche never again approached the heights of his 1987 season. Ninth at the Giro (1989 and 1993) and ninth and a single stage win at the Tour (1992) was as good as it got at the Grand Tours. Elsewhere there was a sprinkling of week-long stage wins but in events without the prestige of Paris-Nice or Romandie.

Roche retired from professional cycling in 1993, going on to run a cycling-holiday business in Mallorca.

MAJOK WINS

Tour de France: 1987
Giro d'Italia: 1987
World Champion: 1987

Sastre, Carlos

ESP

BORN: 22 APRIL 1975, LEGANÉS, SPAIN

Stage 17 of the 2008 Tour was a brute. Running for 210km the stage took in climbs of the Galibier and Croix de Fer before a finish atop l'Alpe d'Huez. It was a stage which had long been identified as a key date for the destiny of the race. As the sun rose on the morning of the stage the CSC-Saxo Bank team, which had entered the race with three potential winners in their ranks (the Schleck brothers – Fränk and Andy – and Carlos Sastre), were well placed. Two of those three co-leaders were in the top five overall: Fränk Schleck was wearing the yellow jersey of race leader while Sastre was just forty-nine seconds back in fourth place. With Australia's Cadel Evans, a better time-trial rider than both the CSC men, sitting third and very much still in the mix with a 53km time trial still to come, the question was how would CSC play their cards on the Alpe to try to secure their first Tour win.

After more than five hours of racing through the mountains, five CSC riders sat on the front of the group of favourites, driving the pace. Sastre was fifth in line, slipstreaming behind Fränk Schleck. Then, as soon as they turned onto the steep initial ramps of the Alpe, Sastre launched his move.

Rabobank's Denis Menchov was the only rider able to initially follow the Spaniard but slowly the leaders crawled their way back. Just as the catch was made Sastre went again. This time Menchov was helpless, as was everyone else. Standing on the pedals, head bowed, teeth bared in effort, Sastre danced away from his rivals, catching the two riders who had led the race onto the climb. Schleck just sat impassively in the group behind, occasionally ramping up the pace to test the legs of Evans. The Australian was now in a bad place, stuck between one rival disappearing up the road and another sat right behind him, waiting to pounce. Any attempt Evans might have made to catch Sastre would simply be used as a launchpad for Schleck.

Despite the undoubted team tension that comes with multiple leaders in the same team, CSC had played a tactical masterstroke. Sastre soloed to a fine win on the Tour's most famous summit finish and took the yellow jersey from his teammate. With a lead 1min 34sec over Evans now in the General Classification, the attack had set Sastre up perfectly for the remaining stages. Defending his lead through a couple of hilly but non-decisive stages, the Spaniard then put in a good time-trial performance on the penultimate day of the race. He still lost time to Evans but nothing like what had been anticipated and Sastre reached Paris with a winning margin of fifty-eight seconds in the bag. Evans was second while Schleck finished sixth, 4min 28sec back.

Sastre later reflected that he had suffered 'like hell' during the first 5km of his attack on the Alpe to secure a decisive gap. 'Beforehand, my soigneur Bengt Valentino Andersen said to me "on Alpe d'Huez, you're going to fight like a lion and fly like an eagle." I kept that in my mind,' he told *Rouleur* in 2018.[1] In Paris he was joined on the podium by his two children. 'Ever since I was a little kid, I've dreamt about winning the Tour de France,' he said. 'Ever since I won my first race, I'd hoped I could go on to win other major stage races. I had to fight for it and gain experience but now I've done it.'[2]

Sastre had grown up around cycling. In the 1980s his father established the Víctor Sastre Provincial Sports Foundation in El Barraco, Ávila, as a way of keeping children off the streets, away from the temptations of drugs and crime. It was there that the young Carlos started cycling aged 8. He rode on the amateur Banesto team for three years, suffering multiple crashes and injuries. Unsure of whether he could make it in the cycling world and not wanting to waste his time if he wasn't good enough, Sastre set himself a target in his final season as an amateur: either do enough to secure a professional contract for the following season or stop cycling completely. At last the results started to come.

The offer of a professional contract duly arrived from Manolo Saiz's ONCE outfit. Sastre, who has remained untainted by the many various investigations that have been undertaken by sport's anti-doping authorities over the past couple of decades, has credited Saiz with being a major influence on his career, this despite Saiz being embroiled in the large-scale *Operacion Puerto* doping investigation into the Madrid clinic of Dr Eufemiano Fuentes (Saiz was subsequently cleared by Spanish courts in 2013). In 2012 Sastre said:

> Manolo showed me the value of hard work and sacrifice and how to earn the respect of my teammates. He was a hard coach, a disciplinarian, very hands-on but he was also a very smart person. He made a lot of mistakes, and he's paying for them now, but I think Manolo Saiz was a revolutionary for cycling. He was controlling everything in the team at the time. No one had a team bus back then, except ONCE, and we had four of them. We had more than 1,000 bikes for the team! There wasn't another team anything like ours.[3]

Sastre rode for Saiz at ONCE for five years, claiming the mountain classification at the 2000 Vuelta. In that time he claimed just one race win – stage 3 at the Vuelta a Burgos in 2001. According to Sastre it was the only time Saiz had put the team to work in support of him and came the day after Sastre had rebuffed Saiz's criticisms for not winning a previous mountain stage, telling his director the blame lay with him alone for not providing the gearing he had requested for the stage.[4]

By the time of Sastre's first professional win he already knew he was moving teams, having agreed terms to join Bjarne Riis at CSC. It was with Riis that Sastre, whose nickname was Don Limpio (Mr Clean), took his career to the next level. Sastre was a man who liked to ride instinctively, with feeling, rather than following strict pre-laid instructions. In a 2012 interview Sastre said that the team complained the first year he joined that his results weren't what they were expecting and that it wasn't until he told the team he would follow his own training plan that things improved. 'I said many times, "Bjarne, I am not a robot,"' Sastre told *Cyclingnews*.[5]

A first Tour stage win arrived in the Pyrenees during the 2003 race. Sastre arrived alone at the finish on Plateau de Bonascre (Ax 3 Domaines). With 100m to go he looked around, put his hand in his jersey pocket and pulled out a baby pacifier. He raised it to the sky for all to see, before putting it in his mouth and crossing the line with his arms in the air. The gesture was for his baby daughter Claudia. 'I had that pacifier in my jersey pocket in every single race for maybe ten years,' Sastre said in 2018. 'Every time I went for a bit of food, my hand would brush it and I would think of them [his children]... I knew that I didn't want to make any mistakes because there were two very important people waiting for me at home.'[6]

Sastre ended his career with three Tour stage wins to his name. He also won a couple of stages at the Giro in 2009. In 2006 he became one of the few riders to have started and finished the Giro, Tour and Vuelta in a single season. In all, Sastre finished in the top ten of a Grand Tour some fifteen times, a record that had his former sports director at Cervélo TestTeam, Gérard Vroomen, proclaim him as 'probably the best GC rider of his generation'.[7]

A rider who is sometimes referred to as the forgotten Tour champion due to his understated public persona, Sastre retired with little fuss in 2011 after serving two years with Cervélo and one year with Geox. 'The moment has arrived to bring this cycle to its close,' he said before revealing he had known the time was right to finish for a while. 'I took the decision last year. I didn't want to make cycling into purely an economic issue for me. I have always wanted to be a professional from the first to the last day. I have known where my limits are.'[8]

MAJOR WINS
Tour de France: 2008

Schleck, Andy

LUX

BORN: 10 JUNE 1985,
LUXEMBOURG CITY, LUXEMBOURG

Andy Schleck was born into a family famous in Luxembourg for their cycling prowess. His grandfather, Auguste, rode in the 1920s twice securing top-three results in the GP Faber while his father, Johny, enjoyed a ten-year career as a *domestique* on the Pelforth and Bic teams, winning a stage of the 1970 Vuelta and helping Luis Ocaña to Tour victory in 1973. Johny also recorded top-twenty finishes himself at the Tour, Paris–Roubaix, Tour of Lombardy and Liège–Bastogne–Liège before retiring from the professional ranks after the 1974 season.

Eleven years later Andy was born, the youngest of three brothers. Fränk, five years older than Andy, would also become a professional cyclist. The careers of the two brothers were intertwined, with Andy riding on the same teams as his brother throughout his professional career.

Schleck signed full professional terms with the CSC team for the 2005 season after impressing team manager Bjarne Riis with his amateur performances and during a three-month period as a *stagiaire* towards the end of 2004.

Two years later and at just 21 years of age Schleck was fighting for victory at the Giro. Despite his tender age he had already developed into a talented climber and during the final week rose into second place overall behind eventual winner Danilo Di Luca after finishing third on the tough stage to the top of the infamous Monte Zoncolan. Schleck held his second position until the race finished in Milan, losing by 1min 55sec to the Italian but claiming the white jersey of best young rider. Di Luca would later return a series of positive doping controls and eventually be banned for life, publishing a book in 2016 that claimed he had first doped in 2001, writing: 'I've no regrets at all. I lied. I cheated; I did what had to do to finish first.'[9] In 2019, in an interview with *Sporza*, Schleck reflected on doping in the sport and losing the 2007 Giro to Di Luca:

We take people who get caught doping, 99% of them stand there and say it was the system, it's not my fault, it was the pressure. That's all excuses, they all stand there in that position like they are a victim but they're not you know. You have to see it from different perspectives. I can say today I didn't win the Giro because Danilo Di Luca was doping which is true in one way. But you know I don't even go there, I haven't said that before, you're hearing me say that now for the first time.[10]

Schleck's first major win arrived in 2009 when he claimed Liège–Bastogne–Liège, escaping on the newly introduced Côte de la Roche-aux-Faucons some 19km from the finish, and staying away over the Côte de Saint-Nicolas to record a win of more than one minute. 'I think there is nothing impossible at this point,' he said afterwards. 'I will try next year for Amstel [Gold Race]. I even think I could go for a race like the Tour of Flanders. Why not?'[11]

While Schleck would never land on the podium at either of those races – his 2009 win in Liège would remain his only major one-day success – it was at the Tour where he was most dangerous, battling Alberto Contador alongside his brother. After debuting at the race in 2008, finishing eleventh overall while claiming the first of an eventual three young riders' classifications, he came second in 2009, 4min 11sec behind Contador. One year later the two riders went to battle again in one of the most enthralling races of the modern era.

Early in that 2010 Tour Schleck took his first stage win, prevailing from a small bunch of climbers that had formed on the climb up to Morzine-Avoriaz. The following day he wore yellow for the first time after finishing in the lead group on a stage that featured climbs of the Aravis, Saisies and Madeleine. He had a lead of forty-one seconds over Contador and held the jersey for six days. Then came 'chaingate'.

On the Port de Balès, Schleck went to attack Contador when his chain dropped. As Schleck stopped to deal with the mechanical issue, Contador launched a counter-move that many held to be against the unwritten rules of the sport. The Spaniard, who later issued a public apology via social media, gained thirty-nine seconds and assumed the race lead. Schleck was furious at his misfortune. 'Now I'm really angry,' he said. 'I will ride on the Tourmalet until I fall from my bike and give everything to this race.'[12]

True to his word Schleck rode magnificently three days later on the stage to the summit of the Tourmalet, duelling with Contador all the way up the famous climb and claiming the stage. Contador had stayed with the

Luxembourger the entire way and so maintained his lead. In Paris Contador's win over Schleck amounted to just thirty-nine seconds, the same margin as he had taken on the stage when Schleck's chain slipped. Schleck reflected in 2019:

> When I was standing on the podium in Paris in 2010 it was probably the podium where I was [most] sad because it was there for me, it was my Tour. I saw that year that I was a little bit above Alberto, it was really the only Tour where we competed for victory where I would say I was stronger than him … I went home thinking this was my Tour, I should have won it.[13]

Two years later the 2010 Tour was awarded to Schleck when the Court of Arbitration for Sport (CAS) imposed a two-year retrospective ban on Contador after a positive test for Clenbuterol backdated to July 2010 (see Contador entry for more). 'It's hard for me to decide if Contador is wrong or if he lied or what the story is,' Schleck said in 2012. 'For me that Tour is forgotten. Maybe it's in the books, but for me it's not a victory. Standing in yellow in Paris is how I would like it.'[14]

Schleck made the Tour podium again in 2011, finishing second behind Cadel Evans, while claiming a memorable stage win on the Galibier. Schleck had attacked on the Izoard, with some 60km of the stage remaining and recorded a 2min 7sec win over his brother at the summit of Desgrange's favourite mountain, 100 years after the founder of the Tour had introduced the climb.

Three years later, suffering with a knee injury, Schleck was forced to retire. He was just 29 years old. 'At the beginning I was just happy to be a pro cyclist,' he said in 2019. 'Being young and being successful can also be very dangerous, sometimes I had the feeling that I jumped some steps in my life, not just my career, in my life.'[15] Today Schleck runs a cycle shop in Luxembourg and works at races as a brand ambassador for Skoda.

MAJOR WINS
Tour de France: 2010
Liège–Bastogne–Liège: 2009
National Champion: 2009

Scieur, Léon

BEL

BORN: 19 MARCH 1888, FLORENNES, BELGIUM

At 7 p.m. on Sunday, 24 July 1921, Léon Scieur was in Paris getting ready to go for dinner with his family. Earlier that day the 33-year-old Belgian had won the Tour, riding into the Parc des Princes with a margin of 18min 36sec over his compatriot and fellow La Sportive sponsored rider, Hector Heusghem, despite being on few observers' pre-Tour list of favourites.

Scieur's family had travelled from Florennes, a small town in the region of Wallonia, to watch his triumphant appearance in yellow. And it had been quite an entrance. Thousands had poured into the famous velodrome to see the twenty-five riders who had made it to the end of the race arrive. Scieur had been photographed, goggles perched on his white cap, surrounded by men in hats all wanting to get a piece of the latest Tour champion. Now, a few hours later, he was happy to be alone at last, ready to spend some time celebrating with his family over a good meal. Then there was a knock at the door.

Standing there was the cycling writer known to readers by his pseudonym Roule-Lacaisse. A reporter for the journal *Le Miroir des Sports*, Roule-Lacaisse wanted Scieur's reflections on the race. The newly crowned Tour champion agreed that he had time before his dinner appointment: 'As I have an hour free, I will try to tell you my modest story,' he said.[16]

Scieur hadn't started riding until he was 22 years old. His family didn't have the money to buy him a bicycle when he was a child and so it wasn't until he was able to save enough from his wages, first as a worker in a glass factory and later as an agricultural worker, that he was able to buy himself a bike and take the first pedal strokes on the road that would lead him to Tour victory.

Encouraged by fellow Florennes resident and professional cyclist Firmin Lambot, who would himself win the Tour twice during his career (see Lambot entry for more), Scieur started his racing career by entering small events in and around his hometown. In 1912 he entered the amateur Tour of Belgium and finished third on the fourth stage before receiving news of his father's death. He abandoned the race and returned home to his distraught family.

Twelve months later and Scieur turned professional. He was 25 years old and signed for Armor, riding alongside Heusghem and the talented but rarely victorious Ernest Paul. He rode his first Tour that year, abandoning on the seventh stage. 'My professional debut was difficult,' he said in 1921. 'I ran into the big pre-war "Aces" ... Victory did not smile on me often.'[17]

Described by Jacque Sys in his book of the top 1000 Belgian riders as 'a powerful rider with great perseverance',[18] Scieur improved in 1914, finishing fourteenth at the Tour and fourth at Belgium's national championship, no mean feat as he placed just behind Louis Mottiat who had won the Tour of Belgium earlier in the year and would go on to win the prestigious Paris–Brussels.

Scieur's own first major win came after the First World War when he won Liège-Bastogne-Liège in 1920, beating future Tour winner Lucien Buysse by three lengths in the final sprint. One month later he claimed his first Tour stage, winning from a four-rider break that formed during the 362km race from Grenoble to Gex, over the Galibier and Aravis climbs, in just over 15hours 30min.

After finishing fourth in Paris, Scieur devoted himself to preparing for the 1921 Tour. Rising at 5.30 a.m., and after eating a breakfast prepared specially by his wife, Scieur rode for 125km every morning through the Belgian Ardennes before returning home for lunch. Afternoons were spent resting – 'like the rich'[19] – to get ready for the next day. It was a programme designed to make sure he reached July primed for action. Early in the season he took things easy, raced sparingly and conservatively, careful not to push himself too much, saving himself for the Tour. 'The Tour de France is, believe it, a work of the devil,' he said after his win. 'If we start this race being already tired by the efforts made in the events at the beginning of the season, [then] there is no level of courage nor will that will hold.'[20]

On the eve of the race Henri Desgrange promised the readers of L'Auto a 'resounding Franco-Belgian duel'.[21] Nothing could have been further from the truth as Belgian riders dominated the race, claiming nine of the fifteen stages and placing seven riders in the top ten overall. Scieur claimed the yellow jersey after the second day, lifting it from his compatriot Louis Mottiat, who had won the opening stage into Le Havre, and keeping it all the way to Paris. Not that Scieur had a particularly easy time of it. On the 333km stage from Nice to Grenoble he punctured and was immediately attacked by Heusghem who gained a five-minute advantage over Scieur on the Allos. Scieur was furious his compatriot had taken advantage of his misfortune and set off in hot pursuit, catching all who had passed him, reportedly giving

Heusghem a lecture on sporting morals as he went by, and winning the stage by more than six minutes.

Then, on the penultimate stage, 433km from Metz to Dunkirk, Scieur broke eleven spokes and was forced to find a replacement wheel. The problem Scieur had was that the race regulations stated he could only replace the wheel if the existing one was confirmed by officials to be beyond repair. With no officials available nearby to verify the wheel's condition, Scieur did the only thing he could: he strapped the broken wheel to his back and carried on for the remaining 300km. The scars on his back where the wheel had dug into his skin remained visible for years to come. 'You have to admit that Scieur, like the previous winners of the Tour, put the odds on his side, never panicking, finding the most logical solution,' reported *L'Auto*. 'But he was pretty lucky too.'[22] Two days later Scieur entered Paris as the winner of the Tour. As he dressed for dinner that evening, Scieur told Roule-Lacaisse:

> I won, because I climbed the passes ... Because the sun has not got the better of me; because in certain stages, I pushed with all my strength to distance my opponents; because I have been well cared for every step ... I won the Tour de France because when you have the happiness, at the beginning of the race, to see fortune coming to you smiling and saying: 'If you are brave, I am yours!' It gives you tremendous morale.[23]

Scieur rode the Tour another three times, never winning a stage nor reaching Paris. During the 1923 race a spectator handed him a drink laced with arsenic. The poisoning forced him from the race and hospitalised him for two months. He never truly recovered.

After retiring Scieur ran a garage, repairing bicycles and cars. He died in 1969 at the age of 81, the perseverance of the rider they called 'The Locomotive' finally at an end.

MAJOR WINS
Tour de France: 1921
Liège-Bastogne-Liège: 1920

Speicher, Georges

FRA

BORN: 8 JUNE 1907, PARIS, FRANCE

'I knew fear only from the moment I wore the yellow jersey,'[24] Georges Speicher said during the 1933 Tour. Speicher meant that once he'd experienced the pride of slipping cycling's most-sought prize over his neck, the fear of then losing it became all encompassing. Luckily for him, despite his fears, Speicher never had to experience that feeling of loss.

Speicher had entered the 1933 Tour as a member of the united and all-powerful France national team. It was a squad that hadn't been defeated at the Tour since national teams had been introduced in 1930 and that had forged a reputation for togetherness despite racing on different trade teams the rest of the year. 'It is a team of friends,' wrote Albert Baker d'Isy, 'even if these friends are not always exactly the same from one year to another and even if some lively words are sometimes exchanged, behind the closed door of a hotel room. Between them, everything becomes simple on the road.'[25]

Alongside Speicher for the 1933 race were the likes of André Leducq, Antonin Magne and Roger Lapébie, each one a former or a future Tour winner. Leducq, who was later credited as discovering the talented Speicher, telling him that: 'Georges, you will one day win the Tour de France: you have to win,'[26] such was his ability, entered the race as the defending champion but would only manage thirty-first in Paris. Such was the strength in the team that Speicher later reflected: 'Truly, between us we had no idea which of us would win.'[27]

L'Auto actually tipped Italy's Learco Guerra for the top spot in Paris before the race, but Speicher would beat him by 4min 1sec. The Frenchman seized the initiative in the midpoint of the race, winning three stages in the space of six days thanks to some terrific descending in the Alps, taking the yellow jersey from his teammate and roommate Maurice Archambaud in Marseilles. Speicher, along with Magne and Lapébie, had followed a move that had been launched by a couple of *indépendant* riders some 100km from the finish and then continued their move when the two protagonists had fallen away. Archambaud had missed the attack because of a puncture and his supporters accused Speicher and co. of treason against the now former yellow jersey. 'I had followed Level and Bernard [the two *indépendants*] to stop them,' said a defensive Speicher. 'I wasn't thinking about the yellow jersey at all, only the stage win. I could not have foreseen that Maurice would puncture.' In their room that night Archambaud told Speicher all was fine. 'My dear Georges, I am glad it was you who took the [jersey],' Archambaud said. 'It is, in short, as if I still had it. I told you so the other day: you are the strongest and it is you who will win the Tour de France.'[28]

Thanks to some fine defensive riding in the Pyrenees and the support of his teammates, Speicher held off the assaults of the Italians as the race headed north towards Paris. The last five stages descended into monotony as no one had any strength left to seriously challenge the leader. Speicher said during the final week:

> In the early stages, riders who are fresh can afford such an effort: we see them emerging from behind and sprinting wildly for some time, hundreds of metres. Now, all my rivals, Guerra and Martano and the others, do not have the necessary strength to get away. Some tried but they took a painful fifty metres and, after a few minutes, completely exhausted, they sat up.[29]

In the Parc des Princes Speicher collapsed onto the concrete track as 50,000 fans chanted his name. 'I could not believe, even in my wildest dreams, a victory in my second Tour de France. I also owe this Tour to my teammates: Leducq, Antonin Magne, Archambaud, Lapébie, Le Calvez and Le Grevès, who were real brothers to me,'[30] Speicher told L'Auto, which had enjoyed a record circulation of 854,000 during the race.

Born and raised in Pantin, in the north-east of Paris, Speicher's first sport had been swimming, with the nearby Canal de l'Ourcq a favoured training spot. He later credited his powerful shoulders to his love of the water.[31] Speicher first rode a bike after taking a job with a local garage. He said:

> I was 17 years old and I needed work. Through the classifieds I saw an advert for a bicycle courier to make deliveries. One problem: I did not know how to ride a bike! Since I needed to make a living, I nevertheless introduced myself. The first few days I followed the pavements as closely as possible, pedalling with my left leg, and balancing with my right on the asphalt![32]

Described variously as a 'dilettante character ... a regular at nightclubs'[33] and a 'dandy who knew how to hurt himself ... very much appreciated by the ladies',[34] Speicher progressed from wobbling around the streets of Paris on a unfamiliar bicycle laden with parcels, to an impressive amateur racer with the Vélo Club de Levallois. In 1931, after serving his military service, he rode as an *indépendant*, within the Thomann team, winning the Criterium des Aiglons and then passing into the pro ranks the following year. He rode the Tour for the first time in that debut professional season, finishing an impressive tenth as Leducq won his second Tour.

Three weeks after Speicher's 1933 Tour win, France hosted the world championship road race for the first time. Held on a racing circuit in Montlhéry (the decision to use a closed circuit was in part motivated by the need to cover the costs of hosting the event, making it easier to charge an entrance fee), France selected a strong team that included both Lapébie and Magne. But one name was missing – Speicher.

Speicher had been busy enjoying himself since his Tour, out celebrating. But when Paul Chocque, a rider some had fancied as France's best chance for victory, fell ill and had to pull out, the call went out for Speicher. He was eventually found, some sources say in a nightclub, others in an old cinema, and told to hurry to Montlhéry to take his place on the start line of a professional world championship race for the first time.

His may have been an ill-prepared introduction, but Speicher imposed himself on to the world championships in spectacular fashion. Somehow, he had retained his form and after being hastily thrust back into action, he would make history as he delivered France's first rainbow jersey.

Speicher ruled a race hit by storms right from the start. After staying at the head of the race from the opening lap he escaped alone with 125km still to ride, pulling out a huge lead. Pierre Chany described Speicher as riding with a sort of aura, without weakness, handling his bike with 'extraordinary dexterity'.[35] After a huge solo effort, Speicher crossed the line more than five minutes ahead of compatriot Magne. France had its first world champion, delivered on home roads with panache by a very popular rider. It was the first time a rider had achieved the Tour/Worlds double, a feat that would not be matched for more than twenty years.

'A champion can win everything,' ran one headline in *Paris-Soir* in the days that followed the race. 'And Speicher is one.'[36] Two years later he returned to the same circuit to record the first of an eventual three national titles – a record haul at the time that he shared with Octave Lapize and Francis Pélissier and not broken until Jean Stablinski claimed four wins during the 1960s.

In 1936 Speicher was controversially credited as the winner of Paris-Roubaix despite it appearing to everyone at the finish (bar the judges on the line) that Belgium's Romain Maes had crossed the line ahead of the Frenchman. The result prompted a huge scandal, both in Belgium and in France. The next day *L'Auto* printed a front-page picture of the pair crossing the line under the headline: 'After seven years of Belgian victories Georges Speicher triumphs for France by taking the 37th Paris-Roubaix.' Yet the photograph appeared to clearly show Maes' wheel crossing the line first. In a piece entitled *The Incident at the Finish*, *L'Auto* reported:

> We interviewed the finish-line judge who told us: 'Speicher just won, but he won. Certainly, if there had been a few more metres, Romain was winning. But before my eyes, it was Speicher. Besides, there were five of us in the judge's cabin, ask these gentlemen, and you'll see what they tell you ... Romain Maes will appeal,' said the judge, invoking the photographic testimony. [But] It doesn't prove anything. It's a question of optics, and it all depends on how the photo was taken ... I have my own conscience and I'm sure Speicher has won.[37]

Speicher rode until 1943. In 1948 he was the national team coach for the 1948 Olympic Games, held in London, once more tasting success as José Beyaert took gold for France. Beyaert later reflected that Speicher had merely told him afterwards he'd done a great thing, adding that he liked people with that approach, 'not blathering on all the time'.[38]

Speicher died in 1978, aged 70.

MAJOR WINS
Tour de France: 1933
Paris-Roubaix: 1936
World Champion: 1933
National Champion: 1935, 1937, 1939

Thévenet, Bernard

FRA

BORN: 10 JANUARY 1948, SAINT-JULIEN-DE-CIVRY, FRANCE

On 13 July 1975 the Tour headed into the Alps for the start of its final week shakedown. It was a Sunday and thousands of fans were spending their day off lining the 217km route from Nice, over the Saint-Martin, Couillole, Champs and Allos, to the summit of Pra-Loup. Millions more sat at home or in bars, eyes locked on the pictures being broadcast live from the Tour. Those pictures were very familiar: Eddy Merckx in yellow and leading the stage.

Merckx had attacked on the Allos and by the time he had reached the bottom of the climb to Pra-Loup he had a lead of over one minute. Chasing behind was the 1965 Tour winner, Felice Gimondi, who was lying fifth overall. Gimondi was chasing alone while further back was a group of three very strong riders: Lucien Van Impe, Joop Zoetemelk and France's Bernard Thévenet.

Thévenet was riding his sixth Tour and was in second overall, only fifty-eight seconds behind Merckx. Two days earlier, as they had started the stage to Puy de Dôme, Merckx's advantage had been 1min 32sec over the Frenchman. During the course of that stage the race's strongest riders – Merckx, Thévenet, Van Impe and Zoetemelk – had remained together, but with a little more than 5km to go, Thévenet and Van Impe had made a move.

For once Merckx couldn't answer the attack, and Zoetemelk was either unwilling or unable to respond as well. Thévenet and Van Impe quickly built a lead with Van Impe eventually going on to win the stage by fifteen seconds over Thévenet.

Further down the climb Merckx had finally managed to put some distance between himself and Zoetemelk and was approaching the line when there was an extraordinary turn of events. With just over 100m to go Merckx was struck twice by spectators. First a woman in a blue coat and white hat leaned over the barriers and slapped him. Then a man in a brown overcoat punched Merckx in his side. Both were apparent expressions of frustration at Merckx's continued dominance of the race who immediately grabbed his side in pain. As Zoetemelk came back, the badly winded Belgian was in agony. The two men crossed the line together, forty-nine seconds behind Van Impe. Merckx changed quickly and then accompanied the police back down the road to find the assailant who was being held by spectators. Charges were filed and the man – a 55-year-old called Nello Breton – was later ordered to pay symbolic damages of a single franc.[1]

Forty-eight hours later on the road to Pra-Loup, Merckx was still hurting. He was bluffing that all was fine by making that signature attack on the Allos and striking out alone but even Merckx was human sometimes. After seven hours of racing his efforts were taking their toll. The pain was becoming too much to bear as the stage was reaching its climax.

Behind Merckx, Thévenet was doing all the work in the chasing group of three, rocking from side to side, head nodding like a pull-along toy dog. He looked behind, slowly reached down and changed gear. He grabbed a bottle from a spectator, took a swig and threw it to the ground before exchanging some words with his sports director, Maurice de Muer, who had pulled up in the Peugeot team car. Then Thévenet pushed harder on the pedals.

Van Impe had no answer to the move and was dropped immediately. Zoetemelk struggled back to the Frenchman before finally yielding to

Thévenet's pace. Soon, France's great hope for a first Tour win since 1967 was alone. Gimondi and Merckx were still up the road but they were now firmly in his sights.

The motorcycle carrying the TV camera operator who had been filming Thévenet's attack then zoomed up the road, keen to find out how far the Frenchman had to go before catching Gimondi. But to everyone's amazement when the next rider came into view it wasn't the Italian they saw. *'Non, non, c'est Merckx!'* came the incredulous shout from the French commentary booth. The Cannibal had finally cracked.

Thévenet, now flying, passed the Belgian and then overtook Gimondi, taking both the stage win and the yellow jersey. His lead over Merckx, who would never again wear the yellow jersey, stood at fifty-eight seconds.

But Thévenet wasn't done. The next day he stormed the Izoard, scaling the legendary climb all alone and with a lead of more than two minutes, knowing that it was here that he could secure his Tour. It was Bastille Day and France was captivated. A fan at the side of the road held a sign aloft: 'Merckx is beaten – the Bastille has fallen!'[2] Louison Bobet, the three-time Tour champion, was jubilant: 'I never felt he could rise to this level,' he said. 'Hats off! It is on the Izoard, on the Casse Déserte more precisely, that the true worth of champions is measured. He will win this Tour.'[3]

It was the first year that the Tour would finish on the Champs-Élysées. Thévenet crossed the finish line on that famous avenue wearing the yellow jersey and with a lead over Merckx of 2min 47sec.

Born into a farming family, Thévenet's parents only discovered he had started racing when they saw the results of a local race in the paper. Preferring their son to spend his time helping on the farm rather than cycling, it took the intervention of the president of his club to soothe the family row that ensued. He turned professional in 1970 after a successful period riding as an amateur with the Paris club ACBB. An invitation from ACBB's head, Paul Weigant, was normally much prized by riders hoping to make it to the professional ranks, such was the pedigree of their former riders, but Thévenet wasn't sure. Thévenet reflected in 2018:

> I had been told that he was killing his riders, that he was asking too much of them. I was doing my military service at the Joinville Battalion at Fontainebleau. Paul Gardet, from CSM Puteaux, ACBB's big rival, came to see me before Weigant. I was looking for a club in Paris during the year of my military service. He told me 'we'll meet again'.[4]

But then Weigant went to see the future Tour champion at home and spent the afternoon talking to him. Thévenet was finally convinced and signed that evening.

It was to prove a decision that would shape his career. 'He was tough, he was authoritative,' Thévenet said of Weigant. 'He also wanted to make his riders men, gentlemen. In everyday life, one had to be polite, correct, that was his philosophy ... deep down, he loved his riders, and he fought to defend us.'[5]

The call to turn professional had come as early as September 1968 but Weigant convinced his 21-year-old charge that it was too soon and that he should spend another year as an amateur. Thévenet agreed to wait, winning a stage of the Tour de l'Avenir in his final amateur season before then joining Peugeot, the team with which he would spend all but two of his twelve-year professional career. Stage success at the Tour came in his debut season. Called into the Peugeot team at short notice because two riders slated to ride had fallen ill – team manager Gaston Plaud had to reportedly phone Thévenet's mother to ask her to track down her son and pass on the message that he was needed quickly – the 22 year old rewarded his team's faith with a fine stage win at La Mongie, escaping from a small leading group on the Tourmalet. More stage wins at the Tour, including on Mont Ventoux in 1972, a national championship title in 1973, and overall victories at the Tour de Romandie and Volta Ciclista a Catalunya, all came his way before his 1975 Tour success.

Thévenet followed that 1975 Tour win with another in 1977 after turning himself inside out on l'Alpe d'Huez to defend his yellow jersey. Van Impe, just thirty-three seconds behind overall, had attacked on the Glandon and ridden onto the lower slopes of the Alpe alone with a two-minute advantage over Thévenet. The Frenchman meanwhile had more than Van Impe to worry about as he was being followed by Hennie Kuiper, himself only forty-nine seconds down.

With 5km to go, and with Van Impe looking imperious and destined to take the jersey, Thévenet was on the limit. Then Kuiper launched a stinging attack to which the Frenchman could not respond. But Thévenet was not a man to throw in the towel and he ploughed on, riding himself ragged in defence of his lead.

As Kuiper powered up the road in search Van Impe, so the Belgian began to suffer, starting to pay for his efforts on the Glandon. Then, disaster. Van Impe was knocked from his bike by a race car. Furious, he remounted and tried to carry on but his rear wheel was buckled. As he raised his hand to call for the team car so Kuiper rode by on his way to the stage win. Now all eyes turned to Thévenet, could he limit his losses to Kuiper enough to retain the jersey?

Incredibly, after looking out for the count, the dogged Peugeot leader dragged himself up one of the Tour's most famous climbs to finish second on the stage, just forty-one seconds behind Kuiper. In one of the most astonishing defences of the yellow jersey that the Tour had seen for years, Thévenet had saved his overall lead by eight seconds. A time-trial win three days later helped boost his lead and six days after his l'Alpe d'Huez heroics, Thévenet stood on top of the Paris podium for the second time. His winning margin was forty-eight seconds.

Thévenet retired in 1981. He later worked as a team manager, journalist and television commentator. In July 2001 he was made a Chevalier de la Légion d'Honneur.

MAJOR WINS
Tour de France: 1975, 1977
National Champion: 1973

Thomas, Geraint

GBR

BORN: 25 MAY 1986, CARDIFF, WALES

When Geraint Thomas was about to win the 2018 Tour the British media went into overdrive. Here was a well-liked and charismatic rider, someone who could always be relied on to provide a good quote or two, a multi-medalled cyclist who lived for more than just the bike, who, perhaps to the surprise of some, was about to claim the world's greatest bike race. As Thomas bore down on Paris, so mainstream media outlets scrambled to get his backstory, eager to find the road this unassuming rider from Wales had ridden to arrive at the very top of his sport.

Their search led them to Cardiff, in particular to the Maindy Flyers Youth Cycling Club and a woman called Debbie Wharton. Wharton had founded the club in 1995 and now, some twenty-three years later, happily opened her photograph album to tell journalists the story of the new Tour champion. Wharton recalled a 9-year-old boy with 'skinny legs'[6] who, after watching a coaching session on his way back from the nearby swimming pool, nervously approached her and asked if he could have a go on the track. The club was not yet a year old but Wharton found a spare bike that was about the right size. Thomas had taken his first pedal strokes on a journey that would ultimately lead to the top step of the podium in Paris.

Soon images started to flash around the world of a young Thomas riding bikes. Two of the photographs stood out. One showed Thomas on the start line of a race, proudly wearing his Maindy Flyers jersey and a red helmet, gloved hands resting on the hoods, a yellow water bottle safely resting in a cage fitted to his red bike. While those around him look around or rest their elbows on their handlebars, Thomas is a picture of readiness. He is looking directly into the camera with steely eyes, a veritable study of calm determination.[7] Another photograph showed a similarly aged Thomas crossing the finish line of a road race. He is wearing the same red helmet but his time one of those gloved hands is clenched into a celebratory fist. On his back is a yellow jersey. Celebrating while wearing yellow – it would be a feeling that would return decades later. 'He was just a normal 10-year-old riding a bike at first,' Wharton said. 'But as he progressed, he started to win and was picking up titles. It was when he won the gold medal at the under-16 level nationals, aged only 14, that we realised he had something special.'[8]

Thomas' performances as a junior included winning a rainbow jersey in the scratch race at the 2004 World Junior Track Championships in California and a win at the 2004 junior Paris–Roubaix. Success on both the track and the road – again a feeling that would return at the elite level. In 2005 he joined the British Cycling Academy. It was there that he honed his craft, realising what it took to be a professional, later reflecting that he learned 'not just about racing but also how to look after yourself'.[9]

One of the lessons dished out to the developing Thomas was particularly memorable for the Welshman. While living at the academy in Manchester, Thomas went out to watch the 2005 champions' league final and to celebrate his 19th birthday. The night became longer and more drink-fuelled than had been first planned and when Rod Ellingworth, then head of the academy, found out he was not happy. As punishment Thomas was stopped from entering the Five Valleys in South Wales, an event raced on his home roads and one he was desperate to ride. It was a lesson that has remained with the Welshman despite all he achieved since. 'I was absolutely gutted. It really hurt,' Thomas reflected in 2015. 'Not only were we not allowed to race, but we were sent off training with Bradley Wiggins and Steve Cummings instead. That was our punishment: six hours in the Peaks with those two.'[10]

While Thomas spent two spells as a *stagiaire* with the road teams Wiesenhof and Saunier-Duval in 2005 and 2006 respectively, and first rode the Tour in 2007 while with Barloworld, it was on the track that he first made his mark. Between 2007 and 2012, Thomas claimed two Olympic gold medals and three world championship titles on the boards as an integral member of Great Britain's imperious team pursuit squad.

Thomas signed for the newly formed Team Sky in 2010. A road national title came later in the year, and after the London 2012 Olympic Games he switched his focus fully to the road. In 2013 he helped Chris Froome win his first Tour, completing the race despite breaking his pelvis during the opening day. 'The next day was the worst day I've ever had on the bike. Just pain,' Thomas later said. 'But the guys in the hospital said it definitely wasn't going to get worse from riding; it was just whether I could put up with the pain. That was encouraging. I definitely didn't want to stop.' Froome later described Thomas' ride as 'the story of the Tour', while Dave Brailsford, Team Sky's principal, said that Thomas could 'go so deep that you need to hold him back a bit'.[11] Soon there would be no holding him back with wins at the Commonwealth Games, Volta ao Algarve, E3 Prijs Harelbeke and Paris–Nice all arriving before the 2017 season.

As well as his balanced persona – 'Obviously, I really want to win but at the same time, it's just a bike race,' Thomas told *Cyclist* in 2015, 'It's not the be-all and end-all. It's not like we're going to Afghanistan or something … We're just really privileged to be in the position we're in,' – one constant in Thomas' career has been his propensity to fall off his bike. Entering the 2017 Giro as one of Sky's protected riders, he was placed second when a collision between riders and a parked motorcycle brought him down and forced him to abandon a few days later. At the Tour he wore yellow after the first day, winning the opening time trial in Düsseldorf, to become the first Welshman to wear the jersey. Yet another crash, again in the second week, forced him out of the race with a broken collarbone. 'I crashed at the Giro on stage nine, and it's stage nine again here. I was lying second overall on both days as well. It's just so disappointing,' Thomas said.[12]

Twelve months on and his disappointment turned to joy. Thomas won the Dauphiné Libéré earlier in the season and quickly rose up through the overall standings at the Tour. Despite Thomas soon enjoying a margin of more than a minute over Chris Froome, who was going for his fourth Grand Tour in a row, it was Froome who initially remained Team Sky's number one rider. It was a point reinforced to Thomas after a particularly warm day early in the second week.

'It was really hot in the hotel but when they put the air-con units on for all eight riders the electricity tripped,' Thomas recounted to Donald McRae in October 2018. 'So they said: "Only one person can have it – Froomey."' It was a sign of where the team's priorities lay. Thomas ignored the warning and switched the unit in his room back on. 'We were fortunate it didn't trip out,' he admitted.[13]

Thomas won back-to-back stages in the Alps, taking yellow by winning the stage to La Rosière and then becoming the first rider wearing yellow to win on l'Alpe d'Huez.[14] The Welshman's winning margin in Paris was 1min 51sec over Tom Dumoulin. Froome finished third. 'The biggest thing with Froomey was that it was never awkward,' Thomas told McRae. 'He would have been gutted because he wanted to win a fifth Tour and three Grand Tours on the trot [sic]. But when he congratulated me, he seemed genuine, and since the Tour we've had a couple of nights out.'[15] His win earned him an OBE and the BBC's *Sports Personality of the Year* award.

After a slow start to his 2019 season, he returned to the Tour focused on a second win. In the end he fell just short, landing on the podium behind his young teammate Egan Bernal (see Bernal entry for more). 'I can be proud and satisfied I've done everything I could to try and be in the best shape,' Thomas said after the race. 'There were a lot of doubters. It's always nice to show what I can do and back it up. If someone else had won, it would be really disappointing, but Egan's won and it's amazing.'[16]

> ## MAJOR WINS
> Tour de France: 2018
> National Champion: 2010

Thys, Philippe

BEL

BORN: 8 OCTOBER 1890, ANDERLECHT, BELGIUM

Nicknamed the 'Basset Hound' because of his short legs and consequent low riding position, Belgium's Philippe Thys, whose career was interrupted by the First World War, became the first rider to record three Tour wins when he claimed the 1920 edition by 57min 21sec over compatriot Hector Heusghem. 'His achievement can hardly come as a shock,' reported L'Auto, 'But for the war this citizen of Anderlecht might have been celebrating his fifth or sixth [Tour victory]. Indeed, it is clear that since Garrigou, cycling has not known so courageous and complete a rider as Thys.'[17]

L'Auto hadn't always been so enthusiastic in its praise for Thys. In fact, in many ways his 1920 win could be seen as a reaction against a personal attack that Henri Desgrange had launched on him within the pages of the sports paper the previous year. Disappointed with the condition in which the then two-time champion had returned to the Tour in 1919, the first held since 1914, Desgrange accused Thys of being decadent, calling him 'un petit bourgeois who had lost his love of the bike.'[18] The Belgian, who had served in the air force during the war, training when he could and racing when on leave – he won the Tour of Lombardy in 1917 by beating Henri Pélissier in a hotly contested sprint that involved jersey-pulling and punch-throwing – had abandoned the 1919 Tour, an act that had prompted Desgrange's missive. Thys was angered by the race-founder's words and set about training for 1920 with renewed vigour, even shaving off his moustache in a bid to reduce wind resistance.

Fourth places at the national championships and Paris–Brussels in the fortnight running up to the 1920 Tour perhaps led some to question whether Thys was really back at his best. While Desgrange still had the Belgian listed as one of six men who could win the race, he ranked France's Eugène Christophe, the man who had so nearly won the 1919 edition, as the main favourite, writing that the Frenchman had 'the necessary morale to overcome all the difficulties of a Tour de France'.[19] As it turned out an injured Christophe would abandon the race in the Pyrenees.

For Thys, however, the Tour was a very different story. He shared the race lead from the end of the second stage and then took over sole custody of the top spot after the stage to Luchon. In all he won four stages and rode a well-managed race, taking time at crucial moments and monitoring his rivals at others. His director at La Sportive – a post war collaboration of bike manufacturers that sponsored many professional riders while the trade rebuilt after the war – was Alphonse Baugé. Baugé had managed Thys at Peugeot and knew how to get the best from his rider. He also knew that an on-form Thys was a very difficult rider to beat over what was nearly a month of racing. And so it proved. Despite a multitude of mechanical issues, Thys rolled into Paris with that huge winning margin. 'My good friend Baugé had told me for so long that I could not be beaten in the Tour de France, that I left with the very clear conviction that it was ready for my taking,' Thys said. 'It was [Baugé] who put me back on my feet. It is to him that I owe this third Tour de France ...'[20]

Le Miroir des Sports, which printed a full-page portrait photograph of a smiling Thys on its front page a few days later, regarded the Belgian's third Tour win as confirmation of his status as the definition of the ultimate cyclist:

Adroit, [a] good mechanic, never leaving anything to chance, he is, moreover, very fast and a good climber ... He has his legs, he has his head: he is the complete man in every sense of the word ... Correct, cheerful, always kind, he knows only friends. He is a champion who honours cycling.[21]

Thys first entered the professional ranks in 1912, signing for Peugeot, riding his first Tour and finishing sixth. He immediately felt comfortable at the race, so much so that when Baugé, newly arrived as the head of Peugeot the following year, asked him in front of his teammates what role he would like at the 1913 Tour, Thys told him that he would win it. While that answer prompted much hilarity among his more experienced teammates, Thys proved good to his word. He took the race lead for the first time in the Pyrenees after winning a monstrous stage from Bayonne to Luchon which passed into Tour legend when Christophe, who had been Peugeot's best-placed rider, was forced to walk down the Tourmalet with his broken bike on his back to find a forge. Christophe arrived in Luchon 3hr 50min behind Thys that day and was then slapped with a further penalty of three minutes because a boy had operated the bellows for him at the forge – such 'assistance' being against the rules.

Thys lost the lead to his teammate Marcel Buysse for two days but grabbed it back definitively after the stage to Nice during which Buysse crashed, broke his handlebars and lost two hours. Thys retained his lead through the Alps and when Lucien Petit-Breton, Thys' nearest rival, abandoned on the penultimate stage to Dunkirk, a day when Thys himself lost some fifty-four minutes to stage-winner Buysse, the way was left relatively clear. Thys finally registered an overall win of 8min 37sec in Paris, a result somewhat clouded by the misfortune of three of his rivals.

While official Tour history records the first official yellow jersey as not being awarded until 1919 (see Lambot entry for more) in the book, *La Fabuleuse Histoire du Tour de France*, Pierre Chany writes that Thys made claims that he had worn a yellow jersey during his 1913 win. In a 1953 interview with the Belgian review *Champions et Vedettes*, Thys said: 'I was the leader of the general classification. One night, Desgrange dreamed of a golden-coloured jersey and proposed I wear it. I refused. I already felt the focal point of everything. He insisted yet I remained steadfast. But he was stubborn, more than me, and kept coming back.' Thys said that a few stages later Baugé persuaded him that it would be good publicity for the Peugeot brand and so they bought a yellow top in the first shop they found that had one. 'It was just about the right size,' he said, but 'it was necessary to cut a larger hole for my head, and that was how I rode several stages in a top with a low and revealing neckline,' he continued. 'It did not stop me winning my first Tour.'[22]

The Belgian made it back-to-back wins the following year beating Henri Pélissier by 1min 50sec. A month earlier the Tour's 145-strong peloton had left

Paris under the dark cloak of night. A few hours later, as the riders continued on their way towards Le Havre, Austria's Archduke Franz Ferdinand was assassinated in Sarajevo. While Thys dominated the race, across Europe all hell was breaking loose.

On the penultimate stage Thys started with an advantage of over thirty-one minutes on Pélissier. During the stage Thys broke a fork and asked for help. He knew getting assistance would mean a time penalty but he was happy to take the consequences. Fewer than twenty minutes later he was back on the road, catching Pélissier and finishing alongside his rival. The Tour organisers slapped a thirty-minute penalty on him but Thys still had an advantage of nearly two minutes. On the final stage to Paris, Pélissier attacked and attacked but couldn't shake Thys, the Belgian holding on to win his second Tour. Two days later, Austria-Hungary declared war on Serbia. The Tour would not return for five years.

Thys rode professionally until 1927. Other notable wins included the 1921 Critérium des As – a race that was in its infancy but would eventually capture France's affections with eleven of the season's best riders receiving invitations to contest a paced circuit race of 100km around Longchamp, Paris. Thys won by half a wheel from his compatriot René Vermandel in a race watched by more than 50,000 roadside spectators.

On retirement Thys worked in a garage and bike shop before entering the world of tourism, bussing coaches full of cycling fans into the mountains to watch the new generation ride the same roads as he had tamed in years gone by. He died in 1971 at the age of 80.

> ## MAJOR WINS
> **Tour de France: 1913, 1914, 1920**
> **Tour of Lombardy: 1917**

Trousselier, Louis

FRA

BORN: 29 JUNE 1881, PARIS, FRANCE

In the early evening of Christmas Day 1900, ten riders took to an indoor track in Paris to compete in a 33km scratch race. It was the first of three similar races to be held in the space of six days on a temporary, 125m-long track, built within the Hippodrome in Montmartre. The *Grand Prix de Noël* was part of a week-long programme of celebrations and sporting entertainment running in France's capital city from 25 December into the new year.

Among the riders competing was a 19-year-old Louis Trousselier who earlier that month had announced his intention to leave the amateur ranks. Making his professional debut that Christmas evening in Paris, Trousselier rode strongly only to clip a pedal on one of the tight corners of the short track with only 4km left to ride. He fell and was forced to change his bike, losing precious time and costing him any chance of a top-three placing. It may not have been the dream start he would have wanted but Trousselier had taken his first pedal stokes as a professional cyclist.

Nicknamed 'Trou-Trou', or 'Le Fleuriste' because of his parents' flower shop, Trousselier came from a cycling family – his brothers Léopold and André also raced, Léopold getting top-ten placings in both Paris–Roubaix and Bordeaux–Paris in 1897 and André winning Liège–Bastogne–Liège in 1908 when it was a race for amateurs. It was Louis, however, who would grow into a true star, taking his first professional road wins in 1902.

The following year Trousselier placed an impressive second at Bordeaux–Paris only to be later disqualified having been found to have ridden in the draft of a car. While his second place was scratched from the records, 'a monstrous mistake'[23] according to his manager, worse was to come with the French Cycling Federation (UVF) handing Trousselier a lifetime ban. 'Let the other riders remember this hard lesson and remember in the future that race rules are made to be observed,' was *L'Auto*'s rather unsympathetic verdict. The UVF's decision meant that Trousselier wasn't able to start the inaugural Tour that started just two weeks after the ban was announced.

Fast-forward more than eighteen months and on 16 February 1905, *L'Auto* ran the following announcement:

Yesterday's mail brought us a sensational commitment to the great Easter test [Paris–Roubaix]. It concerns Louis Trousselier, the young champion, who was disqualified for life last year [sic] and who has just been granted his license back on the occasion of the UVF's silver anniversary. The presence of Trousselier alongside [René] Pottier, [Hippolyte] Aucouturier, [Edouard] Wattelier means it is a sure thing for us that Paris–Roubaix 1905 will be worthy of the races that have gone before.[24]

Thanks to this moment of clemency from the UVF to mark twenty-five years of its founding, Trousselier was back riding in cycling's biggest events. The only problem was he was also in the middle of his military service. Despite having to fit his racing around military commitments, Trousselier would in fact enjoy his most successful season, claiming both Paris–Roubaix and the Tour in the space of three glorious months.

Trousselier's win at Roubaix came ahead of Pottier and Henri Cornet. Cornet had attacked early and at one point had gained four minutes. Just after the race had reached Doullens, there were four leading the way, with Cornet and Pottier joined by Trousselier and the two-time defending champion, Aucouturier. It was Trousselier who would prove to be the strongest of that strong bunch. He finally took a grip on the race and led into Arras, going on to win by seven minutes. L'Auto reported:

A few weeks ago, Louis Trousselier could never have hoped to live the day he did yesterday. Strikingly banned by the France Velocipedic Union, he seemed dead forever to the sport of cycling. But the man is young and did not suffer from this inaction. He was confirmed yesterday a man of first order and exceptional quality for being able to get rid of riders as stubborn as Pottier and Cornet ...[25]

Two and a half months later Trousselier entered the Tour for the first time. After the debacle of the 1904 edition (see Cornet entry for more) Desgrange, who at one point had said he feared the second Tour would also be the last, a victim of its own success, instead opted to make some radical changes. He increased the race distance but added a further five stages, bringing the average stage distance down from 404km in 1904 to 272km. He also changed the basis of the general classification. Instead of elapsed time deciding the winner, points were awarded based on a convoluted calculation that combined stage finishing position and time gaps between riders. The stage winner accumulated one point, with each following rider then accumulating one point more than the rider preceding them. A further point was then accumulated for every five-minute gap between them and the rider before – though the total accumulated points difference was capped at eleven between riders no matter what the time differential. So, a rider finishing second, six minutes behind the stage winner (who accumulated one point) would themselves accumulate three points, calculated as the preceding rider's points tally (one point) plus one point for finishing one place behind (total: two points) plus a further one point for finishing more than five minutes behind the preceding rider (grand total: three points). A rider then finishing third, a further six minutes behind the second-placed rider would accumulate five points, calculated as the preceding rider's points tally (three points) plus one point (four points) plus a further one point because of the six-minute gap (total: five points). The rider with the fewest number of accumulated points after three weeks of racing was the winner. And to think all of that was designed to make judging easier.

Trou-Trou didn't take long to make his mark. He won the race-opening stage, 340km from Paris to Nancy and assumed the race lead. He briefly lost that lead to Pottier, the rider he had beaten at Roubaix in April, but regained it after winning stage three to Grenoble. From there Trousselier never looked back, holding the lead all the way to Paris. He had been due to return to his regiment during the race but opted to continue, believing a Tour win would pacify his superiors. The model of consistency, he never placed lower than fourth on any stage and won no fewer than five. His accumulated points total was thirty-five while Aucouturier, Trousselier's fellow Peugeot rider, came second with sixty-one. It had been nothing short of a mauling.

The race was deemed a triumph, one that put the Tour back on the right tracks – although a reported 125kg of tacks were still thrown onto the roads in a bid to thwart the race. 'I'm not sorry it's over – at least I will be able to sleep until noon,' quipped Trousselier at the finish. 'I owe a vote of thanks to those who have contributed to my victory ... and to *L'Auto* who have placed a modest fortune into the palm of my hand.'[26]

Trousselier (who reportedly used to escape from restaurants without paying by pretending to argue with friends about who was fastest sprinter, then getting the owner to set up a race to settle the matter, explaining that the loser would pay the bill, before they all disappeared into the night on their bikes, never to be seen again[27]), won some 6,950 francs over the course of the 1905 Tour. That prize fund, alongside bonuses from Peugeot and future race appearance money already paid meant that Trousselier's 'modest fortune' amounted to some 25,000 francs. A mischievous and lively character, he couldn't resist a night of post-Tour gambling with a dice on a massage table in the Velodrome Buffalo. By morning Trousselier had nothing of his fortune left.

While 1905 represented Trousselier's best year on paper – it was the first time a rider had won both Paris–Roubaix and the Tour in the same year. If that doesn't sound particularly remarkable given that the Tour was only in its third year at the time, consider that to date only three riders have so far achieved the same feat: Octave Lapize (1910), Eddy Merckx (1970) and Bernard Hinault (1981) – according to Trousselier himself his finest win came three years later when he won Bordeaux–Paris, the very race at which he'd incurred his lifetime ban five years earlier. He won that race by more than twenty-five minutes, breaking the course record in the process. 'I ate fifty chops, three kilograms of rice cake, twenty tarts and I took, with each refuelling, two cans of lemonade,' Trousselier said when reflecting on the race in 1926. 'I can even say that if my pacers had had more energy, my time would have been even better.'[28]

After his 1905 win the Florist would go on to win another seven stages at the Tour. The onset of war in 1914 brought an end to his career and he retired to run his flower shop in Paris. He died in 1939.

MAJOR WINS
Tour de France: 1905
Paris–Roubaix: 1905
Bordeaux–Paris: 1908

Ullrich, Jan

GER

BORN: 2 DECEMBER 1973, ROSTOCK, GERMANY

Stage 10 of the 1997 Tour was 252km, from Luchon to the Andorran ski resort of Arcalis. Jan Ullrich had spent much of the early part of the race riding defensively for his Deutsche Telekom leader and defending champion, Bjarne Riis. But Riis was not riding at the same level as the previous year and the sense was growing that the 23-year-old German was straining at the leash, begging to be let go. After all, he had claimed a stage and finished second himself in 1996, just 1min 41sec behind Riis. That impressive result had come despite it being his first Tour start and being forced to ride as a *super-domestique* for his leader. From the moment he stood on the second step of the podium in Paris it had been clear that one day Ullrich would be freed from his shackles and able to ride his own race.

226 TOUR DE FRANCE CHAMPIONS

It was equally clear that there would be few who could then stay with him. The only question was when that time would arrive.

The answer came on the road to Arcalis. Already sitting 1min 30sec ahead of Riis in the standings despite riding in his service, and with Riis again dropped by the group of favourites, Ullrich drifted to the back the group and spoke with his sports director Walter Godefroot. After a quick chat through the open car window, Ullrich, wearing the jersey of Germany's national champion, rode back to the group and went straight to the front. 'The way he pedalled back to that group there, he made it look so, so easy,' television commentator Phil Liggett observed. 'I think we are looking at Ullrich in the making here, he is so, so strong.'[1]

As recently as that very morning the Telekom team had been insisting that Ullrich would continue to work for Riis. Even if the team management had truly believed what they had said to the press, the truth of what was being seen on the road could be denied no more. Ullrich was demonstrably Telekom's strongest rider and the conversation with Godefroot had finally given him the nod. As Riis suffered so the German flew the nest. On the climb to Arcalis, Ullrich made his decisive move, leaving his group and powering past all those that had been ahead of him on the road. 'He is showing us the class of a rider who we will see for the next ten years,' said Paul Sherwen.[2]

Ullrich soared into the yellow jersey, winning the stage by 1min 6sec over Marco Pantani and taking the overall lead by 2min 58sec, ahead of Richard Virenque. Riis trailed in more than three minutes back, a result which meant he now trailed his young teammate by 4min 53sec. The two men embraced at the finish, acknowledging that the baton of leadership had been passed. 'They say I climbed well,' Ullrich said, 'but I could have gone faster. Even so, I put in a fair amount of effort.'[3]

The jersey never left Ullrich's shoulders for the remainder of the race. He defended his lead resolutely in the Alps, none more so than on the stage to Courchevel when the second-placed Virenque threw everything he had at the German. Virenque and his teammates set a fierce pace on the Glandon, isolating Ullrich, before descending with abandon, building a sizeable lead. Ullrich was in trouble. Realising he could never bridge the gap alone he slowed and waited for salvation to arrive in the form of his team.

Sure enough, help duly came. Riis paced Ullrich up the Madeleine, the penultimate climb of the day, to bring the yellow jersey within touching distance of Virenque. On the final ascent to Courchevel the German sat on Virenque's wheel and while the Frenchman crossed the finish line first, Ullrich was right there with him. After a day of aggressive riding that took in three huge climbs, Ullrich's lead of 6min 22sec had remained intact and the race was as good as his.

Ullrich's final margin of victory was 9min 9sec. He had exploded onto the scene and the bright-eyed, freckle-faced German was surely destined to rule the Tour for the foreseeable future. It seemed to everyone that cycling was about enter a period of Ullrich dominance. At the time it was all but inconceivable that he would never again stand on the top step of the Paris podium, but as it turned out, 1997 would be the one and only time Ullrich tasted Tour glory.

Born behind the iron curtain in East Germany, Ullrich was only young when his father left the family apartment for good. He later wrote that being taught to ride a bike at the age of five was one of the last experiences he shared with his father. 'I also experienced his hot temper and his violence,' Ullrich wrote. 'I was six when my dad beat me once. To this day, a small scar on my head reminds me of it. Only if I wear my hair very short can you see it. It's a reminder of my dad that will stay. Like the memory of my first bike ride.'[4]

Ullrich was a product of East Germany's sport development programme. He joined East Berlin's Kinder und Jugendsportschulen when he was 13 years old. 'The support we received as athletes was very good,' Ullrich told *Cyclist* magazine in 2015. 'My mother wouldn't have been able to afford a road bike for me because it was ridiculously expensive, so having one was something very special.'[5]

The fall of the Berlin Wall exposed Ullrich to Western culture for the first time – 'we could just drive across the old border. I bought a pair of socks. It was exhilarating to buy whatever you wanted,' he recalled.[6] It also opened more cycle racing possibilities. In 1993 he won the amateur world championship road race in Oslo, prevailing in the final sprint during a rain-sodden race, and by 1995 he was a professional riding for Deutsche Telekom.

That Ullrich never again reached the heights of his 1997 season was perhaps due to two factors: firstly, he had a reputation for enjoying the finer things in life too much, returning from the off-season out of shape and battling to control his weight. Nevertheless he still finished on the Tour podium no fewer than seven times during his career, which brings us nicely to the second factor – Lance Armstrong.

Ullrich finished second at the Tour behind Armstrong on three occasions – 2000, 2001 and 2003. In 2005 he was third, again behind the American. Theirs was a rivalry that gripped cycling during the early 2000s, even if Ullrich never overcame Armstrong. He came closest in 2003, a race during which Armstrong famously had to ride cross-country over a mountain pasture to avoid a crash and later hit the deck in the Pyrenees when his handlebars became entangled with a spectator's bag. Ullrich won a time trial, his first stage win since 1998 (when he also finished second overall, that time to Marco Pantani) and pushed Armstrong all the way, losing by only 1min 1sec.

A 1999 win at the Vuelta, Olympic Gold in 2000 and a brace of world time-trial titles (1999 and 2001) were Ullrich's only other victories of real note. While that would be a great return for the vast majority of riders, for Ullrich it meant that a career that had initially promised so much ultimately descended into underachievement, controversy and scandal. In 2002 he crashed his Porsche after a night out and was found to be over the alcohol limit. A few weeks later an out-of-competition test recorded a positive result for amphetamine, resulting in suspension and a fine.

In 2006 Ullrich was implicated in the Operación Puerto doping investigation and fired by his T-Mobile team. He never rode again. In 2013 he admitted doping during his career. 'I didn't take anything which the others were not taking,' he said. 'For me, betrayal only begins when I gain an advantage, but that was not the case. I just wanted to ensure equal opportunities.'[7]

Ullrich's personal life has remained troubled. In August 2018 he was admitted to a psychiatric hospital in Frankfurt after two separate allegations of assault were levied against him, including an alleged attack on a prostitute in a Frankfurt hotel. Ullrich told the German paper Bild that separation from his wife and not being able to see his children had been the start of his troubles:

When the problems really started with Sara [his ex-wife] and I could not see or talk to the kids for weeks, I exploded. I broke some TVs and I pulled the punching ball from the ceiling. To calm down, I took cocaine and amphetamines. But I do not need it now, if I have my children, I do not need drugs.[8]

The incidents led Armstrong to visit his old rival in Frankfurt. 'He was such a special rival to me,' Armstrong posted on Instagram. 'He scared me, he motivated me, and truly brought out the best in me. Pure class on the bike … Please keep Jan in your thoughts and prayers. He needs our support right now.'[9]

MAJOR WINS
Tour de France: 1997
Vuelta a España: 1999
National Champion: 1997, 2001

Van Impe, Lucien

BEL

BORN: 20 OCTOBER 1946, MERE, BELGIUM

The Tour's now famous *maillot blanc à pois rouges*, or polka-dot jersey, was introduced in 1975 when Chocolat Poulain, then the financial backer of the race's mountain prize, asked for a jersey to be designed and awarded to the leader of the classification to aid exposure of their sponsorship.

It has often been claimed that the jersey was designed to reflect the sponsor's packaging, but in his book, *Maillot à pois*, Pierre Carrey writes that the design came from the then co-director of the race, Félix Lévitan. Lévitan had once written an article on the track racer Henri Lemoine who raced from the late 1920s until the 1950s. Dubbed 'the P'tit pois', Lemoine had worn a jersey decorated with polka dots during his career. When it came to design the Tour's new mountain jersey, Lévitan remembered Lemoine and opted to base the jersey of that of the P'tit pois.

So it was that on 20 July 1975 Belgium's Lucien Van Impe became the first rider to wear the new jersey into Paris. Nicknamed 'the Kleine van Mere' because of his small stature, Van Impe had already won the mountain classification twice (1971 and 1972). This time, however, he had a distinctive jersey on his back to mark his efforts. The following year he would take a jersey of a different design and colour into France's capital city.

Perhaps the greatest climber ever to have turned a pedal at the Tour – he would win six Tour mountain classification prizes during his career and once claimed that the only reason he didn't win more was out of respect to Federico Bahamontes, the great climber who had helped the Belgian launch his career in 1969 and who had won six mountain titles at the race himself – Van Impe entered the 1976 edition of the Tour as the leader of the Gitane team. He was thought to have a legitimate, if small, chance of victory. Eddy Merckx, the man whose presence had loomed large over the recent history of the race, was absent through injury, and consequently most had Bernard Thévenet, Joop Zoetemelk and Luis Ocaña as the main favourites. But Van Impe had Tour pedigree. A well as the three mountain titles he had claimed by 1976, he had twice stood on the final podium in Paris – finishing third in 1971 and again in 1975.

In the off season Van Impe had worked on riding against the clock, all too aware of how time won in the mountains could easily be lost in a time-trial. He was also feeling the beneficial effect of the presence in his team of a new sports director. Cyrille Guimard had taken the place of Jean Stablinski at the helm of Gitane and had brought with him new methods, creating, initially at least, a more harmonious environment. 'Last year I had two valuable teammates, [Alain] Santy and Mariano Martinez,' Van Impe said on the eve of the race. 'But they were not fit for the Tour. The team lacked cohesion. Under Guimard's leadership this is changing ... for the first time, I am entering the Tour to win it.'[1]

Van Impe started his assault on the race in the Alps, taking yellow on l'Alpe d'Huez after a famous duel with Zoetemelk on the slopes of the now legendary climb. Van Impe accelerated at the first corner and left everyone standing apart from Zoetemelk. The Dutchman followed and the two went toe to toe, pedal to pedal, all the way up the mountain. Neither rider could shake the other. The next day the French daily *Le Dauphiné Libéré* described the two men as riding in tandem. Zoetemelk managed to take the win on the line after what remains one of the closest battles the Alpe has ever hosted (at the time it was only the second appearance of the mountain in the race) while Van Impe took yellow. The great French hope, Bernard Thévenet, came in eighth but his sports director at Peugeot, Maurice de Muer, was unconcerned saying: 'We think that it is in the Pyrenees that the Tour will play-out, particularly during the stage which, after four passes in 140 kilometres, ends at Saint-Lary-de-Soulon, on Plat d'Adet.'[2]

De Muer would be proved correct, although it wasn't his rider who would profit. Van Impe had lost yellow four days after the stage to l'Alpe d'Huez when Thévenet's teammate, Raymond Delisle, attacked on the stage to Pyrenees 2000, a move that had apparently been made following the suggestion of none other than Van Impe's own sports director, Guimard, who was keen to remove the responsibility of defending the race lead from his team for a few days. Van Impe was reportedly furious after the stage while Guimard simply told his rider to leave the race if he didn't like how he was managing things.

Two days later came the stage to Pla d'Adet that De Muer had predicted would decide the race. With some 80km to go Van Impe followed an attack that had been made by Luis Ocaña who then did much to help Van Impe open the gap on Zoetemelk. Whose idea this move was remains the subject of some conjecture. Guimard is quoted in Ed Pickering's book, *The Yellow Jersey Club*, as having to implore reporters from the Belgian newspaper *Het Volk* to drive up to Van Impe and tell him in Flemish that if he didn't start riding, 'the idiot'[3] would lose the Tour, such was Van Impe's initial reluctance to follow Ocaña. For his part Van Impe is quoted as saying he always knew he could take the jersey on that stage, reflecting simply that his director 'always takes credit'[4] for the move.

Whoever's idea it was to follow Ocaña by the time he reached the lower slopes of Pla d'Adet, Van Impe knew the time to seize the race had come. He launched himself up the mountain, easily distancing Ocaña. Zoetemelk meanwhile had stayed on the wheel of Delisle, his teammate who was in yellow. Finally realising he had backed the wrong horse, Zoetemelk attacked but it was too little, too late. Van Impe won the stage by more than three minutes to take the jersey by 3min 18sec. It was a lead that would grow further on the way into Paris, his final margin standing at 4min 14sec. Van Impe and Guimard had won the Tour together for Gitane in Guimard's first season as a director. But the short-lived harmony in the team had gone. Perhaps unsurprisingly Van Impe moved teams the following season.

Born in Mere, Belgium, it was on the short and punchy hills of Flanders that Van Impe had learned his craft, climbing the Muur van Geraardsbergen 'for example ten, twenty, times in succession ... again, every day'.[5] Having won impressively as a junior and amateur, including claiming the mountains prize at the Tour de l'Avenir, Van Impe turned professional in 1969 with the Sonolor-Lejeune team after Bahamontes had seen the Belgian riding in Spain. Just two days after signing professional terms he was in Roubaix for the start of the Tour. Such a baptism of fire would be unthinkable today, but Van Impe rode impressively, finishing four stages in the top ten and coming a remarkable twelfth overall. Two years later he finished third and claimed his first mountains title despite not winning a stage. He put that right the following year, winning at Orcières Merlette after escaping with Joaquim Agostinho before the final climb, just pipping the Portuguese to the line to take his first Tour stage.

Van Impe was fastidious in his training and diet. Reportedly he wanted a hot bath ready for him on his return from training and his children knew there had to be quiet at the house when he was home, with no friends allowed to come round to play.[6] He constructed his entire career around the high peaks of the Tour, sometimes facing criticism for narrowing his focus so much. But whenever he did widen his sights to include other mountains, he invariably met with success, taking stage wins in both the Giro and the Vuelta and claiming two mountain classification wins at the former.

In total Van Impe rode the Tour fifteen times and finished every one. He retired in 1987, having spent some eighteen years at the top of the sport. At the time of writing he remains the last Belgian to have won the Tour.

MAJOR WINS
Tour de France: 1976
National Champion: 1983

Walkowiak, Roger

FRA

BORN: 2 MARCH 1927, MONTLUÇON, FRANCE

Prior to 1956, Roger Walkowiak, a Frenchman born to a Polish father and a French mother, had taken to the start line of three Tours. In 1951 he finished fifty-seventh, in 1953 he came forty-seventh and in 1955 he abandoned. So it is fair to say that his 1956 race went a little better.

Cycling history has often painted Walkowiak as a virtual unknown prior to the 1956 Tour but that belies the truth somewhat. While no one would ever have considered him a genuine contender for the race – even though the Tour was thought to be wide open in the absence of three-time winner Louison Bobet – Walkowiak had nevertheless made an impression during the eight years he had been a professional. He had picked up some wins and had finished on the podium in Paris–Nice in 1953 and the Dauphiné Libéré in 1955, staying with no less a champion climber than Bobet on the murderous slopes of Mont Ventoux at the latter – a performance that had Bobet lobbying for his inclusion in the French national team for the 1955 Tour, a call that ultimately went unheeded. Walkowiak had also spent the bulk of his professional career riding for some of the biggest trade teams in the sport: Peugeot, Gitane and Saint Raphaël. Add in that just a couple of months before the start of the Tour he had won a stage at the Vuelta while riding for the France national team, and the conclusion must be that while Walkowiak was by no means a fancied rider entering the 1956 Tour, nor was he a completely unknown quantity.

In fact, Walkowiak's Vuelta experience nearly cost him a spot at the Tour. The French team had imploded in Spain. Bobet had abandoned and one by one others followed. Walkowiak joined the exodus, reportedly deciding to catch a train home rather than start a stage. His abandonment infuriated the French team's sport director, Sauveur Ducazeaux, who vowed not to select Walkowiak for the Nord-Est-Centre team that he was going to manage at the Tour (Walkowiak again hadn't done enough to earn a call-up to the national team). In the end it took a letter of apology and the intervention of the experienced and respected Raphaël Géminiani to secure his spot on the regional team.

Early in the race Walkowiak got himself into a couple of breaks that brought him into the top ten overall before the start of the race's seventh stage, 244km from Lorient to Angers. Then he joined a thirty-one-rider breakaway that crossed the line over eighteen minutes ahead of the rest of the field in Angers. Walkowiak was the best-placed rider in the group and took over the race lead. The 29-year-old held the yellow jersey for three days before losing it to Gerrit Voorting of the Netherlands when he lost more than fourteen minutes on the stage into Bayonne. He was now 9min 4sec behind the new race leader. And that looked to be that.

In 2012 Walkowiak told *Bicycling* that losing the race lead was tactical:

Whenever there were attacks, all my teammates would be dropped. I couldn't count on anybody. But I knew I had good legs and would have chances later. I let a breakaway go and lost the jersey, but as a result didn't have to do an ounce of work throughout the Pyrenees and all the way to the second rest day.[1]

Whether losing the jersey was truly intentional or not, Walkowiak started to chip away at his time loss. Bit by bit the Frenchman slowly made his way back up the overall classification and by the time the riders started the stage from Turin to Grenoble, over Mont Cenis, the Croix de Fer and the Luitel, Walkowiak was in second place, 4min 27sec off leader Wout Wagtmans.

Six kilometres from the top of the Croix de Fer, Walkowiak attacked. He dragged with him Charly Gaul and Federico Bahamontes, the greatest climbers in the race and two riders who had been considered favourites for the overall win. Walkowiak couldn't shake the climbing specialists and in the valley they regrouped. On the Luitel, Gaul launched a blistering attack that brought him the stage victory, while Walkowiak stayed with Bahamontes, knowing that his earlier efforts meant that if he could hold on, the yellow jersey would be coming back to him.

Walkowiak finished the stage 8min 9sec ahead of Wagtmans. Slumped over his handlebars, fighting to hold back tears, the Frenchman knew it was more than enough to take the race lead, which he then held for the rest of the race. The reaction though was lukewarm at best. The crowds jeered in Paris while the press berated the French national team, which it accused of again being unable to work together, allowing a rider from a mere regional team to emerge victorious. Despite Walkowiak later claiming he had to fight multiple attacks on the final stage, *L'Équipe* bemoaned the lack of action on the 300km stage into Paris, reporting: 'Riders who had been attacking all out on stages of 200 kilometres, capable of seizing advantages of 15 minutes, didn't even open hostilities to challenge the 1min 25sec lead in 300 kilometres.'[2]

Walkowiak hadn't won a stage and many considered he had prevailed only because he had slipped away on an innocuous stage, taking advantage of tactical errors made by better riders. His win even coined a new term, '*à la Walko*' to mean an upset caused by an unworthy winner.

That reaction defined the rest of Walkowiak's career. The man who had started his cycling life racing friends around a square in his home town before progressing through the amateur ranks, had turned professional in 1949 only after struggling to find regular work on his return from military service. He rode on until 1960, though a second Vuelta stage was the only other result of note in the second half of his career. On retirement he opened a bar before returning to the factory in which he had worked while an amateur. Later he opened a garage and then turned to sheep farming. He maintained a media blackout for more than twenty years, so hurt was he by the accusations that he didn't deserve his win. 'They stole my Tour, they're bastards,' he said in a rare interview during the 1980s. Later he would appear on French television: 'They always said I won the Tour on a flat stage,' he said. 'And when I think of all the effort I made, the pain I endured, which was never acknowledged ... it leaves me speechless.'[3]

Walkowiak has at last begun to receive the recognition he long deserved. 'Walkowiak won that Tour through hard graft. Not everyone is permitted to win the Tour,' Géminiani told *Rouleur* in 2016.[4] 'There are people who say that Walkowiak should not have won the Tour,' five-time winner Bernard Hinault once said. 'He took the jersey, he lost it and he regained it. Then he was there every day. No one has the right to say it was given to him. He was not a thief. The Tour is not a gift.'[5]

Walkowiak died in 2017 aged 89.

MAJOR WINS
Tour de France: 1956

Wiggins, Bradley

GBR

BORN: 28 APRIL 1980, GENT, BELGIUM

On 1 August 2012 Bradley Wiggins sat on a throne in the grounds of Hampton Court Palace with his British Cycling jersey unzipped, allowing a glimpse of his tattooed chest. As the cameras of the world's media captured the image so Wiggins pulled the fingers on both of his hands into a 'V for Victory' sign. His adoring public watched on, many wearing the paper cut-outs of his famous trademark sideburns that had been printed and distributed by two of Britain's tabloid newspapers. Ten days earlier Wiggins had been crowned in Paris as Britain's first male Tour winner. Now he sat in the shadow of King Henry VIII's former palace, firmly established as British cycling royalty.

A little earlier Wiggins had blasted around the 44km Olympic time-trial course, destroying all before him. Silver medal winner, Tony Martin, the reigning time-trial world champion, was over forty seconds back. Wiggins had reigned supreme in London, roared on by the hundreds of thousands lining the road, and bringing the curtain down on what had been a quite remarkable season for the 32-year-old. 'I don't think my sporting career will ever top this now. That's it. It will never, never get better than that,'[6] said King Bradley as he sat on his throne.

Wiggins was born in Gent – his British mother, Linda, had moved to the Belgian city to be with Wiggins' father, Gary, an Australian who was trying to make his way on the Belgian six-day racing scene – but brought up in London after Linda returned to her parents' flat in Kilburn when Gary walked out on the family. In his 2012 book *My Time*, Wiggins recalls how Gary had disappeared from his life before his second birthday, reappearing only when Wiggins was seventeen. Wiggins writes that Gary returned to London with 'four black bin liners' of their things, leaving them at the 'bottom of the stairs', to his Nan and Grandad's flat.[7] The pair hadn't talked for years when Gary died after an assault in Australia in 2008.

It was in London that the young Wiggins discovered a love and talent for cycling – 'I was a kid living in Kilburn in the early 1990s, with pictures of Belgian cyclists on my wall. There has probably never been a kid in Kilburn, before or since, who had a bedroom wall like that,'[8] he told Donald McRae in 2018. A junior world title on the track arrived in 1998 and while he signed professional terms for a number of road teams, including Française des Jeux, Cofidis and Credit Agricole, between 2000 and 2008 Wiggins did his best work in the velodrome, securing three Olympic gold medals and six world titles on the boards in that time (further Olympic golds and world track titles would come in 2016).

Wiggins had still raced on the road in that golden track period, riding the Giro and Tour as well as a number of Classics, collecting a prologue win at the 2007 Dauphiné Libéré. It wasn't until 2009 that he emerged as a real force in stage races, taking a surprise fourth at the Tour (later promoted to third following Lance Armstrong's disqualification) while on the Garmin-Slipstream team. He had entered that race as a support rider for Christian Vande Velde, but with both riders still in the top ten going into the final week, the positions were reversed when Vande Velde fell away on the stage to Verbier. Wiggins, by contrast, scaled the Alps with the likes of Alberto Contador, Cadel Evans, Andy Schleck and Carlos Sastre – the sport's very best climbers. By the end of the Verbier stage Wiggins was third overall, just 1min 46sec behind eventual race winner Contador.

A protracted move to the newly formed Team Sky followed and while his 2010 and 2011 Tour performances – twenty-fourth (later promoted to twenty-second) and DNF respectively – didn't match his 2009 showing, results in other races, including a 2011 overall win at the win at the Dauphiné Libéré, showed his potential as a genuine future Tour contender. Just under two months after he left the 2011 Tour bound for hospital after crashing out, he was back racing, taking third (later promoted to second) at the Vuelta.

With a history as long and varied as professional cycling's there are precious few genuine 'firsts' worth celebrating these days. However, such was the magnitude of Wiggins' 2012 season that he had rewritten the history books before the month of June was out. No rider had ever won Paris–Nice, the Tour de Romandie and the Dauphiné Libéré, three of the most prestigious stage races outside of the Grand Tours, in a single season, before Wiggins did just that in 2012. Cycling legends Eddy Merckx and Jacques Anquetil had won Paris–Nice and the Dauphiné in the same year but not Romandie as well. There, Wiggins stood alone. No wonder then that at the Tour, Wiggins was considered one of the main favourites.

His team had learned as well. Their performance at the Dauphiné had been particularly impressive, marshalling the peloton at key moments and controlling the race. Everything was set up for a Wiggins offensive at the Tour. In a precursor of what would soon become commonplace in France during July, Team Sky were simply too powerful for the rest of the peloton. Wiggins took the yellow jersey on stage seven and never looked like losing it, despite an element of infighting within the team. On the stage to La Toussuire, Chris Froome had ridden so aggressively much to the confusion of Wiggins and the team that he had to be ordered back to his leader. Wiggins later likened the events to a soldier ignoring a battle plan and 'going off and doing his own thing'. He wrote that he had considered quitting the race due to his uncertainty over what the team was trying to do.[9]

Wiggins went on to win both time trials with ease, he defended stoutly in the mountains and then even had the strength to lead out teammate Mark Cavendish, who was wearing the rainbow jersey of world champion, to win the race's final stage on the Champs-Élysées. The Brits had conquered France. Bradley Wiggins was the new king of Paris.

Two years later Wiggins claimed a time-trial world championship title before turning his attention back to the track, claiming the hour record in 2015 and then, in 2016, taking a Madison world title before adding a further Olympic team pursuit gold medal in Rio in 2016. Later that year he brought the curtain down on his glittering career at the legendary Gent six-day race, winning alongside Mark Cavendish in the city of his birth.

Vehemently taking an anti-doping stance during his career – in 2007 he had put his Cofidis jersey in the bin after a teammate tested positive at the Tour, he was 'so sick' by what had transpired[10] – in 2016 the Fancy Bears hack revealed that Wiggins had been granted a Therapeutic Use Exemption (TUE) to use Triamcinolone, an otherwise banned corticosteroid, for medical reasons prior to races in 2011, 2012 and 2013. A later parliamentary select committee report claimed Team Sky had crossed an 'ethical line' in applying for and receiving those TUEs. 'In this case, and contrary to the testimony of [Team Principal] David Brailsford in front of the Committee, we believe that drugs were being used by Team Sky, within the WADA rules, to enhance the performance of riders, and not just to treat medical need,' stated the report.[11]

There also emerged the peculiar case of an unrecorded delivery of a package from the Team Sky/British Cycling shared medical store in Manchester to the Team in France after the 2011 Dauphiné. To date all efforts to conclusively resolve exactly what was in that package and how it was used have failed.

The effect on Wiggins, who has always denied wrongdoing, was huge. His family suffered. 'People have free rein to put their own facts in place,' he said in 2018. 'The whole thing becomes an uncontrolled trial by media. In any other court it would be thrown out because the media have skewed the facts.'[12]

Wiggins remained in cycling after his retirement with the Team Wiggins continental-level cycling team aiding the development of promising talent. In August 2019 it was announced the team was to fold while Wiggins himself said he was pursuing a new career in social care, having enrolled on a degree course. 'I don't give a shit about my cycling career now,' Wiggins said in the Big Issue. 'I'm just detached from it; I don't want to live off the back of it.'[13]

MAJOR WINS
Tour de France: 2012
National Champion: 2011

Zoetemelk, Joop

NED

BORN: 3 DECEMBER 1946,
THE HAGUE, NETHERLANDS

With a career remarkable both for its longevity and consistency, Joop Zoetemelk is rightly considered one of the Netherlands' finest ever riders, yet outside of that country he perhaps never fully got the recognition he deserved. For seventeen years Zoetemelk took his place in the professional peloton, tasting victory in both his first and final seasons as a pro (a stage of the 1970 Paris–Luxembourg race and the 1987 Amstel Gold Race respectively). He landed on the podium at the Tour no fewer than seven times – only Raymond Poulidor has done so more frequently. Twelve years separated his first and final visit to the Paris podium with Poulidor and Jean Alavoine the only riders beating that particular mark, with fourteen and thirteen years respectively.

With a brace of national titles, a Vuelta, three Paris–Nice wins, two Ardennes Classics, a couple of Paris-Tours and a rainbow jersey to his name, Zoetemelk was a very talented rider indeed. His misfortune was that his time bridged the eras of two of cycling's great champions: Eddy Merckx and Bernard Hinault. That meant that for all his ability, Zoetemelk would all too often end up playing second fiddle to the Cannibal and the Badger at the Tour. Twice he finished behind Merckx in Paris; three times he was runner-up to Hinault. He would, however, at least get to stand on the top step once, something Poulidor famously never managed.

That Tour win finally arrived for Zoetemelk in 1980, his first year at the TI-Raleigh team having signed from Miko-Mercier, but his tenth appearance at the race. Hinault, going for his third straight Tour win, started as the firm favourite even if he threatened strike action on the eve of the race due to the inclusion of 40km of cobblestones he branded 'inhuman'.[1] The Frenchman had already won Liège-Bastogne-Liège and the Giro earlier in the year and was regarded by some as virtually unbeatable. Zoetemelk meanwhile only had stage wins at the Dauphiné Libéré and Tour de Romandie, and a win at the GP Pino Cerami on his 1980 tab. 'If Hinault wants to win, win he will,'[2] was the view of Dutch daily *Leidsch Dagblad*.

Sure enough, Hinault took yellow on the first day after winning the opening prologue. TI-Raleigh then won the first of two team time trials, lifting Zoetemelk into the top five for the first time. Hinault meanwhile fell from the top spot with first France's Yvon Bertin and then Belgium's Rudy Pevenage taking over yellow, before France's favourite then reclaimed the jersey midway through the race.

He might have been wearing yellow once again but all was not well for Hinault. He had been suffering with tendinitis in his knee since the start of the race and with four huge Pyrenean climbs on the horizon the pain was such that enough was enough. Despite holding a twenty-one-second lead over Zoetemelk, Hinault and his manager Cyrille Guimard decided that the Frenchman should abandon. In Pau he left the Renault team hotel by the back door, escaping from the kitchen and getting into a car. 'Get going, Hubert,' he told his teammate Hubert Arbes who was driving. 'We can't have anybody following us.'[3] Hinault was taken to Arbes' home near Lourdes to hide out before any journalists had any idea what was going on.

Hinault's abandonment meant that the race lead passed to Zoetemelk. The Dutchman refused to wear yellow the following day once he had learned what had happened but steadily increased his lead over the rest of the race.

Over the course of the remaining ten stages he turned a 1min 10sec gap over compatriot Hennie Kuiper into a 6min 55sec win in Paris. Of course, it wasn't all easy going – he came off his bike in the Alps after teammate Johan van der Velde's gears slipped and the two came together and then was put under intense pressure during the stage to Morzine. He clawed back a two-minute deficit in unbearable heat that day on the Madeleine. Zoetemelk claimed the final time trial to crown his overall win amid a dominant display from his team which claimed no fewer than eleven stage wins in total. 'Zoetemelk-day in Paris,' ran *Nieuwe Leidsche Courant's* front-page headline. 'Tens of thousands of Dutchmen celebrated the entry of Tour de France winner Joop Zoetemelk on the Champs Élysées yesterday afternoon,' the paper reported. Included in that number was the Dutch Prime Minister, Dries van Agt, who was there to congratulate Zoetemelk.

The Dutchman's win was felt by some as coming with an asterisk against it – after all, he still hadn't beaten Hinault. Not that the Frenchman agreed any caveat was needed. After travelling to Paris for the finish, Hinault said:

> Joop was definitely the best ... He did not have to attack. At the time I had to give up Joop had a small lead in the General Classification. He arrived in Paris with seven minutes' gap [sic]. That means he must have made the right decisions. It was up to his competitors to attack.[4]

Zoetemelk was still forced on the defensive though. 'Surely winning the Tour de France or any other sporting event is a question of health and robustness?' he asked. 'If Hinault doesn't have that health and robustness and I have, that makes me a valid winner.'[5]

Zoetemelk had started his sporting life speed skating on the frozen canals of the Netherlands, becoming a teenaged regional champion, before discovering cycling. His amateur career had taken him to the Mexico 1968 Olympic Games where he had won gold as part of the Dutch four-man team time-trial squad, beating the Swedish outfit by 1min 37sec over the 100km course. He had also shone at the Tour de l'Avenir, winning the 1969 edition and catching the eyes of the professional world. In 1970 he signed for Flandria.

Flandria was a team full of talent, with the De Vlaeminck brothers – Eric and Roger – and Eric Leman among the riders on the squad. Wins came quick and fast for the team, particularly at the Classics, which were their main focus. While that meant Zoetemelk found himself working for others during the one-day races, it did offer him some freedom at stage races and later that year he came second at the Tour at the first time of riding, finishing 12min 41sec behind Merckx. In his book *Alpe d'Huez*, Peter Cossins writes that Zoetemelk's sports director at Flandria, Alberic Schotte, had told the young Dutchman to stay on Merckx's wheel as much as possible in order to learn from the master. Soon Zoetemelk would gain a perhaps unfair reputation as a rider who merely followed the lead of others. 'Why did Zoetemelk never get a suntan?' ran a Dutch joke. 'Because he was always in someone else's shadow.'[6]

Of course, such criticism was more than a little unwarranted. Zoetemelk was an intelligent rider who knew his strengths and weaknesses as well as he knew his rivals. '[Other riders] all tried to duel with Eddy,' he once said. 'I was smarter. I refused to force myself. I knew exactly how far my talents reached.'[7]

And those talents took him far. A talented climber and time trialist, he won Paris–Nice in 1974 and 1975, beating Merckx both times (he took a third win in 1979) and won the Vuelta in 1979 claiming two time trials along the way. In 1976 he became the first Dutchman to win a Tour stage on l'Alpe d'Huez, the mountain that has since become synonymous with the Netherlands (see Van Impe entry for more). He took a second stage on that mythical ascent three years later. He also won on Puy de Dôme twice, a feat only matched by Luis Ocaña. He was a tenacious and determined man – a bad crash at the Midi-Libre race in 1974 nearly cost him his life let alone his career. That he returned at all is testament alone to his quiet strength of will.

Five years after his 1980 Tour win, he added the rainbow jersey to his palmarès. Zoetemelk seized the initiative in the closing stages of the 265km world championship race in Montello, Italy, while the likes of Greg LeMond, Stephen Roche and Moreno Argentin were all waiting for the sprint to unwind. Zoetemelk was 38 years and 273 days old. Finally no one could still legitimately claim he was a mere follower. The Dutchman remains the oldest man to have won the road world championship.

Zoetemelk retired two years later to run a hotel in Meaux, France. A statue depicting his signature two-arms-raised victory salute stands today in Rijpwetering, the Dutch village where he grew up.

MAJOR WINS

Tour de France: 1980
Vuelta a España: 1979
World Champion: 1985
National Champion: 1971, 1973

TOUR DE FRANCE PODIUMS

Year	First	Second	Third
1903	GARIN Maurice (FRA)	POTHIER Lucien (FRA)	AUGEREAU Fernand (FRA)
1904	CORNET Henri (FRA)	DORTIGNACQ Jean-Baptiste (FRA)	CATTEAU Aloïs (BEL)
1905	TROUSSELIER Louis (FRA)	AUCOUTURIER Hippolyte (FRA)	DORTIGNACQ Jean-Baptiste (FRA)
1906	POTTIER Rene (FRA)	PASSERIEU Georges (FRA)	TROUSSELIER Louis (FRA)
1907	PETIT-BRETON Lucien (FRA)	GARRIGOU Gustave (FRA)	GEORGET Emile (FRA)
1908	PETIT-BRETON Lucien (FRA)	FABER François (LUX)	PASSERIEU Georges (FRA)
1909	FABER François (LUX)	GARRIGOU Gustave (FRA)	ALAVOINE Jean (FRA)
1910	LAPIZE Octave (FRA)	FABER François (LUX)	GARRIGOU Gustave (FRA)
1911	GARRIGOU Gustave (FRA)	DUBOC Paul (FRA)	GEORGET Emile (FRA)
1912	DEFRAYE Odile (BEL)	CHRISTOPHE Eugène (FRA)	GARRIGOU Gustave (FRA)
1913	THYS Philippe (BEL)	GARRIGOU Gustave (FRA)	BUYSSE Marcel (BEL)
1914	THYS Philippe (BEL)	PÉLISSIER Henri (FRA)	ALAVOINE Jean (FRA)
1919	LAMBOT Firmin (BEL)	ALAVOINE Jean (FRA)	CHRISTOPHE Eugène (FRA)
1920	THYS Philippe (BEL)	HEUSGHEM Hector (BEL)	LAMBOT Firmin (BEL)
1921	SCIEUR Léon (BEL)	HEUSGHEM Hector (BEL)	BARTHÉLÉMY Honoré (FRA)
1922	LAMBOT Firmin (BEL)	ALAVOINE Jean (FRA)	SELLIER Felix (BEL)
1923	PÉLISSIER Henri (FRA)	BOTTECCHIA Ottavio (ITA)	BELLENGER Romain (FRA)
1924	BOTTECCHIA Ottavio (ITA)	FRANTZ Nicolas (LUX)	BUYSSE Lucien (BEL)

25	BOTTECCHIA Ottavio (ITA)	BUYSSE Lucien (BEL)	AIMO Bartolomeo (ITA)
26	BUYSSE Lucien (BEL)	FRANTZ Nicolas (LUX)	AIMO Bartolomeo (ITA)
27	FRANTZ Nicolas (LUX)	DE WAELE Maurice (BEL)	VERVAECKE Julien (BEL)
28	FRANTZ Nicolas (LUX)	LEDUCQ André (FRA)	DE WAELE Maurice (BEL)
29	DE WAELE Maurice (BEL)	PANCERA Giuseppe (ITA)	DEMUYSERE Joseph (BEL)
30	LEDUCQ André (FRA)	GUERRA Learco (ITA)	MAGNE Antonin (FRA)
31	MAGNE Antonin (FRA)	DEMUYSERE Joseph (BEL)	PESENTI Antonio (ITA)
32	LEDUCQ André (FRA)	STÖPEL Kurt (GER)	CAMUSSO Francesco (ITA)
33	SPEICHER Georges (FRA)	GUERRA Learco (ITA)	MARTANO Giuseppe (ITA)
34	MAGNE Antonin (FRA)	MARTANO Giuseppe (ITA)	LAPEBIE Roger (FRA)
35	MAES Romain (BEL)	MORELLI Ambrogio (ITA)	VERVAECKE Félicien (BEL)
36	MAES Sylvere (BEL)	MAGNE Antonin (FRA)	VERVAECKE Félicien (BEL)
37	LAPEBIE Roger (FRA)	VICINI Mario (ITA)	AMBERG Leo (SUI)
38	BARTALI Gino (ITA)	VERVAECKE Félicien (BEL)	COSSON Victor (FRA)
39	MAES Sylvère (BEL)	VIETTO René (FRA)	VLAEMYNCK Lucien (BEL)
47	ROBIC Jean (FRA)	FACHLEITNER Édouard (FRA)	BRAMBILLA Pierre (FRA)
48	BARTALI Gino (ITA)	SCHOTTE Briek (BEL)	LAPÉBIE Guy (FRA)
49	COPPI Fausto (ITA)	BARTALI Gino (ITA)	MARINELLI Jacques (FRA)
50	KÜBLER Ferdinand (SUI)	OCKERS Stan (BEL)	BOBET Louison (FRA)
51	KOBLET Hugo (SUI)	GEMINIANI Raphaël (FRA)	LAZARIDÈS Lucien (FRA)
52	COPPI Fausto (ITA)	OCKERS Stan (BEL)	RUIZ Bernardo (ESP)
53	BOBET Louison (FRA)	MALLÉJAC Jean (FRA)	ASTRUA Giancarlo (ITA)
54	BOBET Louison (FRA)	KÜBLER Ferdinand (SUI)	SCHAR Fritz (SUI)
55	BOBET Louison (FRA)	BRANKART Jean (BEL)	GAUL Charly (LUX)
56	WALKOWIAK Roger (FRA)	BAUVIN Gilbert (FRA)	ADRIAENSSENS Jan (BEL)
57	ANQUETIL Jacques (FRA)	JANSSENS Marcel (BEL)	CHRISTIAN Adolf (aut)
58	GAUL Charly (LUX)	FAVERO Vito (ITA)	GEMINIANI Raphaël (FRA)
59	BAHAMONTES Federico (ESP)	ANGLADE Henry (FRA)	ANQUETIL Jacques (FRA)
60	NENCINI Gastone (ITA)	BATTISTINI Graziano (ITA)	ADRIAENSSENS Jan (BEL)
61	ANQUETIL Jacques (FRA)	CARLESI Guido (ITA)	GAUL Charly (LUX)
62	ANQUETIL Jacques (FRA)	PLANCKAERT Joseph (BEL)	POULIDOR Raymond (FRA)

1963	ANQUETIL Jacques (FRA)	BAHAMONTES Federico (ESP)	PÉREZ José (ESP)
1964	ANQUETIL Jacques (FRA)	POULIDOR Raymond (FRA)	BAHAMONTES Federico (ESP)
1965	GIMONDI Felice (ITA)	POULIDOR Raymond (FRA)	MOTTA Gianni (ITA)
1966	AIMAR Lucien (FRA)	JANSSEN Jan (NED)	POULIDOR Raymond (FRA)
1967	PINGEON Roger (FRA)	JIMÉNEZ Julio (ESP)	BALMAMION Franco (ITA)
1968	JANSSEN Jan (NED)	VAN SPRINGEL Herman (BEL)	BRACKE Ferdinand (BEL)
1969	MERCKX Eddy (BEL)	PINGEON Roger (FRA)	POULIDOR Raymond (FRA)
1970	MERCKX Eddy (BEL)	ZOETEMELK Joop (NED)	PETTERSSON Gösta (SWE)
1971	MERCKX Eddy (BEL)	ZOETEMELK Joop (NED)	VAN IMPE Lucien (BEL)
1972	MERCKX Eddy (BEL)	GIMONDI Felice (ITA)	POULIDOR Raymond (FRA)
1973	OCAÑA Luis (ESP)	THÉVENET Bernard (FRA)	FUENTE José Manuel (ESP)
1974	MERCKX Eddy (BEL)	POULIDOR Raymond (FRA)	LÓPEZ Vicente (ESP)
1975	THÉVENET Bernard (FRA)	MERCKX Eddy (BEL)	VAN IMPE Lucien (BEL)
1976	VAN IMPE Lucien (BEL)	ZOETEMELK Joop (NED)	POULIDOR Raymond (FRA)
1977	THÉVENET Bernard (FRA)	KUIPER Hennie (NED)	VAN IMPE Lucien (BEL)
1978	HINAULT Bernard (FRA)	ZOETEMELK Joop (NED)	AGOSTINHO Joaquim (POR)
1979	HINAULT Bernard (FRA)	ZOETEMELK Joop (NED)	AGOSTINHO Joaquim (POR)
1980	ZOETEMELK Joop (NED)	KUIPER Hennie (NED)	MARTIN Raymond (FRA)
1981	HINAULT Bernard (FRA)	VAN IMPE Lucien (BEL)	ALBAN Robert (FRA)
1982	HINAULT Bernard (FRA)	ZOETEMELK Joop (NED)	VAN DER VELDE Johan (NED)
1983	FIGNON Laurent (FRA)	ARROYO Angel (ESP)	WINNEN Peter (NED)
1984	FIGNON Laurent (FRA)	HINAULT Bernard (FRA)	LEMOND Greg (USA)
1985	HINAULT Bernard (FRA)	LEMOND Greg (USA)	ROCHE Stephen (IRL)
1986	LEMOND Greg (USA)	HINAULT Bernard (FRA)	ZIMMERMANN Urs (SUI)
1987	ROCHE Stephen (IRL)	DELGADO Pedro (ESP)	BERNARD Jean-François (FRA)
1988	DELGADO Pedro (ESP)	ROOKS Steven (NED)	PARRA Fabio Enrique (COL)
1989	LEMOND Greg (USA)	FIGNON Laurent (FRA)	DELGADO Pedro (ESP)
1990	LEMOND Greg (USA)	CHIAPPUCCI Claudio (ITA)	BREUKINK Erik (NED)
1991	INDURAIN Miguel (ESP)	BUGNO Gianni (ITA)	CHIAPPUCCI Claudio (ITA)
1992	INDURÁIN Miguel (ESP)	CHIAPPUCCI Claudio (ITA)	BUGNO Gianni (ITA)
1993	INDURÁIN Miguel (ESP)	ROMINGER Tony (SUI)	JASKULA Zenon (POL)

1994	INDURÁIN Miguel (ESP)	UGRUMOV Piotr (LAT)	PANTANI Marco (ITA)
1995	INDURÁIN Miguel (ESP)	ZÜLLE Alex (SUI)	RIIS Bjarne (DEN)
1996	RIIS Bjarne (DEN)	ULLRICH Jan (GER)	VIRENQUE Richard (FRA)
1997	ULLRICH Jan (GER)	VIRENQUE Richard (FRA)	PANTANI Marco (ITA)
1998	PANTANI Marco (ITA)	ULLRICH Jan (GER)	JULICH Bobby (USA)
1999	[DSQ]	ZÜLLE Alex (SUI)	ESCARTIN Fernando (ESP)
2000	[DSQ]	ULLRICH Jan (GER)	BELOKI Joseba (ESP)
2001	[DSQ]	ULLRICH Jan (GER)	BELOKI Joseba (ESP)
2002	[DSQ]	BELOKI Joseba (ESP)	RAIMONDAS Rumšas (ITU)
2003	[DSQ]	ULLRICH Jan (GER)	VINOKOUROV Alexandre (KAZ)
2004	[DSQ]	KLÖDEN Andreas (GER)	BASSO Ivan (ITA)
2005	[DSQ]	BASSO Ivan (ITA)	MANCEBO Francisco (ESP)
2006	PEREIRO Óscar (ESP)	KLÖDEN Andreas (GER)	SASTRE Carlos (ESP)
2007	CONTADOR Alberto (ESP)	EVANS Cadel (AUS)	[DSQ]
2008	SASTRE Carlos (ESP)	EVANS Cadel (AUS)	MENCHOV Denis (RUS)
2009	CONTADOR Alberto (ESP)	SCHLECK Andy (LUX)	WIGGINS Bradley (GBR)
2010	SCHLECK Andy (LUX)	SÁNCHEZ Samuel (ESP)	VAN DEN BROECK Jurgen (BEL)
2011	EVANS Cadel (AUS)	SCHLECK Andy (LUX)	SCHLECK Fränk (LUX)
2012	WIGGINS Bradley (GBR)	FROOME Chris (GBR)	NIBALI Vincenzo (ITA)
2013	FROOME Chris (GBR)	QUINTANA Nairo (COL)	RODRÍGUEZ Joaquim (ESP)
2014	NIBALI Vincenzo (ITA)	PERAUD Jean-Christophe (FRA)	PINOT Thibaut (FRA)
2015	FROOME Chris (GBR)	QUINTANA Nairo (COL)	VALVERDE Alejandro (ESP)
2016	FROOME Chris (GBR)	BARDET Romain (FRA)	QUINTANA Nairo (COL)
2017	FROOME Chris (GBR)	URÁN Rigoberto (COL)	BARDET Romain (FRA)
2018	THOMAS Geraint (GBR)	DUMOULIN Tom (NED)	FROOME Chris (GBR)
2019	BERNAL Egan (COL)	THOMAS Geraint (GBR)	KRUIJSWIJK Steven (NED)

BIBLIOGRAPHY

This book draws on a wide range of sources. The following are worthy of special mention:

Bacon, Ellis: *Mapping Le Tour*, HarperCollins Publishers, 2013.

Bobet, Jean: *Tomorrow we ride*, Mousehold Press, 2008.

Chany, Pierre: *La Fabuleuse Histoire du Cyclisme*, Editions ODIL, 1975.

Chany, Pierre: *La Fabuleuse Histoire des Classiques et des Championnats du Monde*, Editions ODIL, 1979.

Chany, Pierre and Cazeneuve, Thierry: *La Fabuleuse Histoire du Tour de France*, Éditions Minerva, 2003.

Cossins, Peter: *The Monuments: The Grit and the Glory of Cycling's Greatest One-Day Races*, Bloomsbury Publishing, 2014.

Fife, Graham: *Tour de France: The History, The Legend, The Riders*, Mainstream Publishing 1999.

Fignon, Laurent: *We Were Young and Carefree*, Yellow Jersey, 2010.

Fotheringham, William: *Fallen Angel: The Passion of Fausto Coppi*, Yellow Jersey Press, 2009.

Fournel, Paul: *Anquetil Alone*, Profile Books, 2017.

Friebe, Daniel: *Eddy Merckx, The Cannibal*, Ebury Press, 2012.

Howard, Paul: *Sex, Lies and Handlebar Tape: The remarkable life of Jacques Anquetil*, Mainstream Publishing, 2011.

McGann and McGann: *The Story of the Tour de France Vol 1&2*, Dog Ear Publishing, 2006.

Pickering, Ed: *The Yellow Jersey Club*, Bantam Press, 2015.

Sykes, Herbie: *Maglia Rosa*, Rouleur Books, Bloomsbury Publishing, 2013.

Sys, Jacques: *Top 1000 Belgische wielrenners*, Lannoo, 2018.

Weidenfeld and Nicolson: *The Official Tour de France Centenniel*, Orion Publishing Group, 2003.

Wheatcroft, Geoffrey: *Le Tour,* Simon & Schuster UK Ltd, 2003.
Woodland, Les: *Cycling Heroes,* Springfield Books Limited, 1994.
Woodland, Les: *The Unknown Tour de France,* Van der Plas Publications, 2005.
Woodland, Les: *The Yellow Jersey Companion to the Tour de France,* Yellow
    Jersey Press 2003.

The archives of: *L'Auto, Le Miroir des Sports, The Guardian,* the *Telegraph,* the
*Independent, La Stampa, Le Petit journal, Paris-Soir, Gazette de Lausanne,
Journal de Genève, Le Monde, Leidsch Dagblad, ABC, Corriere della Sera,
L'Équipe, La Gazzetta dello Sport, Coureur, Sporting Cyclist, New York Times,
Ride Cycling Review, Rouleur, Cyclist*

The following websites: cyclebase.nl, cq.com, cyclingnews.com, velonews.
com, procyclingstats.com, bikeraceinfo.com, letour.fr

ENDNOTES

A

1   Woodland: *The Yellow Jersey Companion to the Tour de France*, Yellow Jersey Press, 2003, p. 8.
2   Chany and Cazeneuve: *La Fabuleuse Histoire du Tour de France*, Éditions Minerva 2003, p. 505.
3   *Sporting Cyclist*, September 1964, p.38.
4   *Ibid.*
5   Chany and Cazeneuve: *La Fabuleuse Histoire du Tour de France*, Éditions Minerva, 2003, p. 521.
6   'Cyclisme. Disparition de Désiré Letort', *Ouest-France*, https://www. ouest-france.fr/sport/cyclisme/cyclisme-disparition-de-desire-letort-396277
7   Fournel: Anquetil Alone (Profile Books) 2017, p15.
8   *Ibid.*, p17.
9   Chany: *La Fabuleuse Histoire du Cyclisme*, Éditions ODIL, 1975, p.553.
10 *Ibid.*
11 *Coureur*, September 1957, p.15.
12 Chany and Cazeneuve: *La Fabuleuse Histoire du Tour de France*, Éditions Minerva, 2003, p.456.
13 *Procycling*, October 2014, p.69.
14 Chany and Cazeneuve: *La Fabuleuse Histoire du Tour de France*, Éditions Minerva, 2003, p.477.
15 Howard: *Sex Lies and Handlebar Tape*, Mainstream Publishing, 2008.
16 Chany: *La Fabuleuse Histoire des Classiques et des Championnats du Monde*, Editions Odil 1979, p.770.
17 *Ibid.*, p.114.
18 Howard: *Sex Lies and Handlebar Tape*, Mainstream Publishing, 2008.
19 *Ibid.*
20 Fournel: *Anquetil Alone*, Profile Books, 2017, p.126.
21 'Men Elite Word Records', *UCI*, https://www.uci.org/docs/default-source/ about—discipline/about-track-cycling/men-elite-world-records. pdf?sfvrsn=244fc916_20

B

1   *Coureur*, October 1959, p.6.
2   *Ibid.*, p.30.
3   Chany and Cazeneuve: *La Fabuleuse Histoire du Tour de France*, Éditions Minerva, 2003, p.436.
4   'En la cuesta de don Federico', *El Correo*, www.elcorreo.com/vizcaya/20080904/deportes/mas-deporte/cuesta-federico-20080904.html
5   *Miroir-Sprint*, 27 July 1959, p.1.
6   *Coureur*, October 1959, p.6.
7   'Bahamontes: «Pasé hambre y comí gatos, por eso fui ciclista»', *ABC*, www.abc.es/deportes/ciclismo/abci-bahamontes-pase-hambre-y-comi-gatos-ciclista-201702191707_noticia.html
8   *Ibid.*
9   *Ibid.*
10 *Coureur*, October 1959, p.34.
11 *ABC*, 2 July 1965, p.57.
12 Augendre, Jacques, 'Le Tour de France: Guide Historique 2018', netstorage.lequipe.fr/ASO/cycling_tdf/2018-historical-guide.pdf
13 'Bahamontes : «Ce prix est mérité»', *L'Équipe*, www.lequipe.fr/Cyclisme-sur-route/Actualites/Bahamontes-ce-prix-est-merite/382048
14 Weidenfeld & Nicholson: *The Official Tour de France Centennial*, 2003, p,129.
15 *L'Équipe*, 17 July 1948, p.1.
16 *Le Dauphiné Libéré*, 17 July 1948, p.1.
17 'Bartali honoured for saving Jews during the Holocaust', *Cyclingnews*, www.cyclingnews.com/news/bartali-honoured-for-saving-jews-during-the-holocaust/
18 *The Sunday Times*, 28 July 2019
19 *Ibid.*
20 *L'Équipe*, 6 July 2019
21 'Egan Bernal well on road to recovery after missing Giro d'Italia', *Cyclingnews*, www.cyclingnews.com/news/egan-bernal-well-on-road-to-recovery-after-missing-giro-ditalia/
22 'Bernal rides into yellow', *Team Ineos*, www.teamineos.com/article/bernal-rides-into-yellow
23 'Commentary: Egan Bernal's improbable pathway to the 2019 Tour de France win', *VeloNews*, www.velonews.com/2019/07/tour-de-france/commentary-egan-bernals-improbable-pathway-to-the-2019-tour-de-france-win_498260
24 'Tour de France champion Egan Bernal given hero's welcome in Colombia', *BBC*, www.bbc.co.uk/news/world-europe-49272766
25 'Meet Egan Bernal: Colombia's newest cycling sensation', *CYCLINGTIPS*, cyclingtips.com/2016/04/meet-egan-bernal-colombias-newest-cycling-sensation/
26 *The Guardian*, 29 July 2019

27 'Egan Bernal: "I don't want to only focus on the Tour de France"', *Cycling Weekly*, www.cyclingweekly.com/news/racing/tour-de-france/egan-bernal-dont-want-focus-tour-de-france-434044
28 Weidenfeld & Nicholson: *The Official Tour de France Centennial*, 2003 p.183.
29 *Le Dauphiné Libéré*, 17 July 1948, p.1.
30 *Coureur*, Winter 1955, p.6.
31 Chany and Cazeneuve: *La Fabuleuse Histoire du Tour de France*, Éditions Minerva, 2003, p.386.
32 *Coureur*, Winter 1955, p.6.
33 Bobet, Jean: *Tomorrow we ride*, Mousehold Press, 2008, p.105.
34 Ibid., p.50.
35 Chany: *La Fabuleuse Histoire du Cyclisme*, Éditions ODIL, 1975, p.535.
36 *Cycling*, 26 August 1954
37 *Miroir des Sports*, 23 August 1954, p.3.
38 Chany: *La Fabuleuse Histoire des Classiques et des Championnats du Monde*, Editions Odil, 1979, p.750.
39 *Coureur*, October 1959, p.24.
40 'Ottavio Bottecchia, le maillot noir', *l'Humanite*, www.humanite.fr/node/287999
41 *Miroir des Sports*, 21 June 1927, p.2.
42 *L'Auto*, 23 June 1924, p.1.
43 Weidenfeld & Nicholson: *The Official Tour de France Centennial*, 2003, p.84.
44 *Miroir des Sports*, 21 June 1927, p.2.
45 *Ibid.*
46 *L'Auto*, 6 July 1926, p1
47 *Ibid.*
48 Kerebel: *Le Tour de France et les Pyrenees*, Editions Cairn, 2010, p.51.
49 *Le Petit Parisien*, 8 July 1926
50 Woodland: *The Yellow Jersey Companion to the Tour de France*, Yellow Jersey Press, 2003, p.75.

C

1 'Alberto Contador greeted by huge crowd chanting "one more year" as he returns home after Vuelta', *Cycling Weekly*, www.cyclingweekly.com/news/racing/alberto-contador-greeted-huge-crowds-returns-hometown-vuelta-espana-350874
2 Email interview with author, 15 September 2017
3 'Arbitration CAS 2011/A/2384 Union Cycliste Internationale (UCI)v. Alberto Contador Velasco & Real Federación Española de Ciclismo(RFEC)& CAS 2011/A/2386 World Anti-Doping Agency(WADA)v. Alberto Contador Velasco & RFEC, award of 6 February 2012', *Jurispridence*, jurisprudence.tas-cas.org/Shared%20Documents/2384,%202386.pdf
4 'Contador fights back on Mortirolo to extend Giro d'Italia lead', *Cyclingnews*, www.cyclingnews.com/news/contador-fights-back-on-mortirolo-to-extend-giro-ditalia-lead/

5   Email interview with author, 15 September 2017
6   *Sporting Cyclist*, May 1957, p.22.
7   *Ibid.*
8   *Ibid.*, p.18.
9   *Le Monde*, 24 August 1948
10 *La Stampa*, 23 August 1948
11 *Sporting Cyclist*, May 1957, p.23.
12 Fotheringham: *Fallen Angel – the passion of Fausto Coppi*, Yellow Jersey Press, 2009, p.171.
13 *La Stampa*, 7 July 1952
14 *La Stampa*, 10 June 1940
15 *Sporting Cyclist*, May 1957, p.14.
16 Woodland: *The Yellow Jersey Companion to the Tour de France*, Yellow Jersey Press, 2003, p.93.
17 Fotheringham: *Fallen Angel – the passion of Fausto Coppi*, Yellow Jersey Press, 2009, p.165.
18 *Procycling*, October 2014, p.73.
19 *Cycling*, 3 September 1953
20 Chany: *La Fabuleuse Histoire du Cyclisme*, Éditions ODIL, 1975, p.228.
21 *L'Auto*, 25 July 1904
22 *L'Auto*, 3 December 1904
23 *L'Auto*, 17 April 1915

D

1   *Miroir des Sports*, 23 July 1929
2   Sys: Top 1000 Belgische wielrenners, Lannoo, 2018, p.64.
3   *Ibid.*
4   Chany and Cazeneuve: *La Fabuleuse Histoire du Tour de France*, Éditions Minerva, 2003, p.225.
5   *Ibid.*, p.226.
6   *L'Auto*, 27 July 1929
7   Sys: Top 1000 Belgische wielrenners, Lannoo, 2018, p.18.
8   *L'Auto*, 17 July 1912
9   *L'Auto*, 29 July 1912
10 *Odieldefraeye*, www.odieldefraeye.be/site/blog.php?c=1
11 Sys: Top 1000 Belgische wielrenners, Lannoo, 2018, p.18.
12 Cossins: *The Monuments: the grit and the glory of cycling's greatest one-day races*, Bloomsbury, 2014, Location 3527
13 'Odiel Defraeye vereeuwigd op kerkplein', *Nieuwsblad*, www.nieuwsblad.be/cnt/dmf20120701_00206983
14 'Beginnings', *Pedro Delgado*, www.pedrodelgado.com/eng/biography/beginnings.html
15 'The Great Pedro Delgado', *Peloton Magazine*, pelotonmagazine.com/features/perico/

16 'Beginnings', *Pedro Delgado*, www.pedrodelgado.com/eng/biography/
    beginnings.html
17 *Ibid.*
18 'The Great Pedro Delgado', *Peloton Magazine*, pelotonmagazine.com/features/
    perico/
19 'Battling a Spanish Mafia', *Peloton Magazine*, pelotonmagazine.com/peloton-x/
    battling-spanish-mafia/
20 Beginnings', *Pedro Delgado*, pelotonmagazine.com/features/perico/
21 *El Pais*, 25 July 1988
22 *El Pais*, 17 October 1994
23 'Floyd Landis admits to doping throughout his career', *BBC*, news.bbc.co.uk/
    sport1/hi/other_sports/cycling/8694452.stm
24 'Lance Armstrong on the attack as doping controversy enters final stage', *The
    Guardian*, www.theguardian.com/sport/2012/jun/16/lance-armstrong-drugs-
    tour-de-france
25 'US Anti-Doping Agency's full statement on Lance Armstrong lifetime ban', *The
    Guardian*, www.theguardian.com/sport/2012/aug/24/us-anti-doping-agency-
    statement-lance-armstrong
26 'Lance Armstrong loses his 7 Tour de France titles', *CBC*, www.cbc.ca/sports/
    lance-armstrong-loses-his-7-tour-de-france-titles-1.1148857
27 *Ibid.*
28 'Lance Armstrong & Oprah Winfrey: interview transcript', BBC, https://www.
    bbc.co.uk/sport/cycling/21065539

E

1 Interview with author, 21 October 2016
2 *Ibid.*
3 *Ibid.*
4 '98th Tour de France – An Australian 1st', *Ride Media*, https://www.ridemedia.
   com.au/past-issue/98th-tour-de-france-an-australian-1st/

F

1 *L'Auto*, 11 August 1908
2 *L'Auto*, 8 July 1909
3 *L'Auto*, 14 July 1909
4 Chany: *La Fabuleuse Histoire du Cyclisme*, Éditions ODIL, 1975, p.818.
5 Rendell: *Blazing Saddles*, Quercus, 2007, p.35.
6 Leroy: *Francois Faber – Du Tour de France au Champ d'Honneur*, L'Harmattan,
   2006, Location 647
7 *L'Auto*, 2 August 1909
8 Fignon: *We Were Young and Carefree*, Yellow Jersey, 2010, p.1.
9 *Ibid.*, p28

10 *Ibid.*, p.52.
11 *Ibid.*, p.54.
12 *Ibid.*, p.101.
13 *Ibid.*, p.137.
14 Chany and Cazeneuve: *La Fabuleuse Histoire du Tour de France*, Éditions Minerva, 2003, p.661.
15 Fignon: *We Were Young and Carefree*, Yellow Jersey, 2010, p.119.
16 *Ibid.*, p.32.
17 *Miroir des Sports*, 24 July 1928
18 *L'Auto*, 8 July 1928
19 *L'Auto*, 13 July 1928
20 *Miroir des Sports*, 24 July 1928
21 *L'Auto*, 7 July 1929
22 Banda School Newsletter, 16 September 2011
23 'Froome awarded 2011 Vuelta victory', *Team Ineos*, www.teamineos.com/article/froome-awarded-2011-vuelta-victory
24 'The Kenyan Who Powered A Shy Boy To Glory', *Forbes Africa*, www.forbesafrica.com/sport/2013/09/01/kenyan-powered-shy-boy-glory/
25 'Interview: David Kinjah – the man who made Froome', *Cyclist*, www.cyclist.co.uk/in-depth/3353/interview-david-kinjah-the-man-who-made-froome
26 *Ibid.*
27 Froome: *The Climb*, Penguin UK, 2014
28 'Froome takes cycling's big step', *Cyclingnews*, autobus.cyclingnews.com/riders/2008/interviews/?id=chris_froome_nov08
29 'Chris Froome pays tribute to mother after winning 100th edition of the Tour de France in Paris', *The Telegraph*, www.telegraph.co.uk/sport/othersports/cycling/tour-de-france/10194115/Chris-Froome-pays-tribute-to-mother-after-winning-100th-edition-of-the-Tour-de-France-in-Paris.html
30 'How Froome and Team Sky blew up the Giro', *VeloNews*, www.velonews.com/2018/05/giro-ditalia/froome-team-sky-raided-giro_467556
31 'WADA clarifies facts regarding UCI decision on Christopher Froome', *WADA*, https://www.wada-ama.org/en/media/news/2018-07/wada-clarifies-facts-regarding-uci-decision-on-christopher-froome

G

1 *L'Auto*, 3 July 1903
2 Chany and Cazeneuve: *La Fabuleuse Histoire du Tour de France*, Éditions Minerva, 2003, p.53.
3 *Ibid.*, p.52.
4 Woodland: *The Unknown Tour de France*, Van der Plas Publications, 2005, p.11.
5 'La mort du petit ramoneur', *Alsa Presse*, web.archive.org/web/20050131053838/http://www.alsapresse.com/jdj/01/02/20/MA/article_1.html

6   *L'Auto*, 28 August 1911
7   *L'Auto*, 15 April 1907
8   Cossins: *The Monuments: the grit and the glory of cycling's greatest one-day races*, Bloomsbury, 2014, Location 2370
9   *Miroir des Sports*, 3 April 1934
10 *Ibid.*
11 *Miroir des Sports*, 26 January 1937
12 *Ibid.*
13 *Ibid.*
14 Chany and Cazeneuve: *La Fabuleuse Histoire du Tour de France*, Éditions Minerva, 2003, p.151.
15 *L'Auto*, 1 August 1911
16 'RIP Charly Gaul, 1932-2005', *Cyclingnews*, www.cyclingnews.com/news/rip-charly-gaul-1932-2005/
17 'Charly Gaul' (Obituary), *The Guardian*, www.theguardian.com/news/2005/dec/08/guardianobituaries.cycling
18 *Coureur*, September 1958, p.29.
19 *Ibid.*, p.6.
20 Chany and Cazeneuve: *La Fabuleuse Histoire du Tour de France*, Éditions Minerva, 2003, p.506.
21 *La Stampa*, 15 July 1965
22 Interview with author, 6 June 2016
23 *Corriere dello Sera*, 03 September 1973
24 Interview with author, 6 June 2016
25 *Ibid.*

H

1   Fotheringham: *Bernard Hinault and the Fall and Rise of French Cycling*, Random House, 2015
2   'Hinault, Vendedor de la Vuelta', *ABC (Spain)*, hemeroteca.abc.es/nav/Navigate.exe/hemeroteca/sevilla/abc.sevilla/1978/05/16/103.html
3   Weidenfeld & Nicholson: *The Official Tour de France Centennial*, 2003, p.266.
4   Bacon: *Mapping Le Tour*, HarperCollins Publishers, 2013, p.17.
5   'Classic jerseys: No.9 Renault', *Cyclist*, www.cyclist.co.uk/in-depth/5621/classic-jerseys-no9-renault
6   *Le Monde*, 2 September 1980
7   *La Stampa*, 1 September 1980
8   *Leidsch Dagblad*, 11 April 1983
9   Moore: *Slaying the Badger: LeMond, Hinault and the Greatest Ever Tour de France*, Random House, 2011, p.33.

I

1 'He Is Miguel, of Course', *Outside*, www.outsideonline.com/1886076/
he-miguel-course
2 'CYCLING; It's the Same Old Song: Indurain Wins His Fifth Tour de France in a
Row', *NY Times*, www.nytimes.com/1995/07/24/sports/cycling-it-s-the-same-
old-song-indurain-wins-his-fifth-tour-de-france-in-a-row.html
3 'He Is Miguel, of Course', *Outside*, www.outsideonline.com/1886076/
he-miguel-course
4 *Ibid.*
5 Woodland: *The Yellow Jersey Companion to the Tour de France*, Yellow Jersey
Press, 2003, p.186.

J

1 'Jan Janssen, Cycling's Gentleman Warrior', BikeRaceInfo, www.bikeraceinfo.
com/oralhistory/jan-janssen.html
2 *Ibid.*
3 *Leidsch Dagblad*, 10 April 1967
4 *Leidsch Dagblad*, 22 July 1968

K

1 'Seul un miracle pourrait sauver Hugo Koblet', *Gazette de Lausanne*, www.
letempsarchives.ch/page/GDL_1964_11_06/2/article/2960137/Koblet
2 'Hugo Koblet: This Charming Man', *Rouleur*, rouleur.cc/editorial/
this-charming-man/
3 *La Stampa*, 14 June 1950
4 Chany and Cazeneuve: *La Fabuleuse Histoire du Tour de France*, Éditions
Minerva, 2003, p.365.
5 *Coureur*, Spring 1956
6 *Sporting Cyclist*, December 1964
7 'Kubler et la Press Française', *Gazette de Lausanne,* www.letempsarchives.ch/
page/GDL_1949_08_04/5/article/3198937/Kubler
8 Chany: *La Fabuleuse Histoire du Cyclisme*, Éditions ODIL, 1975, p.505.
9 *Journal de Genève*, 3 September 1951
10 Chany and Cazeneuve: *La Fabuleuse Histoire du Tour de France*, Éditions
Minerva, 2003, p.400.
11 'Ferdy and Géminiani play "telephone"', *Cyclingnews*, www.cyclingnews.com/
features/ferdy-and-geminiani-play-telephone/
12 Chany and Cazeneuve: *La Fabuleuse Histoire du Tour de France*, Éditions
Minerva, 2003, p.400.

13 'OBITUARY: Ferdinand 'Ferdi' Kuebler, Swiss national hero and 1950 Tour de France winner', *Irish Examiner*, https://www.irishexaminer.com/sport/other-sports/obituary-ferdinand-ferdi-kuebler-swiss-national-hero-and-1950-tour-de-france-winner-438900.html

L

1 *L'Auto*, 19 July 1919
2 *L'Auto*, 29 July 1919
3 Sys: *Top 1000 Belgische wielrenners*, Lannoo, 2018, p.20.
4 Clemitson: *The History of Cycling in 100 Objects*, Bloomsbury, 2017, p.40.
5 *L'Auto*, 29 June 1937
6 Woodland: *The Yellow Jersey Companion to the Tour de France*, Yellow Jersey Press, 2003, p.214.
7 *L'Auto*, 23 July 1937
8 *L'Auto*, 23 July 1937
9 'Roger Lapébie, de grandes histoires offertes à la petite reine', *l'Humanite*, www.humanite.fr/node/88187
10 *L'Auto*, 13 June 1935
11 Woodland: *The Unknown Tour de France*, Van der Plas Publications, 2005, p.38.
12 Woodland: *The Yellow Jersey Companion to the Tour de France*, Yellow Jersey Press, 2003, p.215.
13 *L'Auto*, 12 April 1909
14 *Ibid.*
15 *Sport et Vie*, July 1957
16 Chany and Cazeneuve: *La Fabuleuse Histoire du Tour de France*, Éditions Minerva, 2003, p.138.
17 Cossins: *The Monuments: the grit and the glory of cycling's greatest one-day races*, Bloomsbury, 2014 Location 1378.
18 *Miroir des Sports*, 11 December 1928
19 *L'Auto*, 1 August 1938
20 *L'Auto*, 18 July 1927
21 *Miroir des Sports*, 15 July 1927
22 *L'Auto*, 7 July 1929
23 Fife: *The Tour de France: the history, the legend, the riders*, Mainstream Publishing, 1999, p.95.
24 *Miroir des Sports*, 26 July 1930
25 *L'Auto*, 29 July 1930
26 Woodland: *The Yellow Jersey Companion to the Tour de France*, Yellow Jersey Press, 2003, p.223.
27 Interview with author, February 2019
28 *Ibid.*
29 *New York Times*, 24 July 1989
30 Interview with author, February 2019

31 *New York Times*, 30 October 1983
32 *Sports Illustrated*, 3 September 1984
33 *Cycling Weekly*, 31 August 1989
34 *New York Times*, 3 December 1994

M

1 *L'Auto*, 5 July 1935
2 Weidenfeld & Nicholson: *The Official Tour de France Centennial*, 2003, p.120.
3 *Miroir des Sports*, 30 July 1935
4 *Miroir des Sports*, 18 April 1933
5 *L'Auto*, 28 July 1936
6 'Antonin Magne, la gloire et la vertu', *LNCpro*, www.lncpro.fr/Default6_32.aspx?HeaderID=4&ArticleID=Magne_Antonin&DirID=grands-champions&SubtitleID=Equipes%20%3E&TriID=
7 Chany and Cazeneuve: *La Fabuleuse Histoire du Tour de France*, Éditions Minerva, 2003, p.315.
8 *Paris-Soir*, 8 September 1936
9 *Ibid.*
10 Antonin Magne, la gloire et la vertu', *LNCpro*, www.lncpro.fr/Default6_32.aspx?HeaderID=4&ArticleID=Magne_Antonin&DirID=grands-champions&SubtitleID=Equipes%20%3E&TriID=
11 Chany and Cazeneuve: *La Fabuleuse Histoire du Tour de France*, Éditions Minerva, 2003, p.247.
12 Weidenfeld & Nicholson: *The Official Tour de France Centennial*, 2003, p.119.
13 Antonin Magne, la gloire et la vertu', *LNCpro*, www.lncpro.fr/Default6_32.aspx?HeaderID=4&ArticleID=Magne_Antonin&DirID=grands-champions&SubtitleID=Equipes%20%3E&TriID=
14 *Eddy Merckx*, www.eddymerckx.com/eddy-merckx
15 Interview with author, June 2016
16 *La Gazzetta dello Sport*, 1 June 1967
17 Weidenfeld & Nicholson: *The Official Tour de France Centennial*, 2003, p.233.
18 *Procycling*, October 2014
19 'Remembering how Eddy Merckx won at home in the 1969 Tour of Flanders', *The Guardian*, www.theguardian.com/sport/100-tours-100-tales/2014/apr/04/cycling-eddy-merckx-1969-tour-flanders
20 'Eddy Merckx m'a fait cadeau du maillot vert', *Le Parisien*, www.leparisien.fr/sports/eddy-merckx-m-a-fait-cadeau-du-maillot-vert-11-07-2012-2085483.php
21 'Eddy Merckx route', *route you*, https://www.routeyou.com/nl-be/route/view/250164/racefietsroute/eddy-merckx-route

N

1   'Biographia', *gastonenencini*, www.gastonenencini.it/Bio2.html
2   *La Stampa*, 18 July 1960
3   Chany and Cazeneuve: *La Fabuleuse Histoire du Tour de France*, Éditions Minerva, 2003, p.443.
4   *Ibid.*
5   Foot: *Pedalare! Pedalare!*, Bloomsbury UK, Kindle Edition, 2011, Location 3612.
6   *La Stampa*, 5 June 1955
7   'Gastone Nencini: Forgotten Champion', *Rouleur*, rouleur.cc/editorial/gastone-nencini-forgotten-champion/
8   Sykes: *Maglia Rosa – triumph and tragedy at the Giro d'Italia*, Bloomsbury, 2013, p.156.
9   Foot: *Pedalare! Pedalare!*, Bloomsbury UK, Kindle Edition, 2011, Location 3682.
10 Boulting: *The Road Book Cycling Almanack*, The road Book Ltd, 2018, p.104.
11 'How I Won – Nibali on 2018's Milan-San Remo', *inCycle/YouTube*, www.youtube.com/watch?v=jjTmKvsU5xE
12 *Procycling*, January 2019
13 *Peloton Magazine*, June 2017
14 'Vincenzo Nibali: Shark life', *Rouleur*, rouleur.cc/editorial/vincenzo-nibali-shark-life/
15 *Peloton Magazine*, June 2017
16 'Nibali seals Vuelta a España win', *Cyclingnews*, www.cyclingnews.com/races/vuelta-a-espana-2010/stage-21/results/
17 'What we learned from the 2013 Giro', *ESPN*, www.espn.com/sports/endurance/story/_/id/9318868/endurance-sports-learned-2013-giro-ditalia
18 *Ride Cycling Review*, Issue 73
19 *Ibid.*
20 'Vincenzo Nibali: Shark life', *Rouleur*, https://rouleur.cc/editorial/vincenzo-nibali-shark-life/

O

1   *Rouleur*, Issue 31
2   *Cycling Weekly*, 13 June 2019
3   Chany and Cazeneuve: *La Fabuleuse Histoire du Tour de France*, Éditions Minerva, 2003, p.576.
4   *Cyclist*, Issue 84
5   *Rouleur*, Issue 31

P

1 *La Stampa*, 6 June 1994
2 *La Stampa*, 6 June 1999
3 'Conconi acquitted after five year trial', *Cyclingnews*, autobus.cyclingnews. com/news.php?id=news/2004/mar04/mar20news1
4 *The Guardian*, 20 March 2004
5 *Le Petit Dauphinois*, 27 May 1936
6 *Paris-Soir*, 3 May 1935
7 *Ibid.*
8 *Miroir des Sports*, 28 February 1928
9 *L'Auto*, 6 July 1919
10 Chany and Cazeneuve: *La Fabuleuse Histoire du Tour de France*, Éditions Minerva, 2003, p.182.
11 *L'Auto*, 13 July 1923
12 *Le Petit Parisien*, 27 June 1924
13 *Miroir des Sports*, 12 June 1928
14 *Paris-Soir*, 3 May 1935
15 *New York Times*, 14 October 2007
16 'Stage 13: Béziers - Montélimar', *Cyclingnews*, www.cyclingnews.com/races/tour-de-france-2006/stage-13/results/
17 'Oscar Pereiro', *Dopeology*, www.dopeology.org/people/Oscar_Pereiro/
18 'Oscar Pereiro: Spanish cyclist's bittersweet Tour de France victory', *CNN*, edition.cnn.com/2017/10/17/sport/oscar-pereiro-tour-de-france-2006-floyd-landis/index.html
19 'The Gospel According to Floyd', *nyvelocity*, nyvelocity.com/articles/interviews/landiskimmage/
20 'Oscar Pereiro reacts to Landis allegations: "I am innocent"', *VeloNews*, www.velonews.com/2011/02/news/oscar-pereiro-reacts-to-landis-allegations-%E2%80%98i-am-innocent%E2%80%99_158327
21 Woodland: *The Yellow Jersey Companion to the Tour de France*, Yellow Jersey Press, 2003, p.287.
22 *L'Auto*, 15 July 1902
23 *L'Auto*, 11 August 1908
24 Chany: *La Fabuleuse Histoire des Classiques et des Championnats du Monde*, Editions Odil, 1979, p.44.
25 Chany and Cazeneuve: *La Fabuleuse Histoire du Tour de France*, Éditions Minerva, 2003, p.529.
26 'Roger Pingeon, certains jours étincelant...', *LNCpro*, www.lncpro.fr/Default6_32.aspx?HeaderID=4&ArticleID=Pingeon_Roger&DirID=grands-champions&SubtitleID=Equipes%20%3E&TriID=
27 'Roger Pingeon Obituary', Inrng, inrng.com/2017/03/roger-pingeon-obituary/
28 Weidenfeld & Nicholson: The Official Tour de France Centennial, 2003, p.227.

29 'Histoire(s) Anquetil - Stablinski, face à face au " Perroquet vert "', *l'Humanite*, www.humanite.fr/node/288922
30 'The triumph of Roger Pingeon - Stage 9 - Tour de France 2017', *Tour de France/YouTube*, www.youtube.com/watch?v=zxq7gGUeAdI
31 Chany and Cazeneuve: *La Fabuleuse Histoire du Tour de France*, Éditions Minerva, 2003, p.547 .
32 *Miroir des Sports*, 4 January 1923
33 Chany and Cazeneuve. *La Fabuleuse Histoire du Tour de France* (Éditions Minerva) 2003, p.87.
34 *L'Auto*, 9 July 1906
35 *L'Auto*, 2 August 1906
36 'René Pottier, un coeur énorme...', *LNCpro*, www.lncpro.fr/Default6_32.aspx?HeaderID=4&ArticleID=Pottier_Rene&DirID=grands-champions&SubtitleID=Equipes%20%3E&TriID=
37 *L'Auto*, 22 May 1905
38 *Miroir des Sports*, 27 March 1934
39 Wheatcroft: *Le Tour*, Simon & Schuster, 2003, p.26.

R

1 'A formerly great Dane', *The Guardian*, www.theguardian.com/commentisfree/2007/may/25/aformerlygreatdane
2 'Riis confesses doping-tainted career', *Cyclingnews*, www.cyclingnews.com/features/riis-confesses-doping-tainted-career/
3 'Bjarne Riis's year without lying: "Now I feel free"', *New York Times*, www.nytimes.com/2008/05/02/sports/02iht-CYCLING.3.12526552.html
4 'Tour De France 1996 Stage Sixteen Agen-Lourdes-Hautacam', *YouTube*, www.youtube.com/watch?v=2OBrmC6pUNE
5 'Jean Robic, le coq des grands cols', *LNCpro*, www.lncpro.fr/Default6_32.aspx?HeaderID=4&ArticleID=Robic_Jean&DirID=grands-champions&SubtitleID=Equipes%20%3E&TriID=
6 Chany and Cazeneuve: *La Fabuleuse Histoire du Tour de France*, Éditions Minerva, 2003, p.322.
7 Weidenfeld & Nicholson: *The Official Tour de France Centennial*, 2003, p.140.
8 Wheatcroft: *Le Tour*, Simon & Schuster, 2003, p.143.
9 Woodland: *The Yellow Jersey Companion to the Tour de France*, Yellow Jersey Press, 2003, p.310.
10 *Coureur*, September 1957
11 Maulavé: *Le Mont Ventoux*, Editions Alan Sutton, 2010, p.25.
12 Woodland: *The Yellow Jersey Companion to the Tour de France*, Yellow Jersey Press, 2003, p.310.
13 'Jean Robic, le coq des grands cols', *LNCpro*, www.lncpro.fr/Default6_32.aspx?HeaderID=4&ArticleID=Robic_Jean&DirID=grands-champions&SubtitleID=Equipes%20%3E&TriID=

14 Interview with author, May 2016
15 *Ibid.*
16 *Ibid.*
17 *Ibid.*
18 Roche: *My Road to Victory*, Stanley Paul and Co Ltd, 1988, p.7.
19 Interview with author, May 2016

S

1   *Rouleur*, Issue 18.4
2   'Sastre Wins 2008 Tour de France, Steegmans Takes Final Stage', *Cycling Weekly*, www.cyclingweekly.com/news/latest-news/sastre-wins-2008-tour-de-france-steegmans-takes-final-stage-94067
3   'Carlos Sastre exclusive: The forgotten Tour de France winner', *Cyclingnews*, www.cyclingnews.com/features/carlos-sastre-exclusive-the-forgotten-tour-de-france-winner/
4   'Carlos Sastre – the gritty, unglamorous fighter', *Rouleur*, rouleur.cc/editorial/carlos-sastre/
5   'Carlos Sastre exclusive: The forgotten Tour de France winner', *Cyclingnews*, www.cyclingnews.com/features/carlos-sastre-exclusive-the-forgotten-tour-de-france-winner/
6   *Rouleur*, Issue 18.4
7   'Carlos Sastre exclusive: The forgotten Tour de France winner', *Cyclingnews*, www.cyclingnews.com/features/carlos-sastre-exclusive-the-forgotten-tour-de-france-winner/
8   'Former Tour de France winner Carlos Sastre retires', *The Telegraph*, www.telegraph.co.uk/sport/othersports/cycling/8765260/Former-Tour-de-France-winner-Carlos-Sastre-retires.html
9   'Di Luca reveals details of his doping in hard-hitting autobiography', *Cyclingnews*, www.cyclingnews.com/news/di-luca-reveals-details-of-his-doping-in-hard-hitting-autobiography/
10 'Andy Schleck: "Alberto Contador did something he shouldn't have done, even if he denies it"', *Cycling Weekly*, www.cyclingweekly.com/news/racing/andy-schleck-alberto-contador-something-shouldnt-done-even-denies-427584
11 'Andy Schleck solos to victory in 2009 Liege-Bastogne-Liege', *VeloNews*, www.velonews.com/2009/04/news/andy-schleck-solos-to-victory-in-l-b-l_91169
12 'Stage 8, Sunday July 11: Station des Rousses - Morzine-Avoriaz, 189 km', *BikeRaceInfo*, www.bikeraceinfo.com/tdf/tdf2010.html#stage8
13 '2010 Tour De France Winner Andy Schleck Reflects on Career and Retirement', *inCycle/YouTube*, www.youtube.com/watch?v=CoJph6jXRG8
14 'Cyclist Andy Schleck on Tour de France Destiny', *Outside*, www.outsideonline.com/1900611/interview-issue-2012-cyclist-andy-schleck-tour-de-france-destiny

15 '2010 Tour De France Winner Andy Schleck Reflects on Career and Retirement', *inCycle/YouTube*, www.youtube.com/watch?v=CoJph6jXRG8
16 *Miroir des Sports*, 28 July 1921
17 *Miroir des Sports*, 28 July 1921
18 Sys: *Top 1000 Belgische wielrenners*, Lannoo, 2018, p.24.
19 *Miroir des Sports*, 28 July 1921
20 *Ibid.*
21 *L'Auto*, 25 June 1921
22 *L'Auto*, 23 July 1921
23 *Miroir des Sports*, 28 July 1921
24 *Le Petit Parisien*, 24 July 1933
25 Chany and Cazeneuve: *La Fabuleuse Histoire du Tour de France*, Éditions Minerva, 2003, p.254.
26 *Le Petit Parisien*, 24 July 1933
27 Chany and Cazeneuve: *La Fabuleuse Histoire du Tour de France*, Éditions Minerva, 2003, p.254.
28 *Miroir des Sports*, 1 August 1933
29 *Ibid.*
30 *L'Auto*, 24 July 1933
31 'Georges Speicher, viril et novateur', *LNCpro*, www.lncpro.fr/Default6_32.aspx?HeaderID=4&ArticleID=speicher-georges&DirID=grands-champions&SubtitleID=Equipes%20%3E&TriID=
32 Chany and Cazeneuve: *La Fabuleuse Histoire du Tour de France*, Éditions Minerva, 2003, p.257.
33 Woodland: *The Yellow Jersey Companion to the Tour de France*, Yellow Jersey Press, 2003, p.328.
34 'Georges Speicher, viril et novateur', *LNCpro*, www.lncpro.fr/Default6_32.aspx?HeaderID=4&ArticleID=speicher-georges&DirID=grands-champions&SubtitleID=Equipes%20%3E&TriID=
35 Chany: *La Fabuleuse Histoire des Classiques et des Championnats du Monde*, Editions Odil, 1979, p.722.
36 *Paris Soir*, 16 August 1933
37 *L'Auto*, 13 April 1936
38 Rendell: *Olympic Gangster – the legend of Jose Beyaert, cycling champion, fortune hunter and outlaw*, Mainstream Publishing, 2009, p.70.

T

1 'Who Punched Eddy Merckx? The Conclusion', *Bicycling*, www.bicycling.com/racing/a20041531/who-punched-eddy-merckx-the-conclusion/
2 Woodland: *The Yellow Jersey Companion to the Tour de France*, Yellow Jersey Press, 2003, p.364.
3 *Les Alpes et Le Tour* (Dapuhiné Libéré Hors Series) p.74.

4   'Les mythiques de la Mavic - Thévenet : « Wiegant aimait ses coureurs »',
     DirectVelo, www.directvelo.com/actualite/63432/les-mythiques-de-la-mavic-
     thevenet-wiegant-aimait-ses-coureurs
5   *Ibid.*
6   'The Geraint Thomas story: The skinny Welsh kid who made sporting
     immortality', *WalesOnline*,
     www.walesonline.co.uk/news/wales-news/geraint-thomas-story-
     skinny-welsh-14956305
7   *Ibid.*
8   *Ibid.*
9   'Geraint Thomas interview', *Cyclist*, www.cyclist.co.uk/in-depth/219/geraint-
     thomas-interview
10   *Ibid.*
11   'Pain maestro Geraint Thomas won't let broken pelvis shatter Tour De
     France dream', *The Telegraph*, www.telegraph.co.uk/sport/othersports/
     cycling/10539562/Pain-maestro-Geraint-Thomas-wont-let-broken-pelvis-
     shatter-Tour-De-France-dream.html
12   'Tour de France 2017: Geraint Thomas out after crash on stage nine', *BBC*,
     www.bbc.co.uk/sport/cycling/40549428
13   *The Guardian*, 30 October 2018
14   *The Road Book Cycling Almanack 2018*, The Road Book Limited, p.380.
15   *The Guardian*, 30 October 2018
16   *The Guardian*, 29 July 2019
17   *L'Auto*, 26 July 1920
18   Sys: *Top 1000 Belgische wielrenners*, Lannoo, 2018, p.11.
19   *L'Auto*, 26 June 1920
20   *L'Auto*, 27 July 1920
21   *Miroir des Sports*, 29 July 1920
22   Chany and Cazeneuve: *La Fabuleuse Histoire du Tour de France*, Éditions
     Minerva, 2003, p.167.
23   *L'Auto*, 15 June 1903
24   *L'Auto*, 16 February 1905
25   *L'Auto*, 24 April 1905
26   *L'Auto*, 31 July 1905
27   Woodland: *The Yellow Jersey Companion to the Tour de France*, Yellow Jersey
     Press, 2003, p.369.
28   *Miroir des Sports*, 30 June 1926

U

1   'Jan Ullrich ► TdF 1997 ► Stage 10 ► Andorra [15.07.1997]', *YouTube*, www.
     youtube.com/watch?v=N3jRlrknXzM&t=51s
2   *Ibid.*
3   Weidenfeld & Nicholson: *The Official Tour de France Centennial*, 2003, p.324.

4   '"Einen Vater habe ich nie vermisst"', *stern*, www.stern.de/sport/sportwelt/ jan-ullrichs-leben—einen-vater-habe-ich-nie-vermisst—3066386.html
5   'Jan Ullrich : Interview', *Cyclist*, www.cyclist.co.uk/in-depth/155/jan-ullrich-interview
6   Woodland: *The Yellow Jersey Companion to the Tour de France*, Yellow Jersey Press, 2003, p.371.
7   'Jan Ullrich: Former Tour de France winner admits blood doping', *BBC*, www.bbc.co.uk/sport/cycling/23013133
8   'Jan Ullrich: "The problems started when I could not see my kids, I exploded"', *Cycling Weekly*, www.cyclingweekly.com/news/jan-ullrich-problems-started-not-see-kids-exploded-392112
9   *Ibid.*

V

1   Chany and Cazeneuve: *La Fabuleuse Histoire du Tour de France*, Éditions Minerva, 2003, p.615.
2   *Le Dauphiné Libéré*, 5 July 1976
3   Pickering: *The Yellow Jersey Club*, Bantam Press, 2015, p.33.
4   *Ibid.*
5   Sys: *Top 1000 Belgische wielrenners*, Lannoo, 2018, p.273.
6   *Ibid.*, p.275.

W

1   'The Lamentation', *Bicycling*, www.bicycling.com/news/a20010028/pro-cycling-news-4/
2   Weidenfeld & Nicholson: *The Official Tour de France Centennial*, 2003, p.186.
3   *Rouleur*, Issue 66
4   *Ibid.*
5   McGann and McGann: *The Story of the Tour de France Vol 1*, Dog Ear Publishing, 2006, p.219.
6   'Wiggins in hot pursuit of medal record', *Olympic*, www.olympic.org/news/wiggins-in-hot-pursuit-of-medal-record
7   Wiggins: *My Time*, Yellow Jersey Press, 2012, p.25.
8   *The Guardian*, 5 November 2018
9   Wiggins: *My Time*, Yellow Jersey Press, 2012, p.210.
10 *Ibid.*, p.181.
11 'Combatting doping in sport', *Parliament*, publications.parliament.uk/pa/cm201719/cmselect/cmcumeds/366/366.pdf
12 *The Guardian*, 5 November 2018
13 'Bradley Wiggins: "I'm detached from cycling now"', *BigIssue*, https://www.bigissue.com/latest/bradley-wiggins-im-detached-from-cycling-now/

Z

1   Weidenfeld & Nicholson: *The Official Tour de France Centennial*, 2003, p.272.
2   *Leidsch Dagblad*, 25 June 1980
3   Galametz and Bouvet: *The Official Encyclopaedia of the Yellow Jersey: 100 Years of the Yellow Jersey*, Hatchett UK, 2019
4   *Nieuwe Leidsche Courant*, 21 July 1980
5   Woodland: *Cycling Heroes*, Springfield Books Limited, 1994, p.133.
6   *Ibid.*, p. 133.
7   *Ibid.*, p. 134.

You may also enjoy ...

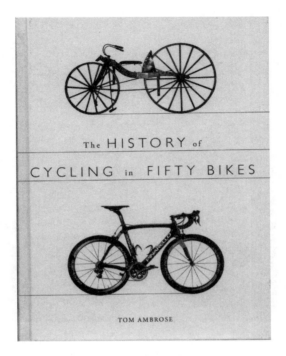

978 0 7524 9944 4

Illustrated in full colour with a wide range of photographs, *The History of Cycling in Fifty Bikes* tells the story of the bicycle through 50 iconic machines, starting with the first primitive wooden two-wheelers through to carbon-fibre super bikes and the designs of the future, celebrating sporting achievements, technological advances and world records along the way.

You may also enjoy ...

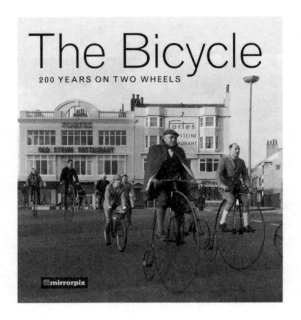

978 0 7509 8005 0

From the eighteenth-century wooden-framed prototype to the penny-farthing to the global phenomenon that is racing, *The Bicycle: 200 Years on 2 Wheels* charts the evolution of the humble bicycle in stunning photographs.

The History Press

The destination for history
www.thehistorypress.co.uk